UNDERSTANDING AUGUSTINE

Other books by John J. O'Meara include

St Augustine: Against the Academics (1950)

The Young Augustine (1954, 1964 US, 1980 paperback)

Porphyry's *Philosophy from Oracles* in Augustine (1959)

Porphyry's *Philosophy from Oracles* in Eusebius's *Praeparatio Evangelica* and Augustine's *Dialogues of Cassiciacum* (1969)

Studies in Augustine and Eriugena, ed. T. Halton (1992)

Eriugena (Oxford University Press, 1988)

Eriugena: Periphyseon IV (with E. Jeauneau, 1995)

The Voyage of St Brendan (Dolmen, 1976 and Four Courts Press, 1995)

Giraldus Cambrenis, *Topography of Ireland* (Dolmen, 1976 and Penguin, 1982)

The Singing Masters (a Memoir, Lilliput, 1990)

Understanding Augustine

John J. O'Meara

FOUR COURTS PRESS

This book was typeset by
Woodcote Typesetters
in 10 on 12 point Ehrhardt for
FOUR COURTS PRESS
55 Prussia Street, Dublin 7, Ireland
e-mail: fcp@ indigo.ie
and in North America for
FOUR COURTS PRESS
c/o ISBS, 5804 N.E. Hassalo Street, Portland, OR 97213.

A catalogue record for this title
is available from the British Library.

ISBN 1-85182-272-0

Printed in Great Britain
by Antony Rowe Ltd, Chippenham, Wilts.

Contents

Acknowledgements

The publisher and author are grateful to the various publishers for permission to reprint the chapters below, which first appeared in the following publications:

1 Introduction to *An Augustine Reader: Selections from the Writings of Augustine*, edited with an introduction by John J. O'Meara (Image Books; 1973).

3 *From Athens to Chartres: Studies in Honour of E. Jeauneau* (Brill, 1990).

4–7 *Charter of Christendom: The Significance of the City of God* (Villanova University, 1961).

8–10 *The Creation of Man in St Augustine's De Genesi ad Litteram* (Villanova University Press, 1950).

APPENDICES

1 *The Irish Ecclesiastical Record*, vol. lxxxv, no. 3 (March 1956).

2 *The Irish Ecclesiastical Record*, vol. cx, nos. 1–2 (July–August 1965).

3 *The Classical Tradition*, edited by L. Wallach (Cornell University Press, 1966).

Preface

I am very happy that Four Courts Press has undertaken to publish this second collection[1] of papers on Augustine. They have something to say on three of his greatest works – the *Confessions*, the *City of God* and *Genesis Understood Literally*. My hope is that one might emerge from reading them with a fairly comprehensive and even fresh understanding of Augustine. I am particularly happy that my lectures at Villanova University on the *City of God* and *Genesis Understood Literally* are being made available to a wider audience, for I believe that they give a just account of the contents of these two important books, which for all their importance have for one reason or another remained insufficiently read: understandably the *Confessions* on the other hand are a lodestar, even for scholars.

Although Augustine is nowadays commonly blamed for what is considered a harsh attitude to the body and sexuality—and he does share many of the anti-body and anti-woman assumptions of his predecessors and contemporaries, both pagan and Christian—the truth is that, while he was profoundly affected by the immaterialist philosophy of the Neoplatonists, he rejected firmly their absolute contention that 'body' could not exist with soul in the afterlife. Whereas Porphyry, the reigning Neoplatonist of Augustine's time, refused to accept the Incarnation of Divinity in Christ and the Resurrection of His or any body, Augustine accepted both and in this acceptance was converted: 'Put ye on the Lord Jesus Christ'.[2] The implications of the precise fulcrum, so to speak, of his conversion were enormous.

From this followed a whole series of positions on the body and sexuality which may surprise our contemporaries: not only, for example, that Adam and Eve, *each* the image of God, were sexually differentiated at their creation, inhabited a Paradise that was earthly, but could have felt *libido* and exercised their sexual roles there. Even more, procreation was not the sole end of marriage, and the exercise of the marriage act without the aim of procreation, though a venial sin, was absorbed in the overriding good of that act: *neque enim quia incontinentia malum est, ideo connubium vel quo incontinentes copulantur, non est bonum*. All of this—and more—is found in *Creation Understood Literally* and *The Good of Marriage*, to which it refers.

Augustine, moreover, had a somewhat greater appreciation and knowledge of Science

1 Cf. *Studies in Augustine and Eriugena*, ed. T. Halton, Catholic University of America Press, Washington, DC (1992), xiv + 362. 2 *Rom.* 13.13.

than one might expect, and entertained some notion of evolution. He was, above all, a man of action, of will, of love. For him one loved God as one loved man—with the full blaze of *amor*, not just in purified *dilectio*.

Voltaire's remark about the *City of God* is well-known: 'it is a great book, no one reads it'. One acquires it for one's library, with the best of intentions. It is in fact very long and very tedious. But for all that it is truly a Charter of Christendom, a Christian prose epic that shows how the Religion of the Hebrews, the Philosophy of the Greeks, and the spreading Empire of Rome are fulfilled in Christianity. There is not one city in question, but two. These are not physical or political, but mystical. They are constituted of two groups of men (and angels), one of which is bound together simply by the love (*amor*) of God: it is the city after which the work is named. The other group is bound together by the love of self, the rejection of God, and is called variously the earthly city or even the city of the Devil. The City of God already exists in heaven and on earth. It is *not* the Church, since some have joined it—such as the Sybil of Cumae—before the Church existed; some who are in the Church now will be rejected; and others, who are not in the Church now, will be admitted. The touchstone of membership is the worship of the one God *only*. The work is, therefore, theological and has little to offer on Political Theory or a Philosophy of History.

It is commonly thought that Alaric's sack of Rome in 410 AD 'caused' Augustine to write the *City of God* as a defence of Christianity. It was the occasion, certainly. But in fact the theme of the work is anticipated in Augustine's works years before, was suggested to him by his own experience (as was often the case with Augustine) and is a version of his *Confessions* writ large for the *whole of mankind*. The defence is not so much against those who blamed the Fall of Rome on the Empire's becoming Christian and so softened as to turn the other cheek, but against the polytheism which still challenged Christian monotheism. More particularly it was one of a series of Christian defences of the Church against Porphyry the Neoplatonist, who had attacked Christianity under various heads and especially its claim that Christ was God as well as man, that He died on a gibbet and that He went bodily to Heaven. Others had also centred their attacks on Porphyry: Arnobius (*fl. c.*300), Eusebius of Caesarea (*ob.*399), Claudianus Mamertus (*c.*474), Theodoret (*ob. c.*466) and Aeneas of Gaza (*ob. c.*518). It was believed for long that their defence of Christianity was against Porphyry's *Against the Christians*.[3] But now it is contended that no such work existed[4] but that, as I attempted to show in my *Porphyry's Philosophy from Oracles in Augustine* (1959), the object of their attack was Porphyry's *Philosophy from Oracles*, which greatly occupied Eusebius, and is named by formal title by Augustine in the *City of God*. Indeed Augustine in his defence of Christianity pitted the Christian 'oracles' of the Bible against those cited by Porphyry: his contention is that they were clearer and more true. From the moment of his conversion in 386 Augustine accepted, as against Porphyry (in whom he found much to approve) the Incarnation and Resurrection of Christ: *induite Jesum Christum*. This acceptance involved a degree of materialism (a 'body', even if 'glorified', as against the total absence

---

3 Cf. 87 below.   4 Cf. P. Beatrice, *Hommage à Jean Pépin* (1992), 355; *Studi in Onore di Ugo Bianchi* (1994), 235.

of any 'body' insisted on by Porphyry, even if he supposed that the soul had some 'envelope', some 'vehicle' or *ochéma*) which had the important implications for Augustine's attitude to the body and sexuality that I have mentioned. Truly the conversion of Augustine had momentous consequences for the Western Church.

But there was a down-side to this understanding of the body. Considerations of the necessary limit of the number of citizens of the *City of God* that would be sufficient to replace the angels that had Fallen, led Augustine to conclude that the majority of men were damned: they were the *massa damnata*. Since they would have a bodily resurrection, their bodies too would be eternally punished. Hence his efforts in the *City of God* to demonstrate that a body could be eternally burned by fire, but never consumed by it. He was oppressed, also, by the carnality of the simple congregation who listened to his sermons, as distinct from those who would read his less controversial and more philosophical works, such as *Genesis Understood Literally*. There was also ever present in his mind the warnings of antiquity, especially of Lucretius and his favourite, Virgil, against following 'love' as opposed to 'duty'. Hence his ambivalence on bodily love.

Time and again, especially in the mature *Genesis Understood Literally*, Augustine admits that there are many things about the soul that he does not know—perhaps, someone else, or even himself later on—may clear up his problems. But he also lets it be known that he is not sure of the body's fate in the afterlife either. Thus he writes: 'let him who can, show that the soul, when it has left this body, has any body. I at any rate do not think so'.[5] After over a decade as bishop he excluded the possibility of anything corporeal in our Vision of God in Heaven (and so shocked a fellow bishop!). At the very end of the *City of God* he does not exclude the possibility of some kind of non-corporeal Vision of God in Heaven,[6] but goes on immediately to develop rather the idea of corporeal participation. Augustine's followers have tended to leave out of consideration his uncertainties in many important matters. They have chosen to teach what he commonly taught to those of whom he had the serious responsibility of pastoral care: this did not allow for alternative answers to subtle questions.

Inevitably in any collection of papers there is bound to be repetition of themes which cannot be eliminated altogether since they are relevant to each paper. Augustine would have understood this, since he constantly repeated themes himself. But I have put in cross-reference as a help, perhaps, to understand why the version of the theme found in each paper is necessary for its argument and can hardly be omitted without loss. Augustine rejected in his conversion—and for always—the immaterialism of Porphyry. The consequence of this was the dominance in the West of the belief in the resurrection of the ('glorified') body. But there was another very important consequence of this anti-Porphyrian espousal of the body by Augustine—an unusually (for his time) sympathetic treatment of the body, sexuality and woman: this should be much better known.[7] While there was some ambivalence in Augustine on these matters, it appears to be related to avoiding the scandalizing of 'the little ones'.

---

5 *De Genesi ad litteram* 12.32, 60. 6 *City of God*, 22.1, 6. 7 Cf. L.B. Richey, *Augustinian Studies* 26 (1995), 130: 'O'Meara has been the dominant voice of the last half-century in arguing for a profound Porphyrian influence on Augustine's thought.' The gist of this argument is given in this volume.

I have included some shorter papers in the Appendices. Two of these are related to the *Confessions* and the third to the *City of God*. They may be considered as something of a *parópsēma*, a side-dish.

Introduction to Augustine

Augustine of Hippo was lucky in his time. At the beginning of the fourth century AD, the century in which he was born in a small town in North Africa, the Christian Church, spreading its influence everywhere, was still subject to a pagan power. By the end of that century the church had for all practical purposes taken over the Roman Empire—and he was a bishop already famous.

There is a well-known and useful line from an epistle of the Latin poet Horace—*Graecia capta ferum victorem cepit*[1] ('Greece, the captive, captured her wild conqueror'). Rome's legions kept marching along the straight and ever penetrating Roman roads; her laws ran everywhere; her prosperity was enjoyed by all. But it was *Greek* art, philosophy, letters, education and even religion that occupied, somewhat unhappily, the mind of Rome. In this sense Arnold Toynbee's characterization of Rome as a late Hellenic rally is evidently true.

When in turn the Christian Church took over the Roman Empire, it too was in danger of being captured by Hellenism. How could it have been otherwise? By now only a minority of Christians were Jews with a Jewish understanding of the Old and New Testaments. The majority were citizens of the far-flung Roman Empire, thinking with the minds of Cicero and Virgil.

Just when the church became the Establishment in the West and had urgent need to politicize its revelation—to make it appear rational—Augustine was at hand to serve. This is what I mean when I say that he was lucky in his time. He set the mould in which Western Christendom was laid: he set it firmly and he set it fully. No one before or since had ever had such an opportunity in this regard. He, moreover, had the desire and confidence to seize that chance although he was not without his uncertainties.

This is one of the reasons why Augustine must be of interest to us. The thought patterns, determining action for fifteen hundred years, were set (not initiated, let it be noted) by him. We nowadays would ask: what were his qualifications for so (in retrospect) momentous a task? His range of knowledge, his experience, his character cannot but be of great interest to us. As it happens, he had an unusual personality and we have his own delineation of it in an extraordinary book—his *Confessions*. This knowledge, experience and character will engage our attention for much of the rest of this Introduction. But

1 *Ep.* 2.1, 156.

we must also examine a little the philosophy, so to speak, which he brought forth from a merging of Hellenistic thought and religion (not excluding demonology) on the one hand and Hebraic revelation on the other.

LIFE

Aurelius Augustinus was born in Tagaste in Numidia—now Souk-Ahras in Algeria, about sixty miles south of Bône—on 13 November, AD 354. His parents, Patricius and Monica, although having connections with Berber stock, were Roman in outlook and Latin was the vernacular of the growing boy. There were at least two other children in the family. Patricius was a modest landowner and town councillor, but was not wealthy. He died in 370, when Augustine was sixteen years of age. Monica was a pious, patient, and insistent woman, whose ambition it was to win both her husband and Augustine to full acceptance of Catholicism. She succeeded and died at Ostia in the year of Augustine's baptism, AD 387. It is often suggested that Monica had undue influence on Augustine.

After local schooling to the age of ten Augustine went some fifteen miles south to Madauros for high school education. This was mainly in the Latin authors Terence, Sallust, Cicero and Virgil. He was taught a little Greek and hated it. At Carthage he subsequently took up the career of rhetorician—in effect a kind of university professor—in which he was to win distinctions in Africa and such success subsequently in Rome and Milan (then the Emperor's court) that he could reasonably entertain the expectation of becoming governor of a province. One should bear very much in mind that his formation and career were almost exclusively in Latin rhetoric, that is in literature and public speaking.

Away from home in the year of his father's death, the sixteen-year-old boy would seem to have succumbed somewhat to the flesh. A little later he took a mistress who gave him a son whom he called Adeodatus—'given by God'. He was faithful to her and she to him for fifteen years—until he planned a regular marriage with another. Then she was sent away, with sorrow in both their hearts. It would seem that her social condition did not allow her to expect or him to offer marriage. He clearly loved her, as he also loved their brilliant son, who, alas, died young. Augustine does not conceal that his own and his mother's worldly ambitions and the social mores of the time made their separation inevitable. He nevertheless tells the story against himself, and this is the plainest evidence that he was deeply attached to her and did not, in the circumstances, treat her— as it is sometimes suggested—brutally. It is simply not fair to apply to him the outlook of our times.

At any rate, the testimony of others, his success in studies, his fidelity to one woman and, perhaps above all, his growing preoccupation with religious and intellectual ideals tend very much to give the lie to his own strictures on these teenage years in his *Confessions*, written nearly two decades later.

In his nineteenth year Augustine felt a strong call stimulated by reading Cicero's *Hortensius* (now lost) to give himself to higher things and condemn mere worldly ambition. The curious result of this was his embracing of Manicheism which promised to teach him all things through reason—unlike Catholicism, which demanded also faith.

Augustine had imbibed Catholicism, as he says, with his mother's milk. He had not been baptized, however, for the baptismal wiping out of sin was thought better postponed until at least wild oats were safely sown. Manicheism was dualistic, positing the existence of two Principles, Good and Evil. While it incorporated many non-Christian elements in its revelation and was actively hostile to Christianity in many ways, and notably to Christianity's acceptance of the Old Testament, it was, in North Africa, nevertheless so 'Christian' in other ways, and particularly in its enthusiasm for St Paul's Epistles, that it was said that one could pass from Manicheism to Christianity or vice versa without any great noticeable change—indeed Augustine the bishop was accused of being a crypto-Manichean all along. Nevertheless Monica was so displeased with her son's joining the Manicheans that she turned him out of her house. Moreover, Augustine's own rigorous controversy with the Manicheans later indicates that for him too at that stage there was a great divide.

Augustine remained a Manichean for nearly all his impressionable and formative twenties, excusing his sins as caused by the Principle of Evil and aspiring to the good. He gradually realized that the Manicheans did not, any more than the Catholics, base their system on reason alone—nor were their lives always exemplary. Still, he tried to spread their gospel while declining to join the higher echelons of the sect. In the end he became so disillusioned with their bizarre beliefs and their exaggerated criticism of the Old Testament that he resumed, at about the age of thirty, the religion of his earlier life. In the meantime, his mother had long before allowed him back. His defiance of her, however, in this—and indeed other—important matters, should not go unnoted.

That Augustine should have subscribed to material dualism in his twenties made his conversion to belief in an immaterial God and his understanding of the problem of evil in the world extremely difficult. What is more, it cannot but have left its mark deeply on him, tainting for him any life of the senses with the suggestion of sin.

By now, about 384, he had abandoned Carthage, his unruly pupils and his mother for Rome (where he found that the pupils did not pay!) and the patronage of Symmachus, a leader of the surviving pagans of the day. He was recommended to a high post, Master of Rhetoric, at the Court in Milan. There the tempo of his life increased: he made important public speeches, he canvassed powerful friends, he kept up the arduous grind of teaching. He put away his mistress and planned for marriage with a girl who had a suitable dowry—but was too young. His search for truth was impatient and despairing. He resolved to join the followers of the New Academy, who professed that one could not know anything and therefore one must assent to nothing. His health was deteriorating. He was so profoundly unhappy that he envied a drunken beggar his intoxication.

But gradually things began to improve. His mother had followed him to Milan, and this led him to attend upon Ambrose, the bishop. Listening for the rhetoric of his sermons, he began to learn that Ambrose was supplying him with the solution to many Manichean and personal arguments against the Bible. Ambrose insisted with St Paul:[2]

---

2 2 *Cor.* 3:6.

'The letter kills, but the spirit gives life'. Scripture was to be understood not literally but allegorically. Even more, he found either in Ambrose's sermons or in the discourse of intellectual friends in Milan an immaterial philosophy that at one stroke enabled him to conceive of a spiritual God, have some explanation of the problem of evil as simply a privation or defect of being and (most wonderful of all) seemed to fit with Catholic teaching, especially on Providence and the Trinity. That philosophy was Neoplatonism and its recent interpreters in Rome were Plotinus (AD 205–270) and his disciple Porphyry (AD 232–305). The excitement of that momentous discovery burned in him as a bright flame for many a long year. He returned again and again to the mystical impulse to ascend the scale of being, from creatures to the One, that Plotinus had given him. Never again could any worldly thing have real value for him. Augustine's attitude was henceforth absolutist: there was no truth, no justice or any other virtue unless it took account first of God. This made an already zealous Augustine zealous beyond measure.

Augustine now felt that intellectually he must become formally a Catholic—but he was held back by the flesh. Part of the problem was undoubtedly created by the differing dualisms of both Manicheism and Neoplatonism. For a Platonist, the body was the tomb of the soul and had to be shunned. How could one aspire to union with the Father while continuing to have truck with the senses? Augustine understood Catholicism to demand the same, at least from him. But he found that his will was sleepy and sluggish, while habit was awake and strong. It took the stories of the conversions of Antony (the father of monasticism) and of the African rhetor Victorinus and other conversions to bring him to a crisis wherein he found himself bidden by the mysterious voice of an unseen child to open the Scriptures and read what his eye first fell on. It was: 'Put on the Lord Jesus Christ, and make not provision for the flesh, to fulfill its lusts'.[3] On the spot his will was adamant. He was converted. Henceforth Augustine was the apostle of grace, unaccountable and irresistible. In 387 he was baptized by Ambrose.

In the following year Augustine returned to Africa with the intention of living in a Christian community and writing a series of Christian literary and philosophical works. Though he became, unwillingly, a priest in 391 and a bishop in 396, engaged till his death in 430 in resounding and extended controversies with successively Manicheans, Donatists and Pelagians, interpreted the Scriptures daily, attended to heavy administrative (some civil) duties, had a vast correspondence (he wrote to many of the notables of his day) and wrote the seminal theological books for Western Christendom, in one way the great adventure of his life was already over. Few authors have so clearly depended on their own experiences to generate their teaching as did Augustine: his life, but above all, his early life, profoundly influenced his teaching.

WORKS

Augustine's works run to over a hundred in number, exclusive of some eight hundred Sermons and over two hundred Letters—some of them the equivalent of books. The

3 *Rom.* 13:14.

Sermons, of course, are mainly exegetical—interpretation of the Scriptures—but they have many a human and sometimes controversial touch. The Letters are testimony to his influence throughout the known world: his opinions and advice were sought by emperors and ministers, popes and saints. They mark his changing interests and are invaluable for understanding the development of his ideas. His works are mainly concerned with his controversies with the Manicheans, Donatists and Pelagians. But the first and third of these controversies are also encountered in the *Confessions* (thirteen books) and the *City of God* (twenty-two books) respectively. The Manicheans we have mentioned very briefly already. The Donatist schism arose in AD 312, when those who had remained constant in a recent persecution refused to have dealings with those who had acquiesced. It is sometimes thought (but this has been questioned more recently) that it was African and rural in outlook as opposed to the official Roman and urbanized church represented by Augustine. In every town the schism was only too apparent— bishop against bishop, church against church. What was involved, therefore, was essentially doctrine on the church itself. Augustine tried every manner of persuasion, in the end resorting reluctantly to physical coercion by the powers of the state, to bring this controversy to a close.

The Pelagian controversy was more serious. Here virtuous and intelligent men— Pelagius, Coelestius and Julian of Eclanum—defended their view of the self-sufficiency of human nature (without the aid of grace) partly from the earlier writing of Augustine himself. Moreover the great questions of free will and predestination were inevitably involved: here Augustine tended to harden his formulas beyond what the church would later accept—all in defence of his preoccupation with grace.

Apart from these pastoral and administrative writings, the more important of his more formal works are the *Dialogues of Cassiciacum*, the *Confessions*, the *Trinity*, the *City of God* and *Genesis Understood Literally*.

The Dialogues (386–7), written after his conversion in a semi-catechetical semi-Platonic manner, discuss knowledge, happiness and order in a manner so philosophical as to have given rise to the idea, now firmly rejected, that Augustine was really converted, not to Catholicism, but to Neoplatonism in AD 386. In fact, they are, for all their philosophy, predominantly based on Christ as the Truth and the Way. Of the three dialogues mentioned, that on Order is the most profound (indeed, it is somewhat obscure) and has a number of anticipations (as has the *Trinity*) of the more mystical speculation of later Western writers subject to Greek theological influence—such as Eriugena, for example. Augustine composed at the same time as these *Dialogues* his *Soliloquies*, which are prayerful, intimate and more personal.

The *Confessions* (397–400) is a great and unique work, rhetorical and emotional, poetic and subtle. It is fatally easy to misunderstand it—to begin with, the confession is not of sin only, but of faith and praise to God. In nine books Augustine outlines in a rhetorical, moralistic and selective way his life, guided as it was by providence and saved by grace, from birth to his conversion at the age of thirty-two: much is taken up with his reactions to Manicheism and Neoplatonism. The tenth book covers more factually the period between his conversion and the time of writing as a bishop some twelve years later. The last three books are a commentary on the first chapter of Genesis. The

Confessions gives rise to great problems in connection with its structure and historicity. But few can read it without being moved and in some way exalted by its obsessive ascent from the dragging body to the soaring mind.

The Trinity (399–419) in fifteen books employs all the resources of exegesis to win from the Scriptures in its earlier part, and from Reason in its later part, some under-standing of this great Christian mystery. Here particularly Augustine exploits analogies with the powers of the human soul to discover in them—mind, knowledge, love; memory, intelligence, will—some faint shadow of Father, Word and Spirit. In this difficult book later writers on creation and mysticism found much help and inspiration.

The *City of God* (413–427), begun after the sack of Rome by Alaric in 410, was in one way or another in prospect for long before. The first ten of its twenty-two books attack in turn the Roman official view that temporal prosperity is dependent upon worship of the many false gods (Books 1–5), and the Greek philosophical view that *happiness in the afterlife* is dependent upon this worship (Books 6–10). It is to be stressed that this part of the *City of God* is against polytheism, not against Roman virtue or Greek philosophy, both of which are commended and considered to be providentially arranged aids to the spread and understanding of the Christian revelation. The final twelve books of the work fall into three equal groups dealing with the scriptural account of the origin of man (Books 11–14), his history (Books 15–18) and final destiny (Books 19–22). The title of the *City of God* is taken from *Psalm* 87:3 and refers not to a political city, but to the society of the saved (both men and angels) here and hereafter. This society is not identical with the Church. The work is equally about the City of Earth (or the Devil), that is, the society of those who will be, indeed are, damned. The work is theological and might be said to give a theological interpretation of history—not a philosophy of it. It has little, moreover, to say on politics. It heralds the coming of the Christian era and explicitly proclaims its Hebraic, Roman and Greek sources. It is a great Christian prose epic— not without its baffling *longueurs*.

Genesis Understood Literally, the best-known work of Augustine down to medieval times under the title, however, of the *Herameron* (the 'Six Days' of creation), is Augustine's last of several attempts to account for everything in the story of creation as far as possible by reason, mainly Neoplatonic reason. It is, therefore, a book of great importance and great interest—especially in our more secular age—but is relatively unknown in modern times. This is due mainly to the unavailability of vernacular translations until very recently.

DOCTRINE

Augustine was not a systematic theologian, though there is much system in his theology. His theological speculation is, however, extensive and has had a dominating influence in the West. He is, therefore, essentially a theologian. He is even less—much less—a systematic philosopher, though he was excited by philosophy in his youth and at the time of his conversion was greatly impressed by it. Nevertheless, although he always retained something of the philosophic manner, related (when convenient) his doctrine to reason, and continued to profess admiration (with certain explicit reservations) for Plato, Plotinus and Porphyry, his stance from the time of his conversion is determined by his acceptance of the Christian doctrines of the Incarnation and Resurrection of the body. In effect, he at least dispensed with the Platonists and in practice often contradicted them. It is, however, anachronistic to distinguish strictly between philosophy and theology in his period. We must, therefore, present his doctrine without such strict distinction.

He has little new or important to give in the theory of knowledge except the seeming anticipation of Descartes's *cogito, ergo sum* (for Augustine, *dubito, ergo sum*), his Neoplatonic emphasis on purification as prerequisite to knowledge, and especially his theory of illumination. This theory is part and parcel of his doctrine on grace. Intellectual ideas (as distinct from ideas arising from sense perception) cannot arise in the mind unless they are illuminated by another (God) as by their sun: God is the only and inner teacher of the soul.

The relation of faith to reason is, of course, a basic problem in Augustine. At the time of his conversion he professed to regard them as two independent ways to—in a sense, revelations of—God which mutually assisted one another. They could be independent (for a very few, however, in the case of reason only). Later he modified his notions on their independence. Since faith depended on verifying the credibility of the testimony one believed in, faith depended upon reason. Reason, on the other hand, operated on its own. It was incapable itself, however, of reaching the truths that revelation proposed for its understanding and was, in time, preceded by faith: to understand anything, you must first accept it. 'I believe that I may understand.'

Christian revelation is verified by reason in four ways: the miracles of Christ, the fulfilment of prophecies, the multitude of believers, the holiness and heroism of Christianity. The sources of faith are the Scriptures, tradition and over all the teaching power of the church.

God exists as the necessarily posited source of all being, all truth and all good. God, however, is ineffable. God's most obvious attribute, to Augustine, is simplicity. Augustine's formulation of his doctrine on the Trinity was a remarkable advance in the West and has endured. Here three points made clear by him are important: the concept of the nature of the Trinity as being before the persons; the attribution of all operations of the Trinity outside itself to the Trinity as one; and the explanation of the procession of the persons in terms of human psychology.

Creatures were made *ex nihilo* distinct from God, and by his will and all at once. While God may intervene at any time, 'new' creatures are but developments of 'seeds' (*rationes seminales*) existing from the one creation. Angels too were created by God, among them the demons, who dwelt in the atmosphere, could sense our thoughts and were skilled and keen to mislead us.

Man's *soul* is immaterial, and man is an unmixed composite of body and soul. Body is a good. Adam's soul was a separate creation. Other human souls would seem in some way to have been associated with generation, if the transmission of original sin was to be explained.

The centre of Augustine's theology and view of history is the *Incarnation*. Belief in the Incarnation was the final challenge at his conversion, the parting of the ways from the Neoplatonists and the unerring and sustaining universal way of salvation. History looked forward and backward to that event, incredible to the proud but believed by the whole world. Christ's predecessors—the Sibyl of Cumae, for example—were saved by Christ whose City of God existed from the beginning. Christ, equal to the Father, is God and is man with a real body and a real soul. In Christ the union is of two natures in one single person.

God's sovereignty over the human will, according to Augustine, is absolute. *Grace*, unmerited, precedes all good actions, including faith. Here Augustine's theories of illumination and grace are at one. Nevertheless, man's *will is free*. God's foreknowledge reconciles both elements in the problem. Adam was punished for his (original) sin by the deprivation of privileges, and his descendants, because of their moral union with him, share his guilt. There is reason to believe that Augustine taught that sensual pleasure in intercourse is the condition for the transmission of original sin to Adam's descendants. Damnation of some kind is the punishment for the original sin *alone* (as in the case of unbaptized infants). Predestination to salvation is absolutely gratuitous, but God, nevertheless, wills to give *all* men the power to save, and the freedom to damn themselves.

Augustine was insistent that 'outside the Church there is no salvation'. But God, Augustine insisted, nevertheless did employ his grace independently of the church. In the last analysis, Christ, who established the church, alone is our teacher. The church's holiness will not be perfect until heaven; here on earth she sanctifies through the sacraments. Her authority is supreme: 'I for my part,' Augustine once proclaimed, 'would not believe in the Gospel, if the authority of the Catholic Church did not bid me to do so'.[4]

Augustine taught that our end in life is happiness, that is, the enjoyment of God, the Supreme End. He as Truth illumines our minds, and we are moved to love him and our fellow men. Evil is not evil nor good good because God forbids one and commends the other: rather is it that he forbids evil because it is evil and commends good because it is good. Charity, or love, is behind every precept. In the afterlife the good will be resurrected and enjoy Heaven, the evil punished in Hell: Purgatory will exist until the Last Judgment.

INFLUENCE

Augustine shares from time to time with Virgil the title of 'Father of the West'—but Augustine's must surely be the greater claim. He was, of course, himself profoundly affected by Virgil. In the pages of Virgil's *Aeneid* he had learned of Love and Mission— of Dido and Aeneas. The struggle in the heart of Virgil was the struggle in the heart of Augustine: love appeared to be the only and all-conquering value. It was also self-indulgent and destructive. Duty must transcend it—obedience to God and the service of his

4 *Contra epistulam quam vocant Fundamenti*, 5.6.

purpose with mankind. Augustine shows all the passion of Dido and all the temptations to weakness of Aeneas. But he follows Aeneas, and consciously. *Mens immota manet, lacrimae volvuntur inanes*[5] ('His mind stays unmoved, tears roll down unavailing'). This was an intellectual struggle for Virgil. It was 'real' for the character Aeneas. It was real also for Augustine.

It is, I think, true to say that the young Augustine is more attractive than the old, that the *Confessions* is his most interesting book and that much of the tension in it disappears on his conversion. Like Aeneas's desertion of Dido and vision of Destiny, Augustine's abandonment of the flesh, and vision of the Neoplatonic-Christian Father marked the end of 'human nature's daily food' and heralded a long campaign, with its endless battles and controversies, to found a holy empire: it is a higher, nobler pursuit—but it may have less human appeal.

To the extent that Augustine followed Virgil and Aeneas in deserting love to found a new Rome, he fell back on the Roman Stoic organization for virtue and public service. Gone for the most part was the beckoning attraction of the flesh; gone too for the most part, Platonic mysticism. They never wholly went. From time to time in the later Augustine (as in the 'later' books of the *Aeneid*) emerge—*veteris vestigia flammae*,[6] 'the scars,' as C. Day Lewis renders it, 'of the old flame'.

At any rate, Augustine's contribution to the *tempora Christiana*, the Christian era, was paramount and enduring. Fulgentius of Ruspe, Isidore of Seville, Caesarius of Arles, Prosper of Aquitaine, Pope Gregory the Great all proclaim their debt to him. Charlemagne conceived his planned Renaissance not with reference to Augustus but to Augustine. In the early Middle Ages Augustine's teaching on predestination was the source of much theological controversy in which Gottschalk and Johannes Scottus Eriugena played important and rather unhappy roles. In the wider field of theology Augustine continued to dominate—'after the Apostles the master of the Churches'[7]—until the thirteenth century and the advent of Aquinas. The *City of God* especially was credited with the prescription of the mutual rights of State and Church—with perhaps little real justification.

In the world of asceticism, the influence of the *Regula Sancti Augustini* (attributed to Augustine and certainly inspired by his influence) grew apace. The foundation of the Canons Regular, Premonstratensians and Dominicans ensured the persistence of Augustine's ascetical ideals; while the abbey of the Canons of St Victor, founded at Paris in 1108 and made famous by its sons, Hugh, Richard and Adam, spread the influence of his spirit of humanism and mysticism.

In many ways Aquinas tended to supplant Augustine in the world of Christian philosophy and theology, if only because he had available to him in a rediscovered Aristotelianism a system that was more adaptable as a rational underpinning for developed Christian revelation than was the dominant Platonism of the era of Augustine. Moreover, Aquinas was much more systematic and acceptable to the Scholastic mode. In fact, of course, Aquinas, a Dominican disciple of Augustine, transmitted the received

5 *Aeneid* 4.449.   6 *Aeneid* 2.23.   7 D.C. Lambot, *Oeuvres théologiques et grammaticales de Godescalc d'Orbais*, Spicilegium sacrum Lovaniense, t. 20 (1945), 327.

inheritance of Christian teaching in the West—and this, as Aquinas makes clear on many an occasion, is mainly Augustinian. It is to be remembered, too, that, whatever his sympathy for Platonism had been in the beginning, Augustine had repudiated its basic tenets that conflicted with the Christian doctrine on the Incarnation and Resurrection. But the Franciscans, through Bonaventure and Duns Scotus and the Order of the Hermits of St Augustine, through Giles of Rome (d. 1316) and Gregory of Rimini (d. 1356), kept the distinctive Augustinian approach alive.

The Reformation marked, in a sense, the return of Augustine to the centre of the stage—especially in its revival of the controversy on predestination. The reformers tended to take the more extreme views of Augustine's interpretation of St Paul's teaching on the consequences of original sin: concupiscence, the powerlessness of man, salvation by grace and justification by faith. It should not be forgotten that Luther was an Augustinian monk whose religious name was Augustine and that he declared not that he had read Augustine but that he had swallowed him whole! In due course, the revival of interest in Augustine and the advent of printing led to the important editions of Augustine's works by Amerbach (Basel, 1508), Erasmus (Basel, 1527–29) and Johann van der Meulen (Antwerp, 1576–77); these editions mark the beginning of a renaissance in Augustinian studies which still endures.

The seventeenth century, especially in France, was the Augustinian century *par excellence*. Cardinal de Bérulle and his spiritual sons St Vincent de Paul, Condren, Olier of St Sulpice and St John Eudes spread the influence of Augustine's spiritual ideals. Unfortunately, the old Augustinian-Pelagian controversy broke out once again on the posthumous publication (Louvain, 1640) of Jansenius's *Augustinus*. The controversy had been gathering force from the time of Baius (1513–89) and the dispute of the Jesuit Molina (1536–1600) with the Dominicans. Now it broke forth with great virulence. The Jansenism of Port-Royal (a name intended, it is said, to remind one of Augustine's see of Hippo Regius), of St Cyran and the Great Arnauld had an immense influence that continued, one might say, until today.

Side by side with these more theological and religious developments, the apparent correspondence of the basic epistemological positions of Augustine and Descartes gave a strong impulse towards the revival of interest in Augustinian philosophical approaches (as seen, for, example, in Malebranche). In this way Augustine has been introduced, so to speak, to the modern age. But indeed one might go further: certain, more mystical, aspects of the work of Teilhard de Chardin suggest that the spirit of Augustine is alive and working powerfully. And some now blame him for the alleged puritanism of traditional Christian attitudes to sex, but we shall say something on this later.[8]

PERSONALITY

In the end, one wants to find out, if one can, the most important thing about Augustine—

8 Cf. 25 and especially 120–30ff. below.

his personality, the kind of man he was. There is no doubt that, for all his luck or circumstances, his impact on the world has been very great. Some would say that it was for good, some for evil. He was a sign to be contradicted. In short, both he and his teaching are complicated, arousing love and hate, or at least like and dislike, in almost everyone who knows them. A totally rounded, consistent picture of Augustine would be suspect.

Some authors see the elements of tension and inconsistency in his birthplace and his birth: Africa made him intense and extreme; his mother gave him goodness and sensibility, especially religious sensibility; his father made him unscrupulous and a bully. All of these elements were in him in one way or another at one time or another in his life. But the assignment of the source or nice calculation of measure can never be more than plausible.

He had other obvious qualities too—a love of ideas and on the whole an even greater and more sustained love of action. He was loyal, persistent, aggressive. He was also disloyal (and to his mother!), indecisive, without confidence. He was methodical and clear in purpose over all: in detail he could be sidetracked and become irrelevant. Were all these inconsistent qualities simply inherited, as some would think, from Monica and Patricius? We can never know.

We can, however, point to evidence of influences more discernible, even if not more fundamental. Augustine was singularly responsive to his environment and experiences. Apart from what may have come to him with his blood and in his home, there were other factors in his life that shaped his outlook and temperament.

The first of these was his intellectual—and religious—formation. This was made up of Latin schooling (as pupil and teacher), Manichean 'reason', Neoplatonic intellectual aspirations and the Bible. All of these marked him deeply and, one is tempted to say (bathetic as it may seem), equally.

Augustine was trained in Latin literature with a dominating, professionally rhetorical slant. This gave or developed in him his finally most obviously realized qualities: eclecticism in ideas and a somewhat detached, indeed, on occasion irresponsibly loyal, absoluteness in moral choice. It also gave him a technique: the technique of persuasion and orderly exposition. But there is more: it gave him the Roman love to serve and rule—which he describes with such sympathy in the fifth book of the *City of God*. God was substituted for Jupiter, Juno and Minerva.

Still, he had the nagging need to get to the bottom of things—to follow the Cicero of the *Hortensius* rather than the Cicero of the *Academica*. Why was there evil in the world? Why do we yield to our baser instincts? Whence do we come? Whither do we go? The Manicheans, while reverencing Christ and St Paul, promised a satisfying rational answer. But Augustine was disappointed by them. Nevertheless there remained with him forever, from this almost ten-year encounter, so overwhelming a conviction that he was utterly powerless before the principle of evil, that the idea of grace, unmerited, became virtually a necessity for him; and pessimism deeply marked his emotional outlook.

Yet his experience of Neoplatonism, of the doctrine of Plotinus and Porphyry, had the opposite effect: from them he got his countervailing optimism that all created nature is good and that evil is no more than the absence or privation of that good. It also enabled him to conceive of a spiritual Being who illumined our minds and arranged all things in his Providence for good. The three Neoplatonic hypostases, moreover, seemed to correspond to the Christian Trinity. Porphyry seemed even to suggest that his Supreme Being was the God of the Hebrews, that grace was given to men and that some Mediator (but Porphyry denied that it was Christ, because of his birth of a virgin and death on the cross), some Universal Way brought man back to God. Above all the reading of Plotinus seems to have stimulated a mystical, visionary flair in Augustine which remained with him till the end. For him the Plotinian return to the Father is inextricably bound up with the New Testament's return of the Prodigal. This spiritual discovery ultimately made possible for him the embracing of the Scriptures and Catholicism, and sustained him in a kind of mystical suspense throughout his life. It would be a mistake, however, to think that Augustine made a profound study or had a profound understanding of Neoplatonism: the lightheartedness with which he stressed the apparent correspondences between certain Neoplatonic and Christian doctrines suggests that he was more interested in discerning and using such possible correspondences than in penetrating them. His great forte was vision. This vision gave a strongly 'salvationist' character to his thought and action, and is the mainspring of his later life. It is to be noted that it involved some departure from an historical attitude. Here we see in Augustine the Aeneas of the later books of the *Aeneid*: the ever willing warrior committed to a goal and the endless battles that come between.

Finally, the Bible became for him literally the oracle of God, peremptory and final. It was his daily food which he shared with his flock. A very large part of his life as a bishop lay in expounding the Scriptures. All other sources of information wilted away before Augustine's consuming passion for God's word.

So much for his intellectual formation. He was formed, too, by the experiences of his life, of which the greatest, the vantage point from which he viewed his own life and the life of every man, was his conversion. This event was marked by such evident intervention of Providence in so many quite improbable ways, that Augustine was ready to see God's finger everywhere. Out of apparent evil had come so much good for him that he felt open to construe any event in a providential light. This gave him a distinctly unscientific attitude to some problems. It also reinforced a detachment from the historical truth of things which is discomfiting. It is to some degree part and parcel of his and his contemporaries' vivid and real belief in demons, dreams and miracles; but it is also an unquestioning acceptance in advance of God's providence, which could always 'intervene' to direct the established order of things. This at once allowed him to adopt positions that were either too extreme or improbable and seem on occasion to us a little irresponsible—notably in relation to grace. But he did this in much simpler things. He advanced, for example, without grounds the theory that the Academic philosophers were not sceptics but crypto-Platonists and then added: 'This theory I have sometimes thought probable. If it is false, I do not mind'.[9] But there are many other instances. In some ways Augustine indulged in make-believe.

Not so, however, in dealing with the Manicheans, Donatists and Pelagians. Here he showed a compensatingly excessive grasp of the practical measures that would ensure

9 *Against the Academics* 3.43.

success. Whatever his initial hesitations and reluctance, he finally used the civil force to bring Donatism to an end in Africa. Likewise with the Manicheans—a recent comment on Augustine's method of controversy with one of them, Felix, is that it was *fort choquante*. Similarly did this hound of heaven, this *procureur général* of the church, pursue the Pelagians. He even insisted too much with Jerome. At best, it is an unattractive trait; at worst it is righteous (perhaps too righteous) bullying. In fact, it was the product of excessive zeal for the best of ends.

Perhaps the quality most associated with Augustine in the popular mind is sensuality, sublimated in later life in the single-minded love of God:

> 'I came to Carthage where all around me roared the sizzle of shameful loves. I was not in love yet, but I was in love with the desire to love, and because of a deep want in myself I hated myself for not wanting enough. I looked around for something to love, in love with loving. I hated a life without trouble and entanglements. To love and to be loved was very sweet to me, especially if I could enjoy the body of my lover. And so I polluted the river of friendship with the dirt of concupiscence and clouded its brightness with the hell of my lust. I threw myself into love in which I wanted to be trapped. I was loved and secretly succeeded in binding myself with pleasure.[10]

Thus wrote the new bishop of his sixteenth or seventeenth year. As an older man he distinguished the city of God from the city of this world on the basis of the love of God and the love of self: 'And so two loves have made two cities—namely the earthly, love of self even to contempt of God; but the heavenly, love of God even to contempt of self'.[11] One of the best-known maxims of Augustine is the apparently very permissive one: *Dilige et quod vis fac.*[12] 'Love, then do what you will!'

The need to love is, undoubtedly, an important quality in Augustine. But it is an exaggeration to claim that the church's traditional attitude and teaching on sex and marriage is mainly traceable to Augustine's reaction from youthful sexual excesses to sublimated love of God.

A strong and professionally competent statement of the case against Augustine appeared in 1963 in an article by L. Janssens in the *Ephemerides Theologicae Lovanienses*,[13] which asserted that Augustine introduced a dualism into married life: his pessimistic attitude to sexual pleasure demanded that he should find justification for its use. This was found both in the need for procreation (*bonum prolis*) and precaution against a partner's adultery (*bonum fidei*). On the other hand, true conjugal love was a *purely spiritual thing* (*bonum sacramenti*), in regard to which sexual relations could have no positive signification whatever.

In fact, carnal desire was for him—the article says—an evil (*malum*) and a disease (*morbus*) and could only be an obstacle to the flowering of conjugal love. The more desire is repressed, the stronger is the *caritas coniugalis*. Hence Augustine, according to Janssens, wishes that all Christian couples could practise complete continence so as to be united not in the flesh but in *caritas*.

Janssens is careful to point out some of the sources of these ideas: Stoics, Neo-

10 *Confessions* 3.1.1.   11 *City of God* 14.28.   12 *Tract in Joh. Ep.*, *P.L.* 35.2033.   13 39. 4, 787–826.

Pythagoreans, Essenes and Gnostics. He is also careful to state that although Augustine was the principal agent in the transmission of these ideas into Christian theology, he was not the only Church Father responsible. There were also Justin Martyr, for example, Athenagoras, Clement of Alexandria, Origen, Ambrose and Jerome. All of these were determined that the Christian view of marriage would be no whit less ascetical than the Stoic or Neo-Pythagorean or what you will. He notes too that of the three great controversies that dominated Augustine's life—with the Donatists, the Manicheans and the Pelagians—the two latter provided him with a field only too favourable for the development of such pessimistic ideas.

It must be admitted that Augustine failed greatly to reduce[14] the age-old Western— perhaps simply human—inhibitions on the vital appetite of sex. His former Manichean beliefs, his Neoplatonic conversion and education in the classics, his personal turning away from the life of the senses to the life of the spirit and, perhaps above all, his stance on the Pelagian controversy, where his need to stress the insufficiency of nature led him to associate original sin with concupiscence—all made it too easy for him to transmit the attitudes of many predecessors. It is to these attitudes rather than to personal reaction to his earlier life *alone* that his role in the transmission of puritan sexual ideas is to be referred.

Augustine did have a loving nature and attracted faithful and loyal friends. He was emotional and responsive. But it is hard to escape the conclusion that his love from the beginning, however it manifested itself, was a consuming love of God: 'Our heart will not rest, until it rests in you'.[15] Here his love joins his mother's, with whom at Ostia before her death in AD 387 he shared the highest mystical experience (so far as we know) of his life. Here is the real key to Augustine. This love is the passion of his life. It explains his embarrassing absoluteness. It is an affair, primarily, of the heart and less of the intelligence.

> Too late I have loved you, beauty old and new! Too late I have loved you. Yet you were within me, while I was outside! There I was searching for you—without any beauty in myself I poured myself out upon the beautiful things you made! You were with me, but I was not with you. Those things kept me far away from you, which if they did not exist in you, would not exist at all. You called me, you shouted to me, you shattered my deafness! You flashed and shone upon and drove away my blindness! You exuded perfume and I drew in breath and smell for you! I taste and have hunger and thirst. You touched me and I burned for your peace.[16]

Augustine has said it himself: *Exarsi in pacem tuam*—he was 'on fire for God's peace'. Fire can be difficult to control.

An aspect of Augustine's passion was its obsessiveness. The enormous extent of his work conceals much circling around what is in the long run a narrow range of ideas. The intensity of his passion and vision sustained him by itself. One might expect that readers, having neither the vision nor the passion, might find in Augustine mere repetitiveness. And yet it is not quite so. For Augustine had an extraordinary power of both memory

14 But see 25ff., 120ff. below.   15 *Confessions* 1.1.1.   16 Ibid., 10.27.38.

and assimilation. The ever-recurring themes have ever-new settings and ever-new treatments. Augustine was undoubtedly an artist, call him poet or musician as you will. Artists have an obsessive quality, a tendency to essay the same thing over and over again in, ultimately, so clearly the same way that we can recognize a piece of Bach—or Gershwin—a painting by Gainsborough—or Kandinsky—almost in an instant. And yet there is always some development, some difference. Augustine might be said to be another Virgil—or another Aeneas (Virgil's *alter ego*); but he had to find expression for his epic intuition in some way that was appropriately contemporary and his own. If his *Confessions* is his *Odyssey*, his *City of God* is his *Iliad*—and they were both necessarily theological and in prose. Van der Meer in his *Augustine the Bishop*[17] has called him simply 'the greatest poet of Christian Antiquity, without ever having written any poetry worth mentioning.' It is a paradox that Augustine himself would particularly appreciate.

17 London and New York (1961).

PART I *Confessions* *

CONVERSION

*For Part I, cf. 17 above. The author's *The Young Augustine*: an Introduction to the *Confessions* of St Augustine (1954, 1964 [US], 1980) is still useful. For the possible connection of two other *Confessions* with that of Augustine see Appendices 1 and 2.

2

Implications of Augustine's Conversion

St Augustine has sometimes been described as the first 'modern' man, and sometimes as a bridge-maker (*pontifex*) between the world of antiquity and the Western world of to-day. The second statement, given the special and important position he achieved in the Christian Church in North Africa at the beginning of the fifth century, is of special interest for us. St Jerome called him the best-known bishop in the whole world; his extensive correspondence was read by high and low with avidity throughout the sphere of Latin influence; his sermons reached a far wider (and more appreciative) audience than his sometimes restless listeners in Hippo; but above all the fame of his conversion as described in his *Confessions*, and the great works that issued from his controversies with the Manicheans, Donatists and especially the Pelagians ensure that the Christian Church in the West, finding its way towards a theological and philosophical system, adequate to its actual dominating role in the Roman Empire, spoke henceforth often with the words of Augustine. To Jerome he was the dispenser of eternal salvation. To Joannes Scottus Eriugena in the ninth century he was one who sometimes disappointed, but who yet was to be revered.

Augustine was a complex, even an ambivalent man. One stream of mysticism in the West finds its Christian origin in him. My colleague André Mandouze spent his life studying the mysticism of Augustine, with ever new results.[1] Another colleague and friend, Paul Henry, wrote an evocative book, *La Vision d'Ostie*,[2] in which he expounded the ecstasy experienced, Augustine says, by his mother and himself at Ostia, just before she died.

This ecstasy was inspired by the *Enneads* of Plotinus, in particular that on Beauty.[3] The philosophy of Plotinus is essentially *immaterialistic*. His disciple, Porphyry, who for the most part transmitted Plotinus's teaching, summed this up succinctly in a phrase that was very well known to Augustine: *Omne corpus fugiendum*—'one should shun every kind of body'.[4] Augustine, who says that throughout all his life he had been unable to conceive of a spiritual, immaterial, deity until he read the Neoplatonists, became, one might say, infatuated by their teaching—for a period. Even when he later controverted them, and to the end of his life, he often spoke in a friendly way about them and used

1. 2 Cf. A. Mandouze, *Augustinus Magister*, 3 Paris (1954), 103ff; *Saint Augustin*, Paris (1968). 2 Paris, (1938). 3 I.6. 4 Cf. *City of God* 10.29 passim.

their speculations where he felt that he could. Immaterialism had appeal for him right to the end.

But there was another side to Augustine—a strong loyalty to, and indeed preoccupation with, the material body. For him the body was exalted by Christ in the Incarnation. It would be glorified in heaven. In attempting to account for a material or sensible body in an immaterial heaven, he distinguished between sensibles that were corruptible (our bodies on earth) and sensibles that were not corruptible (our bodies in heaven).[5] Augustine to a Platonist would have seemed to be hard pressed.

Here I shall say something of the immaterial and material, of the spiritual and corporeal, in Augustine's thought. I should speak rather of the spiral (*spiritalis*), that is of the 'spirit' or 'mind' or '*nous*', rather than of the spiritual, which in the ordinary way has connotations affecting piety, as when people speak of spiritual books. But I do not wish to be too technical. In practice I shall be speaking of Augustine's initial enthusiasm for the immaterialist philosophy of the Neoplatonists and his later fundamental rejection of it. This approach to Augustine is intended to show his cast of mind as it revealed itself in different phases.

Just one hundred years ago, in 1888, Gaston Boissier of the Collège de France and Adolf von Harnack, a great Protestant theologian, quite independently came to the conclusion that Augustine, in writing his *Confessions* after 396, misrepresents his conversion in 386 which, according to them, judging the matter by his writings at the time of his conversion, was to Neoplatonism, not to Catholicism. Le Gourdon in 1900 went further and declared that Augustine was not entirely converted to Catholicism until 400, four years after he had become a bishop.[6]

One needs to explain that this was not so improbable then as it might appear now. Synesius of Cyrene, for example, who was nearly a contemporary of Augustine and lived in North Africa too, was elected bishop of Ptolemais by his countrymen for material services rendered, but on the express condition laid down by him that he should continue to hold views, influenced by Neoplatonism, on the pre-existence of the soul, the eternity of the world, and the resurrection of the body—which he took to be merely allegorical. This 'Platonist in the mitre' may not have been baptized when he was elected, and in any case remained in his heart more a Neoplatonist than an orthodox Christian. What Synesius did was not, of course, necessarily done by Augustine, even if the latter was not far removed in time and region. But neither should we automatically assume that to Augustine none of this was a possibility.

One of the most thorough examinations of Augustine's Neoplatonism was made by Prosper Alfaric in his *L'évolution intellectuelle de saint Augustin* I (1918). Here is the gist of his conclusion: 'Doubtless (Augustine) accepted the Christian tradition, but considered it only as a popular adaptation of Platonic wisdom. it wasn't until much later that he came to submit reason to faith'.[7] There have been, however, many books written since

5 *Retractationes* 1.4, 3.   6 Cf. my *Against the Academics*, Ancient Christian Writers 12 (1950), 19ff and notes 159ff. Cf. 71 below.   7 399; cf. viii, 515, 527.

Boissier, von Harnack and Alfaric arguing, on the whole successfully, that Augustine was sincerely converted to Christianity, even if he also hoped for a time that Neoplatonism would afford rational explanations for his Christian beliefs. It is appreciated, nevertheless, that the measure of Augustine's enthusiasm for the immaterialistic doctrine of the Neoplatonists before his conversion was very great.

The sermons of St Ambrose had already disabused Augustine of the whole campaign of the Manicheans against the Old Testament, when he insisted that 'the letter kills, but the spirit gives life'. The Old Testament, with all its scandalous tales of the Patriarchs and its, from time to time, patent incredibility if interpreted strictly according to the letter, became acceptable, if it were taken allegorically. This raised a grievous burden from off Augustine's mind in relation to the religion inculcated by his mother. And the revelation of Neoplatonism to him, whether in Christian or pagan circles in Milan, allowed him for the first time in his life to conceive of a spiritual deity, and seemed to promise a great deal more: the three Neoplatonic hypostases—the Father, Word and Soul—had been plausibly paralleled with the Christian Trinity. Neoplatonism went to his head:

> But lo! when certain books full to the brim, as Celsinus says, had wafted to us good things of Arabia, when they had let a very few drops of most precious unguent fall upon a meagre flame, they stirred up an incredible conflagration—incredible, incredible—beyond even what I would believe of myself. What honour, what human pomp, what desire for empty fame, what consolations or attractions of this mortal life could move me then?[8]

These words were written not long after his reading of the Neoplatonist books, and after he had renounced both a promising marriage and the prospect of the governorship of a province at least, for which he had so long driven himself so feverishly.

Later in the *Confessions* he censured in a frigid phrase his excess of enthusiasm for Neoplatonism at this time: 'I prated as if I were well skilled, but if I had not sought Your Way in Christ, our Saviour, I would have been killed, not skilled.'[9]

So much for his immaterialism. But to continue for a moment with the story of his conversion: in the meantime he wrestled with continence until, in a dramatic scene in a garden in Milan in the summer of 386, he emerged 'victorious' and converted. Although his description of the carnal sins of his life up to then might appear to suggest that he had been a great *roué*—when we have made allowance for strong rhetoric in the service of a bishop anxious to stress that, no matter how great our sins, Grace can conquer them, we have little to conclude more than that he suffered the normal storms of adolescence; was, by comparison with his peers, a serious and ambitious young man; and had entered into a stable relationship of then socially acceptable concubinage for over a dozen years with a woman by whom he had a son of whom he was proud. As his mother had not favoured marriage earlier, lest it should hamper his career, so she it was who now got him to dismiss his mistress, when she thought that the time for an improving marriage had come. The separation from his mistress was very painful for

8 *Against the Academics* 2.5. 9 7.20, 26.

both Augustine as well as for her. And he does not conceal from us in the *Soliloquies* how the victory of Continence did not remove from him all interest in women.

Augustine reports that his conversion was worked, so to speak, as had Antony's, by a text of Scripture. Antony chanced to hear the text 'Go, sell what you have, and give to the poor, and come follow Me,' and had on the spot followed the injunction. For Augustine the text was 'Not in revelling and drunkenness, not in debauchery and licentiousness, not in quarrelling and jealousy—but put on the Lord Jesus Christ, and make no provision for the flesh, to gratify its desires'.[10] The corresponding positive injunctions here are: abandon the flesh and put on Christ. Of these the one pertaining to the flesh—because of the earlier emphasis on his difficulties with the flesh—has tended to distract attention from the more crucial putting on of Christ. It was the putting on of Christ that enabled him through the Grace then afforded to put off the flesh. But the putting on of Christ had also a special significance for him.

In putting on—in accepting—Christ, Augustine was in one sense doing no more than following the logic, indeed yearning, of his whole life since, as he says, he drank in the name of Christ with his mother's milk. Of any new system of philosophy or religion that attracted his support, he asked if Christ's name was in it? Thus the enthusiasm aroused in him at nineteen years of age by Cicero's *Hortensius*, an exhortation to philosophy, where Christ was not mentioned, yielded immediately to the professedly rational system of the Manicheans, where Christ seemed to be held in honour. When he abandoned the Manicheans finally in his early thirties, he was attracted by the sceptics of the New Academy, but he did not commit himself to them either, because their philosophy was without the saving name of Christ: and so he decided 'to continue as a catechumen in the Catholic Church, commended to me by my parents' (in effect, his mother). When he had listened to the sermons of Ambrose a little later, he says that he drank in more and more of the faith of Christ, so firmly fixed within his heart. When he came soon to read the Neoplatonists he was astonished how nearly their teaching approached that of the Prologue to the Gospel of St John. But he complained again that neither the birth of Christ—who claimed to be the Mediator between God and man—nor his death was to be found there. And in *Against the Academics*, written between his conversion and baptism, he speaks of his conversion as no more than like looking back from the end of a journey, as it were, to that religion which is implanted in us in our childhood days and bound up in the marrow of our bones: 'she was drawing me unknowing to herself.[11] The conclusion of A.D. Nock—no mean scholar in this matter —is that Augustine's conversion rests in the last resort on the permanence of an early impression and of the religious atmosphere with which his mother had invested his childhood.[12] This, given the evidence, is a wholly tenable—and even perhaps sufficient —conclusion.

Here I cannot but advert to the inevitable question of the influence of his mother on him. In the *Happy Life*, written just after his conversion, he attributes everything he is to her: *cuius meriti credo esse omne, quod vivo*.[13] Passing remarks here have already hinted at the enveloping persistence of her purpose of converting him. There is much more

10 *Rom.* 13.14; cf. *Confessions* 8.12, 29.   11 2.5.   12 *Conversion*, 1933, 266.   13 6.

that could be said on this. But what is its significance? Should we follow the Freudian Charles Kligerman[14] in holding that Monica transferred her erotic needs from an incompatible husband to her son, an incestuous affection translated into the frustrating demand on his divided loyalties, the end result of his conversion being the experience of identification with his mother and a passive feminine attitude to the father displaced by God? Or should we follow another Freudian, James Dittes, in concluding that Augustine's thought is not only monistic, but also 'mom-istic'? According to him, Augustine's dependence on his mother is to be described in terms of oral preoccupation, supineness ('a cowering mama's boy'), narcissism, self-abasement; and the hint of homosexuality. 'After years of the most vigorous assertion of his independence, Augustine submitted. He surrendered to his mother, and to her church and to her wishes. He abandoned, in short, the effort to be a father. Instead, he became an obedient son.'[15] This is psychology having its way, paying insufficient attention to the controls of the historical texts. Eric Dodds's assessment is at least a little more restrained in its terms: Augustine elected for misogyny and asceticism, the permanent effects of his abnormal love for his mother.[16] I for my part, without accepting that his love for his mother was as outlined in these opinions, cannot but regard her influence on him as great and inevitably restrictive, but not misogynic.[17] It is impossible to deny that his attitude to religion was, as he says over and over again, deeply influenced up to his conversion by the religion she inculcated in him; and the indications are that after her death it continued to be so.

To return to the significance of Augustine's putting on Christ as enjoined by the verses of St Paul—in another way Augustine was creating a problem for himself with the Neoplatonists, the great immaterialists, and with Porphyry in particular, who rejected Christ as the Mediator and Way of Universal Salvation, and insisted that he was no more than a man of excellent wisdom. But Augustine in the *Dialogues*, written within a few months of his conversion, explicitly asserts that Christ is God and Christ is man. He may well not have understood—given the state of the theology of the Incarnation at the time—the relations of the Father and the Word; but he clearly accepted that the God-Word was flesh. And so he can speak of his hopes that what Revelation teaches, Neoplatonism will explain: 'I, therefore, am resolved in nothing whatever to depart from the authority of Christ—for I do not find a stronger. But as to that which is sought out by subtle reasoning—for I am so disposed as to be impatient in my desire to apprehend truth not only by faith but also by understanding—I feel sure at the moment that I shall find it with the (Neo)platonists, nor will it be at variance with our sacred mysteries.[18] Augustine supposes that there was now at last a synthesis between reason and faith, that is between Neoplatonism and Christianity, the one for the few, the other for all. Even as late as 390, in *True Religion*, he says that 'with the change of a few words and statements'[19] the Neoplatonists would have become Christians.

14 *American Psychoanalytic Association Journal* 5 (1957), 469–84. 15 *Journal for the Scientific Study of Religion* 5 (1965), 130–40. 16 *The Hibbert Journal*, 26, 472. 17 See 109ff. below. 18 *Against the Academics* 3.43. 19 7.

But Porphyry, the reigning Neoplatonist of Augustine's time, *was* a problem. Augustine had read an attack of his on the notion of Christ's being God, in which he scoffed at the birth of God from a virgin and the crucifixion of God on a Cross. Augustine attributed Porphyry's blindness, as he saw it, to his pride and worship of demons. *Hence his putting on of Christ and belief in the Incarnation was a conscious rejection of Porphyry and his slogan 'omne corpus fugiendum', 'one should shun every kind of body'.* We know that Porphyry intended his slogan for the need of purification indeed in this life, but also and principally in reference—doubtless with the Christians in mind—to the notion of a deity or a soul in heaven being joined to a body. Augustine's *Retractationes* indicate that before his baptism he accepted the resurrection of bodies in heaven, if in a glorified state: they would *not* be corruptible and they would be without concupiscence. In the *Greatness of the Soul*, written one year after his baptism, he writes: 'we shall see also such great transformations and changes of our corporeal nature that we shall hold the very resurrection itself of the flesh, which partly is reluctantly, and partly altogether not believed, with such certainty, that it cannot be more certain to us than that when the sun sets, it will rise again. In this case death, the ultimate flight and escape from the body (*omne corpus fugiendum*), is desired as the greatest boon.'[20]

Augustine, then, from the time of his conversion deliberately supported against, or rather alongside of the immaterialism of the Neoplatonists, what would have seemed to the Neoplatonists materialist claims for the body. One wonders why? Was it, for example, his background in materialist Manicheanism throughout his impressionable twenties? Some accused him in later life of never having ceased to be a Manichean. Or was his mother's religion, the environment of the whole of his first thirty years, in which he could not even conceive the idea of anything that was not material, responsible? Or was there something within his own personality that elevated the flesh?

To illustrate how he departed not only from Porphyry in choosing to espouse the body in a particular way, but also has been seen to differ even from Ambrose, his spiritual father, as he calls him—who was also an important theologian writing in Latin—we may anticipate a little of the chapter following. The espousal of the body by Augustine as against Ambrose has had the most serious consequences for theology as it affects body—in sexuality, in the nature of the resurrection of bodies and in other important matters. For the ninth-century Eriugena and Ambrose (and others of course) man was created and placed in an Eden that was wholly spiritual. The sexual differentiation between male and female was an anticipation of the consequence of sin as foreseen and so provided for by God. Man's body in Paradise was wholly spiritual. Augustine on the other hand held very firmly that Paradise was corporeal as well as spiritual, that man's body was animal, and that sexual differentiation was intended by God from the beginning and was not a consequence of sin. Even more, Adam and Eve could exercise their sexuality and experience *libido*, but a *libido* that did not escape obedience to reason: *libido non est bonus et rectus usus libidinis—the good and correct use of libido* is not *libido*. Sexuality, Augustine contended contrary to what some of the Fathers had suggested, had nothing to do with the first sin of man: that was a sin of disobedience. But the

20 75.

condign punishment for this in man, as he now is, is the escape of *libido* from obedience to man's will.[21]

Eriugena, anxious to excuse Augustine from holding such extraordinary (in his view) propositions, wants to believe that in fact in his *True Religion*, completed four years after his conversion, Augustine does hold that Eden was wholly spirital—thus agreeing with Ambrose. He is oppressed, however, by the overwhelming evidence of Augustine's views having been otherwise and supposes, as often, that Augustine, while holding other views himself, was but adapting his teaching to an audience capable of carnal thinking only. And so also for the animality of man in Eden. 'I do not cease to be amazed,' writes Eriugena, 'why he calls that body animal.'[22]

In relation to Augustine's belief in the resurrection of human bodies in a glorified condition, Eriugena is staggered: 'When I read of such things in the books of the Holy Fathers (he is careful to spare Augustine's blushes) I stagger, so to speak, amazed and horror struck.'[23] These Fathers (including Augustine), he says, by the power of contemplation have risen above the whole sensible world themselves. They must have been considering only carnal men who, if they were to be told that there was to be no body in heaven, could conclude only that there would be nothing. So it was, Eriugena thinks, that such great men taught that earthly bodies would be transformed into heavenly and 'spiritual' bodies. Ambrose's teaching, however, was that the change was not from an earthly into a heavenly body, but *a complete passing into* pure spirit: man's body, soul and mind will, according to Eriugena's understanding of Ambrose, be one spirit, one Mind.[24]

Augustine's teaching that Christ's resurrected, immortal body was 'subject' to spatial limitations, as it had been on earth, also caused Eriugena great unease. Once again he can only suppose that Augustine is writing in a manner suited to the limited intelligence of his audience than that 'this most skilful enquirer into all things human and divine should have been in disagreement with Ambrose and Gregory.'[25]

This topic of Augustine's inclusion of the corporeal (even if incorruptible and not subject to concupiscence) body in situations where Ambrose and Greeks such as Origen totally eschew any intrusion of the corporeal—as surveyed by Eriugena, who is more than just sympathetic to Augustine—will be pursued presently somewhat further. One should discount absolutely the excuse resorted to by Eriugena that Augustine thought otherwise than as he spoke or wrote. What he wrote, he wrote—and did so in very many books intended for and read by the intelligent Christians of his day. But enough has been said to illustrate Augustine's departure, not only from such as the Greek Origen, to whom he is indebted in *Genesis Understood Literally*, but significantly from Ambrose. In that departure Augustine not only blocked off Neoplatonism from being a dominant influence in the West, but also put an emphasis on the human body which some consider to have had both fortunate and unfortunate consequences. It is only fair to add that on one occasion in *Genesis Understood Literally* Augustine does declare: 'whether [the soul] has some kind of body when it goes out from this body, let him show who can; for my part I do not think so'[26]—*ego autem non puto*. But this is quite exceptional for him. Still

---

21 Cf. 109ff. below.   **22** *Periphyseon* 805B.   **23** Op. cit., 986B.   **24** Ibid. 987B.   **25** Ibid., 992A.
26 12.32, 60.

one might remark that these words were written towards the end of a *non-controversial* book, in which he was committed, for a final time, to employ reason as far as was possible in the understanding of *Genesis*.

There is a connected matter on which Augustine chooses to follow earlier, indeed pagan, emphases on the physical rather than recent Christian refinements, that is in the use of the term *amor*—love. In classical Latin *amor* was used both in a higher sense (for example, in philosophy) and equally in a lower (in comedy). The word *diligo* was used of love with the connotation of esteem or regard. In the Vulgate, however, *amo* is comparatively rarely used, while *diligo* and the noun *caritas* are very frequently employed: this is presumed to be because of the low associations of the term *amor*. Augustine is fully aware of this distinction. The matter arises for discussion particularly in connection with the text in St John's Gospel (21.15f.) where Christ asks Peter if he *loves* him. Twice Christ used the term *diligo*. Peter replies twice using the term *amo*. On the third occasion Christ changes from the term *diligo* to *amo*, while Peter of course continues to use *amo*. Ambrose expressed surprise that Christ, speaking of love, should on the third occasion, as a climax, have resort to the term *amo*. He must conclude that the term *amo* is in *this instance* more perfect than *diligo*, as indicating that Peter loved Christ not only with his soul but with the ardour of his body—but this is a view he did not regard as normal.[27]

Augustine, going against Ambrose's general view and, it would seem, the majority of Christians of his time, refuses to allow any distinction between *amo* and *diligo*: *amo* is not, in his view, reserved to body, much less was it restricted—on that account—to a bad kind of love. *Amor* and *dilectio* are one and the same.[28] Augustine *exalts* bodily love.

Love, mental *and* physical, is indeed the great motivation in Augustine's life. He is a man of intellect, it is true, but he is even more a man of will, a man of love. The poet in him wrought prose, rhetorical indeed, but instinct with the incantation of poetry:

> I was not yet in love and I loved to love. With a hidden want I hated myself for not wanting enough. I looked around for something to love, loving to love.[29]

Or again (in Pusey's old-fashioned translation):

> Too late loved I Thee, O Thou Beauty of ancient days, yet ever new! Too late I loved Thee! And behold, Thou wert within, and I abroad, and there I searched for Thee. Thou calledst and shoutedst, and burstest my deafness. Thou flashedst, shonest, and scatteredst my blindness. Thou breathedst odours, and I drew in breath and pant for Thee. I tasted, and hunger and thirst. Thou touchedst me, and I burned for Thy peace.'[30]

How physical that famous passage is; how full of the five senses!

In the *Confessions* the soul (an immaterial thing) is portrayed as having a head, eyes, a back, thighs and a belly; the heart has a mouth and ears, and suffers the toils of labour.[31]

---

27 Cf. *Bibliothèque Augustinienne* (= *B.A.*), Oeuvres de saint Augustin, Desclée de Brouwer, Paris, vol. 35, 530. 28 Cf. *In Joan tract* 123.5: *unum atque idem esse amorem et dilectionem.* 29 *Confessions*, 3.1. 30 Op. cit., 10.38.3. 31 *B.A.* 13, 1962, 227f.

And it is our heart, not our mind, that in a famous phrase is restless until it rests in God. Of course this is only metaphoric, but it reveals a cast of mind.

Nevertheless, in *spite of his espousal* of the material body Augustine is *ambivalent about love and about the body* which gives it physical expression. His attitude reminds one of Virgil, who, according to the *Confessions*, made a very deep impression on him as a child, and whom he professionally interpreted right up to the time of his conversion. Virgil appears to have been by far the major literary influence upon him.

Virgil[32] was drawn inescapably to the theme of love: the *Aeneid* is indeed the epic of Rome, but it is most remembered (as Augustine himself remembered it) for the story of the fatally love-sick Dido. The *Georgics* celebrate fecundity and have a remarkable passage in the third book on the destructiveness of love as it affects animals, who are expressly depicted as having the same experience (of love) as man. It ends with the haunting and tragic story of Orpheus, who brought destruction on Eurydice and himself through the madness of love. The *Eclogues* sing of many loves and end with:

'*Omnia vincit Amor: et nos cedamus Amori.*'[33]

—'Love conquers all: let us too yield to love.'

But Virgil did not yield to Love. He had inherited through Lucretius from Greek literature a scarifying account of love, which he passed on most powerfully. Witness Dido herself: for her, love is represented by Virgil as an enemy, a wound, a plague, a disease, an evil, a poison; it is painful, sad, unhappy, anxious, hopeless, fearful, weakening; it is cruel, savage, deceitful, hard, intolerable, shameful; it is a slavery, it is blind, it is incurable, it is invincible. And so the list goes on. It was better to follow Lucretius's advice and keep away from all but the casual exercise of love (which Lucretius, patently, had not done). Philosophy and the cult of marriage (in which the mother played an important *family* role) were competing, and for the most part successful, rivals of love in the Graeco-Roman world. Virgil had his experiences, his *Lives* tell us, and does not conceal his fascination with the theme of love; but he lived his life, not as did his near contemporary Catullus, amidst the hazards of romantic love at Rome, but in a circle of *poets* and *philosophers* at Naples.

So too Augustine loved the body, yet still was ready to consign it to eternal punishment. He exaggerated the carnal excesses of his life up to the time of his conversion, although he was undoubtedly a sensual man. His attachment to the body was reinforced but redirected by his conscious acceptance of belief, that in Christ God had taken into union with Himself a human body—such as that which Augustine had himself. As Christ's, so *his* body would be resurrected and become immortal: 'take away death, and my own flesh shall be one dear friend throughout eternity.'[34]

But Augustine, as Virgil, also treated love as destructive. When, as a very mature bishop, he came to explain why Adam yielded to the temptation represented by the proffering of the apple to him by Eve, he explains that Adam was fully aware that in tasting the apple he would commit the greatest possible sin, the direct disobedience of

32 Cf. the author's *Studies in Augustine and Eriugena*, ed. by T. Halton (1992), 59–117. 33 10, 69. 34 *Sermon* 155.15.

an express injunction of the Almighty. Yet he took the apple through too much attachment to Eve: 'Adam did not wish to sadden her. He was afraid that without his comfort, and estranged from his mind, she would pine away and even die.'[35] Orpheus and Adam, unlike Aeneas, listened to the instinct to *love*, rather than the *dread command* to obey. The result for Adam and all of us, according to Augustine, was a Fall into incalculable misery.

Augustine insists that the unity of the human race could have been achieved in a merely 'friendly' union of Adam and Eve, but this unity was the better achieved and the more intimately because of 'the lying together of Adam and Eve and the mingling of their flesh.[36] As unity between Adam and ourselves was so welded by God in such intimacy, so the sin, original sin, Augustine says, is transmitted to us in effect by the carnal concupiscence that attends our conception. Concupiscence itself is, however, a sin only after a manner of speaking (*modo quodam loquendi*).[37] Yet through original sin mankind as a whole has been condemned, destined to perdition.[38]

While Augustine sees in Christ's Redemption of the human race great opportunity for some even to improve upon man's state before the Fall (hence it could be called a *felix culpa*, a fortunate fault), yet he conveys the chilling message that the majority of men will be damned. Augustine was the first Father to have clearly indicated the character of guilt inherent in the sin that has passed from Adam to all mankind. He also clearly related its transmission to the body. If the saved will be possessed of their bodies, glorified, that is incorruptible and without concupiscence, in heaven, so the majority of men will possess their bodies to be physically tormented in hell. He reports that some believe that the fire in question affects only the soul, while others believe that it affects the body too. For his part he prefers to believe that the fire is intended expressly to affect the body only, while it is implied that pain is suffered by the soul also. He goes to much trouble to 'show' how it is not impossible for a material body to be subjected to fire for all eternity and never be destroyed.[39] Augustine chose the age-old pagan path trodden also by Virgil:

> Hell's river of fire. . . . Within can be heard the sounds of groaning and brutal lashing.[40]

Virgil was using what for him was probably no more than a colourful and, for literary purposes, useful mythology. But for Augustine and his successors hell was no mere mythology, no just useful allegory, no 'milk' to nourish only the weak. He chose this emphasis on the body and he especially has been followed in the West. Once again Eriugena follows another tradition which sees in the damnation of any created humans, never mind the majority, an unacceptable failure of the Incarnation and Redemption. For Eriugena all human nature returns, good and evil, equally to God; the good and the evil will, however, have differing phantasies, of felicity on the one hand and of sorrow on the other. Not even Eriugena fully escapes the Styx.

---

35 *Genesis Understood Literally* 11.42, 60. See 128ff. below.   36 *The Good of Marriage* 1.1. See 124ff. below.   37 Cf. *Augustinus Magister* 1954, 3, 252f.   38 *City of God* 21.12. 39 *City of God* 21.2.   40 *Aeneid* 6.550f.

Two tendencies were opposed within Augustine. The philosophic-ascetic drive which led him when in doubt to seek in an immaterialist philosophy the answer to many fundamental questions, and which led him also to pursue asceticism in relation to things of the body: the use of concupiscence even within marriage should be moderate or, better, restrained altogether; for himself he pursued a chaste celibacy.

On the other hand in his bitter controversies with the Donatists and Pelagians Augustine manifested a very pragmatic, non-philosophic and non-ascetic spirit. In the case of the Donatists he championed the cause of those who *did not claim to be purists*, and he even used force, if only in the end, to overcome these opponents. Against the Pelagians he championed the cause of those who relied wholly on God's Grace, accepting that they could merit nothing of themselves. The exercise of virtue did not attract that Grace; the neglect of virtue did not repel it. Peter Brown in his book *Augustine of Hippo*, speaks of Augustines's writings against the Donatists and Pelagians as a significant landmark in the process by which the Church had come to embrace, and to tolerate, the whole lay society of the Roman world, with its depressing resilience of its pagan habits.[41]

In the pursuit of this practical aim Augustine was active and resourceful as the leading bishop in North Africa. From being one who had looked askance at miracles, he became promoter of the miracles wrought by the relics of the Protomartyr, St Stephen. He subscribed to belief in dreams, visions and especially demons as did so many of his contemporaries. He may have accommodated his real beliefs to the weak understanding of an audience; he may have used figures of speech that enabled him to say even the opposite of what he meant; he may well have had such a lively belief in Providence (and Grace) that he felt assured that God would have His way, no matter what the preacher might say or leave unsaid. But all of these approaches, understandable perhaps in relation to being pragmatic in those times, hardly commend him as primarily an intellectual. Here we see Augustine the extreme pragmatist and 'materialist'.

It would be surprising if at the end of his life this intelligent, sensitive, alert, eager and loving man did not reflect upon the truth or falsity of some of what he had written. In a late review of his life's works and writings, the *Retractationes*, he was troubled that in church he had not been quick to *listen*, and slow to *speak*. He was troubled too, in view of the huge bulk of what he had written, by the words of Scripture which declared that it was impossible not to sin in the use of many words: he had no doubt that in his works there was much that was not necessary or perhaps even false. In the last ten days of his life he insisted on being alone for the most part so that he might read over and over again the penitential Psalms, crying all the while from the depth of his heart.

This account does not necessarily suggest that Augustine regretted what he had taught. He had been undoubtedly intelligent, loving and sincere. But the materialist religion of his childhood (which did not make it possible for him for so long to conceive of an immaterialist being), Manicheism (which was wholly materialistic), and the bitter controversies in which he too willingly engaged (in which he appeared to tolerate imperfection) led him to a materialistic approach in certain areas of his teaching. Because of his clear dominance at a crucial time, this materialist approach—rather than the more allegorical of Ambrose, for example—has had the major influence in the Christian West. The church did refuse to follow the most chilling of his formulations on Predestination. But Augustine's election for the material over allegory and symbol, in many matters pertaining to the body, met with little opposition.

To finish on a point on which our generation is particularly curious—why, if Augustine so honoured the body in accepting the union of a body in the Incarnation and the glorification of a body in the Resurrection, did he not take a more lenient attitude to sexuality? Was it not he especially who, at the least, transmitted to us the negative attitude to sexuality, which has been such a problem in the West?

Yes, it was he, principally, who because of his time and position transmitted much of this: for that attitude did already exist in Christians, and pre-Christian groups alike and, indeed, may respond to something deep in our nature. He did this eagerly. His own asceticism, affected, no doubt, by reaction to his past as described in his *Confessions*, made this transmission too easy. On the other hand his glorification of the body, as in the Incarnation of Christ and our own Resurrection in no way enlightened or helped him in handling the problems of sexuality. His teaching here was that in Eden the exercise of sexuality was under control and sinless; while in heaven there would be sexual organs but no problems of sexuality. Neither of these situations, nor the life of Christ (a virgin, born without sin) gave guidance in the problems of sexuality. But his preoccupation with the body and ambivalence in its regard allowed him to fix on the concupiscence of sexuality in conception the transmission of the guilt of original sin. This in the end was his contribution.

It is necessary to emphasise how different the views of important Greek Fathers were from those of Augustine on the question of the non-survival or survival of *bodies* in the resurrection. Even in the West Augustine's own spiritual guide, so to speak, St Ambrose, has this to say on the subject: 'Death has no interest for us—for it is the separation of soul and body: the soul is freed, the body is dissolved. What is freed, rejoices: what is dissolved into its earth, feels nothing. What feels nothing, has no interest for us.'[42] On the other hand Augustine insists: 'my own flesh shall be my dear friend throughout eternity.'[43] While the flesh in question for Augustine is 'glorified', the body for Ambrose, dissolved and feeling nothing, has no interest for him. Augustine's rejection of Porphyry's 'one should shun every kind of body' (in the afterlife), and embracing of the union of Divinity with body in Christ's birth and Resurrection, had incalculable significance—given Augustine's dominating position—in the Western church.

The following chapter is intended to illustrate an alternative view of the afterlife held by some Christians in the West, but especially in the East. It was almost completely overwhelmed by the view of Augustine.

42 *The Good of Death*, 31.   43 *Sermon* 155.15.

3

Contrasting Approaches to Neoplatonic Immaterialism and Materialism in Augustine and Eriugena

I have elsewhere[1] drawn a contrast between Augustine and Joannes Scottus Eriugena[2] in their fundamentally different approaches to the interpretation of an important text from Genesis: *et divisit deus lucem a tenebris*[3]: For Augustine this signifies, Eriugena says, either the difference between the perfection of form on the one hand and the confusion of 'informity' on the other; 'or the separation of the faithful from the fallen angels'. Eriugena here interprets Augustine as understanding that the 'reasons' or causes of things are eternal in God and in being created, from being light, become darkness. Eriugena for himself, however, takes so to speak, a diametrically opposite view of the matter. For him following, he says, Dionysius, 'darkness' signifies the incomprehensibility of the eternal reasons in God as well as God himself; and light signifies the *declaratio,* manifestation or 'theophany' of these reasons in the effects that we see. This difference between Eriugena and Augustine, signalled by Eriugena himself, is fundamental. There is a profound and perhaps revealing difference between looking at darkness as a symbol of something transcendingly superior to light (Eriugena's approach) and on the other hand greatly inferior to it (Augustine's).

This kind of fundamental difference of approach is, I venture to suggest, also to be discerned in Eriugena's handling of the question of predestination. His over-riding view of the problem is, again, God-orientated—there can be no predestination: God's simplicity precludes it. But he does address himself to Augustine's opinions, and strains argument to discover a few texts in which Augustine appears to teach that there is only one predestination, to salvation, and to interpret the *de facto* overwhelming number of Augustine's declarations on the subject (to the effect that there was predestination to salvation and damnation) through the employment of the figure of speech known as antiphrasis or *a contrario:* Augustine, he suggests rather desperately, actually means the opposite of what he says.

Repeatedly Eriugena gives this kind of unsatisfying explanation for texts of Augustine that he considers unworthy of his 'Father'. A singular and important instance of this Eriugenian difficulty arises, as we shall see presently, with the question of Augustine's teaching on the resurrection of bodies. This is a test-case of the real allegiance of each

---

1 'Magnorum Virorum quendam Consensum Machinari', *Eriugena: Studien zu seinen Quellen*, ed. W. Beierwaltes (1980).   2 Cf. *Periphyseon* 691A–693C.   3 1.4.

of them to purer Neoplatonic doctrine, and a possible reason for the actual general rejection of Eriugena in the West.

There is no doubt that at or shortly before his conversion in the summer of 386, Augustine was infatuated with Neoplatonism, particularly with the Plotinian description of the elevation of the soul to the One. Pierre Courcelle[4] has little difficulty in descrying three or four passages in Augustine's *Confessions* where, according to him, Augustine attempts, vainly, Plotinian ecstasy. Augustine was undoubtedly single-minded and not easily inhibited in his ambition to achieve whatever he thought desirable —although to attribute to him attempts to achieve ecstasy may savour of some exaggeration. But his contemporary account of the effect on him of reading certain 'Platonist' books leaves little room for doubting its intensity: 'when they (the 'Platonist' books) had let a very few drops of most precious unguent fall . . . they stirred up an incredible conflagration—incredible, and perhaps beyond even what I would believe of myself. What honour, what human pomp, what desire for empty fame, what consolations or attractions of this mortal life could move me then? Swiftly did I begin to return entirely to myself'.[5] Though it cannot be said that Augustine's enthusiasm for the Platonists remained at this white heat to the end of his life, nevertheless with, perhaps, some ambivalence, he appeared to follow their *immaterialistic* views from time to time, and had constant recourse to Greek Fathers and their Neoplatonically inspired commentaries in his extensive interpretation of *Genesis*. Even in the last pages of the *City of God* he puts forward an immaterialist view of the *Visio Dei*, if only to give clear preference to a more material one that might appeal more to his carnally-minded flock.

One wonders, then, about Augustine's ardent espousal of the body (while seeking very much to control it) and some consequent infidelity to Neoplatonic *immaterialism*. It is to us, inheritors of belief in a spiritual God, almost incredible that Augustine could not, well into his thirties, even conceive of such a being. But so it was. Something within himself, perhaps, something also in the religion imparted to him and inculcated by his mother; something undoubtedly arising for him in Manicheism, the religion of his twenties, may give some explanation. Later on as a pastor thinking primarily of guarding and nourishing his flock, he gave them, Eriugena suggests, the carnal solutions which they preferred. It is a type of 'economy' always in practice everywhere, and not least in the late Graeco-Roman world. It is impossible to escape the conclusion that Augustine throughout his pastoral life used it more and more.

Morever his obedience to the injunction of St Paul 'Put on the Lord Jesus Christ',[6] which was the positive direction in the scriptural text that, so to speak, wrought his conversion in the garden at Milan, was a deliberate acceptance of Christ's Incarnation (God's becoming material flesh) in conscious rejection of the characteristic teaching of the best-known and most influential of contemporary Neoplatonists, Porphyry. For Porphyry the notion of God becoming flesh, or of Christ's or anyone's body persisting in any way in an after-life, was anathema: *omne corpus fugiendum*—'one should shun every kind of body—was the battle-cry of Porphyry, constantly rejected by Augustine.

4 *Recherches sur les Confessions de saint Augustin* (1950), 157ff.   5 *Against the Academics*, 2.5.   6 *Rom.* 13.14

But these doctrines of the Incarnation and Resurrection of the body Augustine accepted on his conversion, even if he may not have wholly penetrated their implications for Catholic theology which in any case on these matters was still uncertain.[7]

One of the few details we know of Eriugena's life is that he enjoyed no ecclesiastical distinctions whatever. There is no evidence that he was entrusted with the care of souls. Apart from any other factor involved, this may well have affected his use of Neoplatonism. Augustine on the other hand had this care, took it very seriously, and was so active and apparently successful in the practical mission of the Church that he was looked to for leadership throughout the whole of North Africa and well beyond. This engendered in him, if he did not possess it already, a somewhat aggressive and combative spirit, which showed itself rather more than eager in the great controversies with the Donatists, Manicheans and Pelagians. In these he behaved savagely ('*atrociter*') showing himself willing to insist on extreme positions, and even to acquiesce in the use of physical force to compel belief in doctrine. These controversies coarsened his sensitivities, but he persisted in, even if he was oppressed by, them—all for his idea of the good of the Church.

The attitudes he gradually took in doctrinal matters due to his leading pastoral position manifest a decreasing intellectualism and greater tolerance of the sensible. This is seen in his changing from an initial scepticism about miracles to his whole-hearted enthusiasm for the plethora of them that he describes in the *City of God*;[8] in his easing of his views on the total invisibility of God by corporal eyes in the after-life, to His indirect visibility;[9] and most of all in his *personal and deliberate preference* for belief in a physical Hell where bodies, as he seeks to illustrate, for us so pathetically, can be eternally burned, without ever being consumed. He was not the only influential thinker of his times to retreat from the sober teachings of science: his failure, in spite of Plato and Pliny the Elder and his own unusual (for the times) science in selective areas, to maintain the existence of the Antipodes, which appeared to him to threaten the notion of the unity of mankind, is regrettable. But Neoplatonists too, in their kind of mysticism, diverted men from the scientific approach, which thereupon was greatly weakened.

Peter Brown, as we have seen,[10] sums up something of Augustine's part in this in his *Augustine of Hippo*, where he declares that Augustine's writings against the Donatists and Pelagians were a significant landmark in the process by which the Church had come to embrace, and to tolerate, the whole lay society of the Roman world, with its depressing resilience of its pagan habits. In the instances given by Brown, Augustine's writings that concerned the Donatists can appear to have been against those that had not betrayed the faith; and those concerned with the Pelagians, against them that tried to avoid sin: grace and imperfection seemed to be preferred to effort and virtue.

The figure of Ambrose, Augustine's proclaimed spiritual father and one appealed to often by Eriugena as more acceptable to him in particulars than Augustine, is part of the context of Augustine's development. Ambrose's insistence that 'the letter kills, but the spirit gives life' had much influence in making the Scriptures acceptable to Augustine. Indeed Augustine's commendation of allegory in the *Confessions* is impressive. But though he may never have forgotten the warning that the letter kills, given by Ambrose,

7 Cf. 24ff.   8 E.g. 22.8.2–22.   9 Cf. *B.A.* 37.853ff.   10 Cf. 30 above.

he may not always have borne it in mind. One wonders what Augustine's spiritual career might have been if he had remained in Milan, near Ambrose and Neoplatonizing Christians, pursuing a life (as he had proposed), uninvolved in disputes in Africa beyond the sea ? It is an interesting speculation. But I believe that for all his impressive interest in them Augustine's bent was not *overwhelmingly* towards contemplation or philosophy: his actions speak louder than his words.

It all goes back to one's conviction about the use of Philosophy. When I was working on Augustine's *Against the Academics* and later on *Porphyry's Philosophy from Oracles in Augustine*,[11] I was deeply impressed by the emphasis that Augustine put upon the liberal arts when he was writing the *de ordine*, that is during the interval between his conversion in 386 and baptism in 387. It was evident, as Ilsetraut Hadot[12] demonstrated later, that he was much indebted to Porphyry in this. Augustine at this time believed that reason, trained in the liberal arts, was a way to the understanding of whatever truth was taught by Revelation, and one that was quite independent of it. He believed that a genuine synthesis had been achieved between Neoplatonism and Christianity, between reason and Revelation. All the same be declared even at this early stage that he would follow Christ *above all*, for he could not find a superior authority. In the meantime he expressed confidence that the Neoplatonists would afford him what enlightenment he needed, and that that would not conflict with, as he says, 'our sacred mysteries'.[13]

Although Augustine continued to look to the Neoplatonists for ideas up to the end of his life, he gradually gave his unquestioned allegiance to Authority only. There is not much room for an appeal to reason in one who writes: 'I would not believe in the Gospel, if the authority of the Catholic Church did not bid me to do so'.[14]

Eriugena's early approach to reason and the liberal arts may have been rather similar to that of Augustine in 386, but unlike Augustine's it persisted. He made his own for always the phrase of the young Augustine in his *de vera religione: est humanae salutis caput, non aliam esse philosophiam, id est sapientiae studium, et aliam religionem:*[15] Scripture was not for him to be accepted at, so to speak, word-level. It needed interpretation and it was reason precisely that interpreted it.[16] Neither was any authority unquestioned. Authority had to be approved by reason.[17] It was not Eriugena's experience that reason could solve every problem, could plausibly interpret every word of Scripture. Then one fell back on negative Theology.

Reason, of course, as understood by Eriugena was not or was not merely the discursive reason of traditional philosophy. Reason was the *anima* and at the highest level was intelligence; but it was also continued downwards through the interior sense so as to become sensation.[18] As there were modes of being (indicated with emphasis by Eriugena at the very beginning of the *Periphyseon* and too quickly forgotten by readers), so there were modes of perception. Both involved non-reciprocal relationships: the perfection of the lower depended on its contemplation of the higher: the imperfection of the higher arose from its contemplation of the lower.

11 Paris (1959).   12 *Arts Libéraux et philosophie dans la pensée antique* (1984).   13 Cf. the author's 'St Augustine's View of Authority and Reason', *Irish Theological Quarterly* (1951), 338ff.   14 *Contra ep. Manichaei q. vocant Fundamenti* 5.6.   15 5.8.   16 *Periphyseon*, 511C.   17 Ibid., 513B.   18 Ibid., 754C-D.

Reason, therefore, could be vision. It might at another level be described as mystical. Eriugena's writing is instinct with this adequating sense of reason. The abstraction involved is sustained throughout his work. It bears the reader up with a near-sublimity that rarely flags. Sometimes it issues in passages that one must describe as elevated and highly spiritual. On a few occasions it breaks forth in simple, abandoning prayer. The spirit of Voltaire is totally foreign to the 'rationalism' of Eriugena. Philosophy for him supposes a God and is one with Theology, not hostile to it.

We return, then, to the great test-case as between the materialistic or immaterialistic ways of Augustine and Eriugena of viewing things—their attitudes towards the resurrection of the body. For Augustine, just as Adam was animal in Eden, so would his corporal body, glorified, be with the soul in heaven: 'my own flesh shall be my dear friend throughout eternity'.[19] It has to be said in parenthesis that in *de Genesi ad litteram* he thinks that the body will not be with the soul in heaven.[20] This is one of a number of instances where Augustine expresses a view at variance with the one he overwhelmingly espouses. Eriugena is aghast and horrified that so great a Father should appear to believe in the existence of any body whatever in heaven: Augustine, he suggests—as he does frequently in these recurring situations—was accommodating his views (which must actually, he may presume, be like those of Ambrose, which appeared or were made to appear similar to those of Eriugena himself) to his audience which could comprehend only carnal things. But it was hardly so.[21]

For Eriugena the whole sensible creature will at the end of the world be unified and then transformed into the intelligible. Then the unification of the created nature will be effected with the nature that was not created. Eriugena would like to think that the eternal damnation of which the Scriptures speak will consist in *the total abolition of wickedness and impiety*. But if the good will hereafter enjoy the phantasies of divine contemplation, and the wicked suffer phantasies of mortal things, nevertheless the good and the wicked will be one nature and will be saved as such. Difference in phantasies is to be accepted in the simplicity of the Catholic faith. For 'who has known the mind of the Lord, or who has been his counsellor?'[22] Not even the Neoplatonists could account for everything.

The difference, then, in the approach of Eriugena and Augustine to materialism and a 'Neoplatonic' immaterialism is very marked and sustained. Eriugena's many professions of his general allegiance to his 'Father', Augustine, tends to conceal this, as do his many explanations on points where they, according to him, may only *seem* to differ. But he does not conceal where they differ seriously, and notably in relation to the fundamental question of materialism and immaterialism in connection with the human body. Indeed he underlines it. Just as he writes: I do not cease to be *amazed* 'why he (Augustine) calls that body (of man in Eden) animal', so he professes to be staggered[23] when he reads of such things in the books of the Holy Fathers: 'I stagger, so to speak, amazed and horror struck!' He may have been amazed, but they were Augustine's ideas that prevailed in the West.

19 *Sermon* 155.15.   20 12.32, 60.   21 Cf. G. Madec, *Jean Scot et ses auteurs* (1988), 62.   22 *Rom.* 11.34. 23 Cf. 37 above.

PART II: *City of God*

CHARTER OF CHRISTENDOM

4

Context and Structure of the *City of God* [1]

'As man amongst creatures, and the Church amongst men, and the Fathers in the Church, and St Augustine amongst the Fathers, so amongst the many precious volumes, and in the rich store-house of his works, his books on the *City of God* have a special pre-eminence.' So wrote W. Crashawe in a dedication to the Earls of Pembroke, Arundel, and Montgomery. So some might commend the *City of God* still as of all books, other than the Bible, the most significant and valuable for the understanding of Western Christendom.

Christopher Dawson in his *The Historic Reality of Christian Culture* (1960), in making a plea for the creation of chairs and courses in our universities in Christian Classics, writes: 'The success of the old classical education was largely due to the fact that it limited itself to a single cultural tradition and was able to study it thoroughly. Nevertheless, the classical tradition was not the only unifying element in Western culture. The tradition of Christian culture is even more important and reaches far deeper into the European consciousness. For it is this and not science or humanism which was the spiritual bond that transcended the divisions and antagonisms of race, class and nationality and created that society of peoples which was the community of Western Christendom.'[2]

The following pages are intended to illustrate not only how important the *City of God* can be for an understanding of our past but also what comfort and help it can afford in these critical times and in face of an uncertain future.

Few are the books that have given rise to so much misconception as the *City of God*. By some it is thought to give a philosophy, by others a theology of history. By some it is thought to contain well-developed political theories, to be hostile to the State as such and in particular to the Roman Empire, and to outline the provinces of an Established Church and Christian State. By others it is understood to be so dominated by Platonic idealism that it led to a reaction against the scholastic philosophy of the Church and inspired thereby the Reformation. Again, it is considered to be primarily a Christian reply to the charge that Rome had been sacked because it had become Christian, as identifying the City of God with the Church, and as teaching that justice is not essential to the definition of the State.

More serious still: the teaching of Augustine on predestination, never accepted in its

1 Cf. 18 above.   2 109.

full rigour by the Church, is grim and sombre in the *City of God.* The Pelagian controversy had tended to force him into some exaggeration, at least in his expressions, in relation both to Nature and to Grace. Yet when one has studied Augustine's life and works for long, one finds it difficult to believe that he was entirely a pessimist. One must expect, and indeed welcome, clear evidence of a countervailing optimism in keeping with so vital a person and one so unreservedly generous in the service of man.

The *City of God* is no more purely theoretical than it is purely theological. It is, of course, mainly theological; but it is also founded upon Augustine's own experience. It will be seen that it is an application of the theme of his own development and conversion, as described in the burning pages of the *Confessions,* to the broader, less immediate, canvas of man's destiny. Augustine's reflection upon his experience, especially at the time of his conversion, both in outline and in surprising precision in detail, is the key to much of his characteristic teaching.

We should take warning from this: however much he might regret some of the ingredients of his past, he was happy to recognize that through it and them Providence had brought him to where, humanly speaking, he felt more secure. His attitude, therefore, to these things could not be wholly negative and full of condemnation. On the contrary he formed from the pattern of his life a theory of providential economy that to many might seem both too living and too tolerant. If Rome and the philosophy of the Greeks could, for all their error, not only not prevent him from accepting Christ and the Christian Revelation, but actually lead him to do so, why should they not be as useful to others—to all mankind? It might seem paradoxical, for example, that the bitterest enemy of the Christians, Porphyry, should through his writing play a significant role (along with other Neoplatonists) in Augustine's conversion. This, however, was a fact, and Augustine was willing to take account of it in his notions of the dealings of Providence with men.

It can be said that although the scope of Augustine's writings is immense, they are animated by a few central ideas that came to him from the sensitive brooding on his own life. Thus the leading ideas of both the *Confessions* and the *City of God,* as we shall see presently, are anticipated in his first extant works. There we can see clearly how close life and thought come in the mind of Augustine.

It is a commonplace to say that the age of Augustine was very like our own. We should remember that our view of his times is distorted by our looking at it from the vantage of over fifteen hundred years of Christian domination. Our view of our own times is too close to be in focus. We may not be able to see the present and the future as they are and will be; but at least we can make some attempt to strip the past of the encumbrances to our vision added later.

Some now speak of our living in post-Christian times, and seem to imply that Christianity as a force in the world can but decline. When one contemplates the defection from Christianity and the scandal of its disunity on the one hand, and on the other the emergence upon the world's stage of the seething populations of non-Christian peoples-peoples who are as likely to assert their independence of Christianity as they are impatient of Western political power—one cannot feel a firm human confidence in the future of Western Christendom.

And yet, when Augustine was writing the *City of God*, his confident reading of the future cannot have seemed so justified to many of his contemporaries as it is to us now. The prospects of Christianity in the first quarter of the fifth century may have seemed bright to us; but we tend to forget that until that time the Church's history had been one, for the most part, of bare toleration and frequent persecution. Even within Augustine's own life there had been the pagan reaction under Julian the Apostate (AD 361–363). Even in the fifth century pagans had not lost all countenance. Again the decline of the powerful and closely integrated Empire of Rome, evident to all and admitted by Augustine, must have struck its citizens with a greater chill than that which affects in our day the loosely associated West.

We should, then, note that the comparison of our situation to his is closer than, perhaps, is ordinarily realized. And we should take hope from his calm confidence at such a crisis in consciously drawing up in the *City of God* the charter for a Christian future not only for Rome but for all the world.

The West is now sometimes tempted to despair. Should it not rather trust that the very qualities that made it dominant in the past among the nations of the world will help it to survive the competition of great and ancient peoples now feeling their strength and anxious to body forth their cultures and traditions? The great lesson of the *City of God* is that out of all things comes good. Augustine saw clearly that in his time both Christianity and Rome would each benefit by the good that was in the other, and by any good from wherever else it might come. For Christianity assimilation meant acceptance that was universal in the context of Augustine's time. For Rome it meant a new birth and an even longer future. For Greek thought it meant transmission and development. The keynote of the *City of God* is fulfilment, not destruction.

In our time observers predict for the future either domination by one culture or a kind of democracy of cultures. Christopher Dawson writes: 'Any claim on the part of the ancient world-cultures to possess a tradition of universal validity represents a kind of cultural imperialism which is no less unpopular than the military and economic imperialism of the Great Powers. In its extreme form [the] idea of "cultural democracy" is obviously unacceptable. We cannot regard the culture of a particular Melanesian people or even the Melanesians as a whole as in any sense equivalent to the culture of China or India. Nevertheless the tendency to cultural relativism is strong among the scholars who have made a lifetime's study of the problems of civilization. We see a striking example of this in the case of Arnold Toynbee, whose whole work is based on the philosophical equivalence of cultures and who rejects the idea of the unity of civilization as a one-sided simplification of history due to the pride and provincialism of Western historians'.[3]

One must obviously follow Dawson in trying to work towards a middle way between the domination of one culture and a proletariat of cultures. Here it would be wrong of us to think that the culture of the Christian West should not suffer accidental change.

3 Op. cit., 102. Cf. Appendix 3 below.

One might ask oneself if the very first followers of Christ could have imagined the Christendom that was ushered in in Augustine's own period. Augustine's attitude to its future in turn was in no way static: he did not believe that the end of the world was at hand; he did not believe that Christianity could not profit, in a human way, from other things. Christianity was a leaven, an acorn. Who could say that it was not at work within the mass? Who could say that the tree was fully grown and that it had taken its final unalterable shape?

The practical problem with which Augustine had—and Christianity still has—to deal was the problem of a spiritual Church in a secular world: the city of God in the city of this world. It is of the first importance to understand that he did not condemn out of hand the city of this world. It was God's creation. It was used by God for His purposes. It was not only availed of by the citizens of God's city but was also intended by God to give compelling example to them of what efforts they should make in their striving for something greater and something higher. Out of that world and what good it had to offer, Christians should take the 'spoils of the Egyptians' and should make them their own. They should profit from secular philosophy (which in its own way was a kind of revelation); they should learn from secular history (which in its own way threw prophetic light upon the future).

Absolutely, according to Augustine, if things were to be judged *only* by the canon of the service and worship of the true God, what the Hebrews achieved in their temporal history, the Greeks in their academies, and the Romans in the virtues of their worthies, was evil. For evil was merely not-to-do-that-service-and-give-that-worship. In this way what looked like virtue was really splendid vice. But *relatively*, or in our ordinary way of speaking, all these things were good and should be used by Christianity. Christianity had changed superficially, was no longer the religion of a few fishermen, was in fact the religion of an Empire accepting its intellectual responsibility. This superficial change wrought through assimilation, absorption, reaction and, it might be, rejection was the law of its life. The Leviathan that challenges Christianity now is greater than it has ever been. The weapons must ever be the same.

Almost the only thing that could not be accepted from Rome was her official religion, polytheism. Insofar as the *City of God* is against anything, it is radically against that. It is unfortunate that Augustine in placing the positive part of his argument in the final twelve books of his work and the negative in the first ten, gives the impression that he is opposed to Rome and Greek philosophy. If he had stated the basis of his positive doctrine first, it would be seen that his attitude to Rome and Greece and his general outlook is positive.

Augustine's message for Christianity in an expanding and secular world, if judged by the *City of God,* would be to seek the good in what is secular, to seek the good in other cultures, to adopt a constructive and sympathetic attitude to State and world. Christians sometimes give the impression that they lack confidence in God's providence and the goodness of creation. Sometimes too they show little evidence of Christian hope. Without that confidence and that hope they bring less than they should to a world in need and distress.

THE RELEVANT HISTORICAL SITUATION

Augustine, born and reared in Roman North Africa in the second half of the fourth century, grew up in an Empire that was in evident decline. Rome's marble city, her invincible army, her wide-flung administration, her riches garnered from every corner of the world, but above all her spirit and very heart were failing. The fatal blow came quickly. On a day in August in AD 410, Alaric with his Christian-Arian Goths sacked the great city that had not known violation by a foreign enemy for eight hundred years.

One does not need much imagination or sensibility to understand how symbolic of impending doom Rome's fall might appear to be. Even two years afterwards St Jerome was still so affected by it that he could not dictate his commentary on Ezechiel. He had, he complained, lost the memory of his own name and could but remain silent knowing that it was a time to weep: with Rome had perished the human race. This was the reaction of a Christian—but, it should be added, an emotional Christian. Another Christian, Orosius, a contemporary of the event and the chief source of information on the sack of Rome, judges soberly that the damage to the city was not great.

It is well to bear in mind that, while the sack lasted but three days and was marked by the relative clemency of the conquerors, the overthrowing of the official Roman religion, a form of polytheism, had been prolonged, bitter, and serious in its consequences. From the time of Constantine onward there bad been a succession of edicts against paganism, twenty of them in the last twenty years of the fourth century, and as many as four in the last year of that century, as if it had been determined that with the century paganism should pass from the Empire forever: idols were to be dethroned; temples to be laicized; judges were to be supervised in the enforcement of the edicts; and bishops were to report any laxity in the carrying out of these instructions.

There had, of course, been opposition to such a policy. An instance of this can be seen in the short-lived respite in the reign of Julian the Apostate (361–363). The symbolical event, however, in this spiritual struggle is usually seen in the confrontation of Symmachus, the Prefect of Rome and the outstanding professed pagan of his day, with St Ambrose of Milan on the question of the Altar of Victory in 384.

The great goddess Victory, associated with Jupiter (chief of the Roman gods), and with Mars (god of war), worshipped by the army (the instrument of Rome's dominion), and intimately related to the felicity of the emperor, had been furnished with an altar, the Altar of Victory, within the very Senate House itself of Rome. There she had stood, presiding over the prosperity of Rome, an earnest and an omen of continuing success. This altar had been removed by Constantius, the father of Constantine, replaced by the pagans in due course, removed again under Gratian in 382, replaced for a brief period by Eugenius (397–394), and perhaps on a final occasion by Stilicho, who died in disgrace in 408.

Of Augustine's acquaintance with one of the protagonists, St Ambrose, in the symbolical confrontation on the Altar of Victory, it will not be necessary to say anything here. On the other hand we should remember that, when Augustine came to teach Rhetoric in Carthage in 374 and had some acquaintance with official circles there, Symmachus was not only in residence as proconsul of Africa but had also been one of the most successful rhetors of his time. It is not unlikely that they met then, but in any case Symmachus knew of Augustine at least later in Rome; for it was he, the most prominent pagan of his day, who recommended Augustine for appointment to the office of Master of Rhetoric at the Imperial Court, then at Milan, the See of St Ambrose. It is well to pause and reflect on the significance that this situation, pregnant as it was to be, must have had for Augustine. Here he was in Milan, an unconvinced Christian as yet, recommended by the champion of the pagans—perhaps for the very reason, among others, that Augustine was not a Christian—at a court subject to the influence of the champion of the Christians. Augustine arrived in Milan in the autumn of 384 only a month or two after the dispute on the Altar of Victory.

Symmachus's part in the affair is represented by a petition for the restoration of the altar, removed, as we have seen, in 382. This petition is extant.[4] As Prefect of the city of Rome and Pontifex Maximus, he stressed the necessity for prudence: no one knew the final secret explanation of Rome's prosperity; it was therefore unwise not to preserve the institutions that had presided over her success; it was perilous to disown them for something new. He brought Rome herself forward to plead her cause: she is old; she has no desire to change her pieties; her religion has civilized the world, driven the Gauls from the Capitol and Hannibal from the city.

St. Ambrose, however, was a doughty opponent, as his domination of the Arian Empress Justina in 385–386 and of the Emperor Theodosius (with the imposition of a public penance in 390) was soon to show. His argument[5] was that the valour and virtues of the Romans themselves were sufficient explanation of their successes. Was it not foolish to pretend to believe that the Empire depended on some 'power' that one must imagine but could not see? To restrict the future through reverence for the mere past was to retard progress and civilization. Christianity had, moreover, a positive contribution to make: it held truth and salvation, while polytheism led to perdition and error.

The Christian cause prevailed, and paganism was clearly and definitely, if not finally, defeated. Prudentius, the Christian poet, describes[6] how the Senate in plenary session formally banished Jupiter and the other gods in favour of the Christian God. The senators, many of whom were known to be dissembling, yielded to mounting public approbation of Christianity and abandoned for monotheism the gods of their forefathers. They made haste to disown their ancient pride, submit to baptism, and pay reverence at the tombs of the Christian martyrs.

The ordinary people were not slow to show their satisfaction, and soon the temples were mouldering in desolation. Theodosius in his time was relentless in his enforcement of the edicts against polytheism throughout the Empire, and particularly those against sacrifice to the gods. Some indeed in their zeal, fearing that shrines that were merely empty might one day be restored, hastened to destroy the temples themselves, some of them splendid edifices. A few of them were converted to Christian use, the most famous of these being the Pantheon, the temple in Rome of all the gods, which to this day stands as it ever stood.

---

4 *Monumenta Germaniae Historiae, Auctores Antiqui*, ed., O. Seeck (1883) 6.1.   5 Cf. *Ep.* 18.   6 *C. or. Symm.* 1. 608.

The decrees of Theodosius, however, reached further even than destruction of the buildings. Sacrifice to idols and divination by inspection of entrails—the commonplaces of public life in earlier Rome—were declared to be high treason and were to be punished by death. Even the most trivial trafficking in garlands and libations was suspected and became liable to fines and confiscation of property.

The collapse of polytheism was in the end sudden, universal within the Empire, and absolute. Its absurdity as a religious system had long before been accepted by the intelligent. Now the wholesale assault on buildings and institutions, with evident impunity and no retaliation from the ousted and enfeebled gods, delivered the masses from any feelings of fear or obligation. The dismemberment of the statue of the great god Serapis at Alexandria met with no revenge in either the death of a Christian or the refusal of the Nile to grant its annual and blessed inundation. Truly the gods had lost, and Christ had won:

> *Et dubitamus adhuc Romam, tibi, Christe, dicatam*
> *In leges transisse tuas?*[7]

Augustine was by his very circumstances a close observer of this stupendous transformation. As he was torn between the loyalties he owed first to Symmachus and then to St Ambrose, so his feelings and thoughts were divided between sympathy for the Rome that was and the vision of a Christian future. Nevertheless his evident delight, for example, at the destruction of the pagan temples at Carthage by Jovius and Gaudentius,[8] and his approval of even punishment by death for pagan sacrificing,[9] leave no doubt, if doubt were possible, where his final loyalty lay. He was not unaware that the recent desertion en masse from an enervated polytheism meant that there were Christians, even many Christians, who had yielded to Christ for unworthy motives—to save their lives or canvass official support for their careers and ambitions—but for all that he felt an overflowing happiness in the visible victory of the Christians.

It is hardly surprising, then, if Augustine's distress at the sack of Rome in 410 was not only much less pronounced than that of St Jerome but was compensated for by a greater optimism. If the pagan historians Zosimus and Rutilius Namatianus, writing of the period, say not a word of the disaster—possibly because they did not find it an attractive topic—we can understand that Augustine's fondness for a theme, about which he was sometimes twitted, was prompted more by its wider significance, as marking a stage in the conflict between Christianity and paganism, than by any preoccupation with the material decline and fall of Rome. The theme was with him an old one, even before the sack of Rome.

The question was, however, raised for him directly by a Christian official in Africa, Marcellinus—to whom in fact the *City of God* is addressed—in a letter[10] in the year 412, the year before Augustine began his greatest book. Marcellinus mentioned the view put forward by some of his friends that the miracles wrought by Apollonius and Apuleius were greater than those of Christianity. He asked how, if God had been satisfied with the type of sacrifice described in the Old Testament, He could, without changing (which

7 Ibid., 587f. 8 *City of God* 18.54. 9 *Ep.* 93.10. 10 136.

in God is impossible), be dissatisfied with it in the New? Finally there arose the problem of why it was that the Empire appeared to decline, when it came to be governed by princes that had forsaken the old, tried, religion and embraced a new one that inculcated precepts of toleration of offences and submission to injury. This did not seem to go well with the interests of Empire.

One should note carefully that, although this letter was written about two years after the sack of Rome, and purported to give the views and complaints of pagans, there is not one word about the event in question, but rather the whole emphasis is on miracles, sacrifices, and religion as causes or explanations of success in Empire or failure.

Augustine replied in a letter to a friend of Marcellinus[11] and in a further one to Marcellinus himself.[12] The themes of these two letters foreshadow very clearly themes of the *City of God*, and some of them must be briefly mentioned: the Saviour came when the time was ripe for His coming; that coming was foretold not only by the prophets but also by secular philosophers and poets; the true Mediator delivered man from the false mediators, the demons; Christ superseded Moses, who was greater than any pagan; the truth of Christianity is seen in its fulfilment of prophecy and its confirmation by miracles; the world appears to be declining and to be in its last age; Christians are multiplying everywhere and await the eternal happiness of the heavenly city (*aeternam civitatis coelestis felicitatem*).[13]

Letter 138 concentrates more on the question of religion and Empire: the gods of polytheism, being by definition many, were discordant and inimical to concord, which was the constituting element of the (Roman) State; this discord issued in civil wars; the gods favour the evils that corrupt men; Christianity, on the contrary, makes men better as soldiers, better as parents, better as children, better as masters and better as slaves, better as princes, better as judges, better as taxpayers and better as taxgatherers—in short, Christianity was the great salvation for the State; it goes, however, beyond this life below and the harmony of the State, and provides entry to eternal salvation and the heavenly and divine republic of a certain eternal people; the splendid success of the Romans, achieved without the true religion, is perfected in their becoming citizens of another city. The letter goes on to insist that the pagan gods are less powerful than even Apollonius or Apuleius; the demons caused damage to the State and aroused hostility to Christianity; prosperity with the worship of the true God was seen in the temporal history of the Hebrews, whose dispersal, even as enemies of Christianity, aided its spread; the miracles of Christianity are incomparably superior to any others.

Augustine ends this second letter by admitting that he has not managed to treat of all the points that he would wish. If Marcellinus writes for more, he will make it his business to reply either in a letter or in a book.

In the event he wrote a book for Marcellinus. It was the *City of God*, was begun in 413, the following year, and deals with essentially the same topics and with the same attitudes.

11 137.   12 138.   13 *Ep.* 137.

ANTICIPATIONS OF THE THEME IN AUGUSTINE

Of the last stages in the conflict between polytheism and Christian monotheism, Augustine could not but have been conscious at least from the time of his being recommended by Symmachus to Milan, where he encountered St Ambrose. What happened to himself in 386, when he was converted, represented in his own regard a victory for Christianity. It would not be surprising, then, if in the earliest compositions of Augustine there were adumbrations and preliminary formulations of what was later the dominating theme of the *City of God*.

A study has been made of the various anticipations in Augustine of this later theme;[14] but here we shall confine ourselves to a very few only, and these from his first extant works, which reflect very strongly his own personal experiences at the time of his conversion. Our purpose is to show how the main theme of the *City of God* had already taken on a special significance for him as he reflected upon the pattern of his own life. Even at that stage he had begun to think that what was true for him was true for mankind at large.

We must ourselves at this point anticipate in assuming that the dominating theme of the *City of God* is salvation and the means to it: the worship of the one true God, involving the rejection of all false gods.

Whereas salvation in the *City of God* is represented by citizenship in a city (*civitas*)— an image explicitly taken from the Scriptures—it is in the earliest formulations represented as arriving at harbour (*portus*), or at the fatherland (*patria*), or being upon the way (*via*). These images are, of course, borrowed from the stock in trade of philosophy, particularly Platonic philosophy, in its eschatological aspects. Other variants used by Augustine at this time are the land of desire (*optatissima terra*), the land of happiness (*beatae vitae regionem solumque*), the happy land *(terra beata)*, and the shining home (*luculentam domum*).

The first few pages of Augustine's first extant work, the *Against the Academics*, written after his conversion in 386, speak of the harbour of wisdom (*portus sapientiae*), to which Providence, making use of misfortune that seems to be but evil, brings us. Special emphasis is laid upon the irrelevance and instability of temporal prosperity. Here Augustine alludes directly not only to the apparent misfortunes of the person to whom the book is addressed, but to his own: prosperity had almost entrapped him, but he had been compelled by illness to give up his profession and betake himself to philosophy, which, as the work makes clear, means philosophy subject to the authority of Christ.[15] One can suppose that Augustine's views, on the irrelevance of prosperity and the use made by Providence of misfortune, might be applied by him to the Empire as much as to mankind in general or himself and his friend.

The image of the harbour is used again in the first five sections of the *Happy Life*, composed at the same time as the previous work. The major image here, however, is the land of desire. There are two ways to this land, both across a sea. One is the way of reason, which, possible only for the few, brings men to the harbour of philosophy, which

14 A. Lauras and H. Rondet, 'Le Thème des deux Cités dans l'oeuvre de saint Augustin' *Études Augustiniennes*, Paris (1953) 99–160. 15 3.43.

is the harbour of the land of desire. The other way is the way of Providence which uses the storms of adversity to bring men, resist and wander in ignorance and folly as they may, to the same harbour. Those who are apparently most successful in life have need of the greatest storms. Some are brought to sanity, however, by the reading of books written by the learned and the wise. And some make their way to the fatherland partly by their own use of reason, and partly by providential adversity.

One great hazard threatens all who approach the harbour—a high mountain at the front of the harbour itself. It is so enticing that it lures to it not only those approaching the harbour, but even some that had already been in the harbour. The people living on this mountain are full of conceit, and fear that others might share their glory; hence they impress on those approaching the difficulty, because of submerged rocks, of joining themselves, but are happy to advise them how they can get to the land of desire. In this way they are destroyed within sight of the shining home.

Finally—a most important point—the harbour is wide, and one may still fail to put ashore and so not achieve one's goal.

There are significant anticipations of the *City of God* here. The very term 'citizens' (*cives*) is used, and the phrase 'on pilgrimage from their fatherland' is that characteristically applied in the later work to the citizens of the heavenly city in their life on earth. The illusions of prosperity and the transcendent role of Providence in its use of adversity are here fully emphasized. Of particular significance, however, is the special mention of the envious and proud, who help others to safety, but are themselves destroyed within sight of the fatherland. This, of course, must refer especially to certain Neoplatonists, who approached Christianity, helped others to become Christians, but rejected Christianity themselves. It is to be noted that not all mankind reach the harbour, and those who are there may still be lost: so too might Christians fail to persevere.

What is of special interest for us here is Augustine's explicit relation of this theme and image to the circumstances of his own life at the time. Here indeed he gives a summary autobiography, parallel to that given in the *Against the Academics*,[16] and later to be expanded in the *Confessions*. It is clear that the theme, as set out in the *Happy Life*, is inspired by his own life: the providential use of illness, the effect of reading certain books (a very precise detail that he repeats and applies without hesitation to other men), his own part use of reason and part guidance by Providence, the illusions of prosperity, and the help of the proud Neoplatonists, who did not benefit from their own wisdom.

In short we have here the opportunity of seeing how the theme of the *City of God* is revealed by himself as constructed from the details of his own conversion. To put it another way, the *City of God* is the application of the *Confessions* to the history of mankind. The inspiration of Augustine's theme is in his life.

The image of the way (*via*) is found first in Augustine in, again, the *Against the Academics*.[17] Here we are given the story of two men travelling to the same destination, one of whom has too much and the other too little credulity. At a crossroads they meet a humble shepherd whose directions the one accepts without question and proceeds to

16 2.4f.   17 3.34.

follow. The other ridicules such credulity and does not move. By the time an elegant gentleman came along on horseback he had found his waiting tedious, and accordingly acted upon the directions now given, although be did not accept them as necessarily true and they conflicted with those given by the shepherd. In the event he got lost in the woods and trackless mountains—for the horseman was an impostor—while his companion was resting at his destination.

The source of this image may have been epistemological, but Augustine explicitly refers its use here to the deeds and behaviour of men. Philosophers and those interested in religion had done so before him, and amongst those was one especially well known to himself, Porphyry. Porphyry's search for a universal way to salvation and his rejection of Christ as that way is the high point of the tenth book of the *City of God* and, indeed, of the work as a whole. Although Augustine's use of the image of the way is undoubtedly at a later stage influenced by Moses's leading of his followers to the promised land and by the description of the Magi's return by another way into their own country, his treatment of it in the *Confessions*[18] and the *De Trinitate*[19] is basically the same as here in the *Against the Academics* and later in the *City of God*:[20] the contrasting attitudes of the proud with the humble, and the simple and credulous with the pretentious impostor. The *Confessions* mark the point well: 'I might discern and distinguish between presumption and confession, between those, who saw whither they were to go, yet saw not the way, and the way that leadeth not to behold only but to dwell in the beatific country. For it is one thing to see the land of peace, and to find no way thither, and in vain to essay through ways impassable, opposed and beset by fugitives and deserters; and another to keep on the way that leads thither'.[21]

Unlike those in the image of the harbour in the *Happy Life*, the Neoplatonists are here represented as seeking direction but being deceived. Both images complete the treatment of them in the *City of God* where they are shown as helping toward the truth, but also as being deceived.

It will not be necessary for our purpose to linger further on other anticipations of the main theme of the *City of God*. The clearest and fullest is to be found in the *True Religion*[22] which was begun at the same time as the works we have been discussing, but was not finished until four years later in 390. Inasmuch as the *City of God* is a discussion of religion (*disputatio religionis*), both works share the same topic. The *De Moribus Ecclesiae Catholicae*, written in 388–390, has this striking passage on the 'way', which is, at the same time, a summary statement of one aspect and much of the contents of the *City of God*: 'the way which God built for us in the segregation of the Patriarchs, the bond of the Law, the foretelling of the Prophets, the sacrament of the Man assumed, the testimony of the Apostles, the blood of the martyrs and the entering into possession of the gentiles. Let us heed the oracles (of Scripture) and submit our puny reasonings to divine inspiration'.[23] Here the gradual revelation of the way is emphasized. Finally the *De Catechizandis Rudibus*, written in 399, speaks plainly of two cities, one the devil's, the other Christ's.

18 7.26f. 19 4.13ff. 20 10.32. 21 7.21, 27, Pusey's translation. 22 Cf. 48ff 23 1.11f.

What we have wanted to stress was not so much the anticipation of the theme of the *City of God*, thereby showing that it was not necessarily dependent upon Alaric's sack of Rome, but even more the rooting of that theme in Augustine's own experience. This will be found to be of use in the understanding of the theme as it was later set forth. As Providence had used adversity to help him, so does Providence dominate the life of every man and every Empire. This might be a banal teaching of a philosophical school, but for Augustine it was also a personal realization, and so it tended to colour and affect all his thoughts and all his theories. Implicit in all this is some regret for that prosperity from which Providence tears us; but there is compensation in the assurance afforded by the fulfilment of prophecies, the miracles of the saints, and the conversion of the multitudes. Even at the temporal level an Empire must benefit from the improved moral character of its citizens, once they were Christians.

If, then, there is sorrow and regret for the past, there is also joy for the future; and if there is sombre pessimism, there is also unbounded hope. The thoughts and images that Augustine uses reflect the experience and life of an artist, the complicated tension of whose anxious spirit reveals to us his large humanity and ardent sensibility.

AUGUSTINE'S DESCRIPTIONS OF THE *CITY OF GOD*

H.I. Marrou, one of the greatest Augustinian scholars of our day, while rightly insisting that salvation is the central drama of the *City of God*, chides[24] us for persisting in the effort to find there the answers to many problems: the rights and duties of the State, the relations of Church and State, the possibility of a Kingdom of God on earth, the explanation of the Reformation, the transmission of Platonism, a philosophy of history, a theology of history—and much else besides. He points to Gilson's book, *Les métamorphoses de la Cité de Dieu*,[25] as a veritable inventory of these 'caricatures' of the true subject of Augustine's work.

With some of these not unfairly labelled 'caricatures' we shall deal in appropriate places. It will be useful at this stage, however, to put the reader in immediate contact with Augustine's *own* descriptions of his book. Whether he was writing a letter to the priest Firmus,[26] or engaged in the opening chapters of certain stages of the work, or reviewing it as a whole when he came to publish his *Retractationes*, his general outline and description are both accurate and unvarying. Here we shall give without comment his over-all description in the *Retractationes*, followed by his explanations at various important points of the book as it proceeded.

Retractationes 2.69 (426–7, AD):
In the meantime Rome had been swept by an invasion of the Goths under the leadership of King Alaric and the impact of a great disaster; and the worshippers of the many false gods, to whom we commonly give the name of pagans, attempting to attribute this visitation to the Christian religion, began more sharply and more

24 *Augustinus Magister* (1954), 3.202.   25 Paris (1952).   26 *Revue Bénédictine*, 51, 109–21.

bitterly than usual to blaspheme the true God. Burning with the zeal of God's house, I decided to write against their blasphemies and errors the books on the *City of God*. This work engaged me for some years because many other matters intervened that I could not conscientiously postpone, and kept me busy completing them first. At last, however, this huge work on the *City of God* was brought to a conclusion in twenty-two books.

The *first five* books *refute* those whose interest in *the welfare of mankind* is bound up with the belief that this *depends on the worship of the many gods* whom the pagans were wont to worship, and who maintain that the misfortunes in question owe their existence and magnitude to the prohibition of that worship. The *next five books*, again, *are an answer to* such as, though they admit that mortal men were never in the past spared such misfortunes nor will be in the future, and that ill fortune is sometimes greater, sometimes less as it affects different regions, eras or individuals, yet maintain that the *worship of many gods, in which sacrifices are made to them, is advantageous because of the life that will be ours after death.* In these ten books, then, are refuted those two false notions that are contrary to the Christian religion.

But lest someone reply that we have only argued against the opinions of others but have not stated our own, this is attended to in *the second part* of this work, which comprises twelve books. When need arises, however, our own position is also stated in the first ten books, and opposing views are also refuted in the twelve later books.

Of these twelve succeeding books, the first four contain the origin of the two cities, the one of God, the other of this world; the second four, their course or progress; the third and last four, their appointed ends. And so all twenty-two books, though they dealt with *both cities, yet took their title from the better,* with the result that they were called by preference the *City of God*.[27]

The text of the *City of God* itself is furnished with a set of headings for every chapter of the work. This goes back to medieval times and is sometimes attributed to Augustine himself or said to have been composed on his instructions. A perusal of it will acquaint the reader with the actual matter of the work.

Augustine reviews the progress of the work at special junctures–such as Books 2. 2; 3. 1; 4.1–2; 6. Preface and 1; 11.1; 12.1; 18.1. Of these a few are as follows:[28]

Book 6. Preface and 1   In the five preceding Books, I have, I hope, sufficiently refuted those who think that many gods are to be venerated and worshipped . . . in order to gain advantages for this mortal life and men's temporal affairs . . . which (worship) is due to the true God alone. Christian truth makes clear that these gods are false, that they are useless idols, or unclean spirits, or dangerous demons, or, at best, mere creatures and not the Creator.

. . . My next purpose, then . . . will be the refutation and instruction of those who hold that the gods of the pagans, which Christianity rejects, are to be worshipped . . . with a view to life after death. The starting point . . . will be the revealed truth (*veridico oraculo*) of the holy psalm. . . .

---

27 2.69: McCracken's translation in the Loeb Series.   28 The reader may not require this documentation.

Book 11.1   The expression, 'City of God', which I have been using is justified by
that Scripture whose divine authority puts it above the literature of all other people
and brings under its sway every type of human genius . . . not by some casual
intellectual reaction, but by a disposition of Divine Providence. For, in this Scripture,
we read: 'Glorious things are said of thee, O City of God'.[29]

Through this and similar passages too numerous to quote, we learn of the existence
of a City of God whose Founder has inspired us with a love and longing to become
its citizens. The inhabitants of the earthly city who prefer their own gods to the
Founder of the holy City do not realize that He is the God of gods—though not, of
course, of those false, wicked and proud gods who, because they have been deprived
of that unchangeable light which was meant for all, are reduced to a pitiful power
and, therefore, are eager for some sort of influence and demand divine honors . . .
[but] of those reverent and holy 'gods'[30] who prefer to obey and worship one God
rather than to have many others . . . worshipping them.

. . . Now . . . realizing what is expected of me . . . to discuss . . . the origin, history,
and destiny of the respective cities . . . which . . . are at present inextricably inter-
mingled, . . . first, I shall explain how these two cities originated when the angels
took opposing sides.

Book 12.1   . . . we must now proceed to the creation of men and see the beginning
of the cities so far as it concerns the kind of rational creatures who are mortal.
First, . . . there is no real difficulty or impropriety in speaking of a single society
composed of both men and angels . . . therefore, it is right to say that there are not
four cities or societies . . . but only two, one of them made up of the good—both
angels and men—and the other of those who are evil [i.e. evil angels and evil men].

There is no reason to doubt that the contrary dispositions . . . among these good
and bad angels are due, not to different natures and origins, 'for God the Author and
Creator of all substances has created them both', but to the dissimilar choices and
desires of these angels themselves. Some, remaining faithful to God, the common
good of all, have lived in the enjoyment of His eternity, truth, and love; while others,
preferring the enjoyment of their own power, as though they were their own good,
departed from the higher good and common blessedness for all and turned to goods
of their own choosing . . . preferring . . . pride to . . . eternity, the craftiness of vanity
to the certainty of truth, and the turmoil of dissension to the union of love . . . they
became proud, deceitful, and envious.

Since the happiness of all angels consists in union with God (*adhaerere Deo*), it
follows that their unhappiness must be found in the very contrary, that is, in not
adhering to God.

Book 15.1   . . . I think I have said enough on the really great and difficult problems
concerning the origin of the world, the soul, and the human race. In regard to
mankind I have made a division . . . those who live according to man . . . those who
live according to God. And . . . in a deeper sense, we may speak of two cities or two

29 *Ps.* 87.3.   30 i.e. angels.

human societies, the destiny of the one being an eternal kingdom under God, while the doom of the other is eternal punishment along with the Devil. (*In duo genera distribuimus, unum eorum, qui secundum hominem, alterum eorum, qui secundum Deum vivunt; quas etiam mystice appellamus civitates duas, hoc est duas societates hominum, quarum est una quae praedestinata est in aeternum regnare cum Deo, altera aeternum supplicium subire cum diabolo.*)

Of the final consummation of the two cities I shall have to speak later. Of their original cause among the angels, whose number no man knows, and then in the first two human beings, I have already spoken . . . therefore, I must deal with the course of the history of the two cities from the time when children were born to the first couple until the day when men shall beget no more . . . as distinguished from their original cause and final consummation, I mean the whole time of world history in which men are born and take the place of those who die and depart.

Now, the first man born of the two parents of the human race was Cain. He belonged to the city of man. The next born was Abel, and he was of the City of God. We all experience as individuals what the Apostle says: 'It is not the spiritual that comes first, but the physical, and then the spiritual.' The fact is that every individual springs from a condemned stock and, because of Adam, must be first cankered and carnal, only later to become sound and spiritual by the process of rebirth in Christ. So, too, with the human race as a whole, as soon as human birth and death began the historical course of the two cities, the first to be born was a citizen of this world and only later came the one who was an alien in the city of men but at home in the City of God, a man predestined by grace and elected by grace. By grace an alien on earth, by grace he was a citizen of heaven.

For as for his birth, it was out of the same corrupted mass that was condemned from the beginning (*ex eadem massa quae originaliter est tota damnata*); but God could make 'from the same mass one vessel for honourable, another for ignoble use'. The first vessel to be made was 'for ignoble use'. Only later was there made a vessel for honourable use[31] . . . as I have said, with the individual . . . comes the clay that is only fit to be thrown away, with which we must begin, but in which we need not remain. Afterwards comes what is fit for use, that into which we can be gradually moulded and in which, when moulded, we may remain. This does not mean that every one who is wicked is to become good, but that no one becomes good who was not once wicked. . . .

Now, it is recorded of Cain that he built a city, while Abel . . . a pilgrim on earth, built none. For the true City of the saints is in heaven though here on earth it produces citizens in whom it wanders as on a pilgrimage through time looking for the Kingdom of eternity. When that day comes it will gather together all those who, rising in their bodies, shall have that kingdom given to them in which, along with their Prince, the King of Eternity, they shall reign for ever and ever.

31 *Rom.* 9.21.

Book 22.30 [This, the last chapter of the *City of God*, gives a summary of Augustine's view of the history of mankind in the past and for the future.] There is a clear indication of this final Sabbath if we take the seven ages of world history as being 'days' and calculate in accordance with the data furnished by the Scriptures. The first age or day is that from Adam to the flood; the second, from the flood to Abraham . . . not identical in length of time, but in each there were ten generations. Then follow the three ages, each consisting of fourteen generations, as recorded in the Gospel of St Matthew . . . to Christ's nativity. . . . Thus, we have five ages. The sixth is the one in which we now are . . . an age not to be measured by any precise number . . . since we are told: 'It is not for you to know the times or dates which the Father has fixed by his own authority'.[32] After this 'day', God will rest on the 'seventh day', in the sense that God will make us, who are to be this seventh day, rest in Him.

. . . this 'seventh day' will be our Sabbath and . . . will end in no evening, but only in the Lord's day—that eighth and eternal day which dawned when Christ's resurrection heralded an eternal rest both for the spirit and for the body. On that day we shall rest and see, see and love, love and praise. . . .

THE STRUCTURE OF THE *CITY OF GOD*

There are a few observations one should make about the structure of the *City of God*. The final twelve books deal in the main with the history of time and eternity as given in the Bible, which is of Jewish provenance. Of the first ten books the second five deal mainly with Greek philosophy, more particularly Platonism, and especially with the Neoplatonists Plotinus and more particularly Porphyry—with lengthy consideration of the views of the latter. The first five books deal in the main with the polytheism of Rome, with special reference to Varro. Here are the three great themes of the work: the Bible, Greece, and Rome. Augustine himself draws attention to this explicitly in one of the most dramatic sections of the work:

'Who is this God of yours, and how do we know that the Romans were obliged to adore Him with sacrifices to the exclusion of other gods?' One must be blind indeed to be asking at this late date who our God is! He is the God whose Prophets foretold things we see realized under our very eyes. He is the God who gave the reply to Abraham: 'In thy seed shall all the nations of the earth be blessed' . . .[33] this promise has been made good in Christ, born in the flesh of Abraham's seed—a fulfilment which those who have remained opposed to Christ's name know so well, though they like it so little. He is the God whose Spirit spoke through Prophets whose predictions are now realized in our visibly world-wide Church and which I quoted in previous Books. He is the God whom Varro, the most learned of Romans, thought was Jupiter, however little he grasped the import of his words. It is at least worth mentioning that a man of his learning was unable to think of our God as despicable or non-existent. . . . Varro identified Him with his own conception of the supreme deity.

32 *Act* 1.7.   33 *Gen.* 22.18.

Finally, our God is the one whom Porphyry, most learned of philosophers and bitter enemy of Christianity, admits to be a great God, and this on the strength of pagan oracles.[34]

The first sentence in this excerpt indicates Augustine's standpoint in the whole of his inquiry: the Roman world.[35] His attitude is not negative; on the contrary he is concerned for that world's future. Rome was to bring together within herself the revelation in the Bible, the wisdom of Greek philosophy, and what was good in her own tradition. Augustine is fully conscious of the fusion of the elements that in fact went to make up the civilization of the West that has endured to this day. In this sense his *City of God* is a, if not the, Charter of Christendom, and in this lies its greatest significance.

The Bible, Greek philosophy, Roman speculation on religion all pointed to one God, the God of the Hebrews. This God should now be accepted as the God of Rome. The prophecies in their fulfilment, and the Church in its extension, its martyrs, and its miracles, left no doubt possible on this. The aspirations of Hebrews, Greeks, and Romans were to be fulfilled in a Christian Rome. The Christian Era, the *tempora Christiana*, was already a reality. Even if some evils endured, it was a blessed reality.

Augustine may have come to these pregnant views through reading or argument; but it is most unlikely that once again his own personal experience did not influence him here also. His was a life led in a Roman environment, based on Roman education, drawing importantly upon Greek philosophy at a time most critical to his development, and resting in the main after his conversion on the Christian Scriptures. His *Confessions* not merely testify to this in contents: in very form they too describe a Roman's background and education,[36] the contribution of Greek philosophy,[37] and life according to the Christian revelation. In particular the last three books of the *Confessions* cover in part the same ground as is later covered in the fuller and richer canvas of the last twelve books of the *City of God*.

There are rudimentary traces of the same progress from Rome to Greece to the Scriptures in others of Augustine's works. The *Against the Academics* proceeds from Cicero to the *schola Plotini*, but puts the authority of Christ above that again.[38] The preface to the *Happy Life,* with which we have already dealt, implies a similar progression. The contemporary *On Order* in its turn discusses more explicitly[39] a system of education based on the same lines.

In the pages that follow we shall take our cue from Augustine and consider the *City of God* from the three angles indicated by himself: its interpretation of the Bible; its attitude to Greek philosophy, in effect to Platonism, or more precisely Neoplatonism; and its attitude to Rome.

---

34 19.22.   35 Cf. *City of God* 3.1.   36 1–7.12.   37 7.13–9.   38 3.43.   39 2.25.54.

5

The Bible

Augustine's first and final evidence on any point in the *City of God* is the declaration of the Scriptures: 'We ought first to place the divine testimonies as it were in the foundation of the building'.[1] In his view the authority of Scripture is the most exalted, and is pre-eminent over everything else whatsoever.[2]

This is not an idle declaration; with it corresponds Augustine's practice. The whole approach of the book is from the viewpoint of the Scriptures, and the matter of the larger second part is, in addition, taken from the Bible.

Such confidence, Augustine believed, was justified by the fulfilment of its prophecies, by the miracles of Christianity, and by the flocking, as it seemed, of all mankind to the feet of Christ. Revelation had been gradual, proceeding more slowly in the beginning, becoming much clearer in the election of Abraham, and finally manifested in the coming of the Saviour. Among the many passages dealing with this theme, a few might be considered representative,[3] of which the first will be taken from outside the *City of God*:

I shall begin the description of His (God's) deeds among men from (the time of) Abraham. For to him a manifest promise was made through an angelic oracle (*angelicum oraculum*), which we now see being fulfilled. For to him it was said: 'In your seed shall all the nations be blessed':[4] from whose seed is the people of Israel, whence the Virgin Mary, who bore Christ, in whom are blessed all the nations let those now dare to deny who can. And not in the Christian era, but long before, was that predicted which is being fulfilled by Christians: 'to Thee shall the nations come from the end of the earth'.[5] Behold now it is happening; behold the nations are now coming to Christ from the end of the earth, repeating these words and breaking idols.[6]
. . . these things were not done and recorded without some prefiguring of what was to come and . . . they are to be referred only to Christ and His Church, which is the City of God. . . .[7] . . . it is in these oracles (*oracula*) (to Abraham) that the utterances of our God, Who is the true God, begin to have a clearer reference to the chosen people. . . .[8] . . . of all the truths they preached the chief is this: that Christ rose from the dead and was the first to reveal that immortality of resurrection in the flesh. . . .[9]

1 20.1. 2 11.1, but see 20 above 3 Cf. 7.32; 10.8, 17; 17.16; 18.27ff., 50f.; 22.5–8. 4 *Gen.* 22.18.
5 *Jer.* 16.19. 6 *De Consensu Evangelistarum* 1.39f. (400 AD). 7 *City of God* 16.2. 8 16.30. 9 22.10.

Among the miracles, used to confirm Scripture, the one which was pre-eminent was Christ's resurrection.[10] This, one can see, was of special significance in Augustine's work.

It will have been noticed that in the quotations just given the Scriptures are referred to as oracles. This is not otiose or an accident: it is frequent and deliberate throughout the *City of God*. There are, for example, a dozen instances of it in Books 16–18. The reason for this is not far to seek. Augustine, in confronting a book of Porphyry's entitled *Philosophy from Oracles*,[11] was facing pagan oracles of considerable repute. These oracles he repudiated—but not so as to deny that they might convey some truth. God's revelation was not confined *solely* to Scripture, and Augustine was ready to recognize that God might reveal His truth as He pleased. The God we worship chose certain spirits and gave them the power of foresight, and through them He makes prophecies.[12]

His confident contention, however, was that the oracles of the Christian Scriptures were not few and obscure as were those of the pagans.[13] The foreknowledge God gave to demons was unsure, and the demons themselves could be deceived.[14] This could not be said of the Scriptures, which were oracles many and clear.

The consideration of the Scriptures from this angle, that is, in contrast with, and as superior to the oracles of Porphyry, lends special significance to Augustine's treatment of his topic in this way. Since his declared doughtiest opponent was Porphyry, he would engage him not only directly in argument but also in his use of oracles.

Apart from Augustine's confident recourse to Scripture for truth and his assurance of its evident superiority over pagan oracles, there is one other point affecting his attitude to the Bible that must at this stage be mentioned: the problem of its interpretation. Here we are not so much concerned with the ordinary aspect of this problem-this is, in a general way, the understanding of the application of the text from St Paul quoted so often, and with such effect in relation to Augustine, by St Ambrose: 'For the letter killeth, but the spirit quickeneth'[15]—but rather with attempting to show that what Augustine (among other Christian authors) was doing was likewise part of a persisting and long-established tradition in the Platonist schools.

Philo Judaeus (*c.*30 BC–AD 45) of Alexandria is credited with innovating the technique of applying Greek philosophy to the Hebrew Scriptures.[16] His method was that of the elaborate and extended commentary upon the text. His chief device in the application of Platonism to Scripture was allegory, an instrument used long before his time in the interpretation of Homer and Hesiod, and similarly used after his time by, for example, Porphyry. Porphyry also used this method in his *Philosophy from Oracles*, which comprised the text of the oracles and his comments upon them.

By Augustine's time this kind of commentary had to an extent supplanted the older vehicle of philosophical speculation, the dialogue. It is, therefore, a cause of no surprise that at an early stage of his career he should have thought of devoting his life to commenting upon the Scriptures, that in fact a great deal of his books are scriptural commentaries, and finally that the last twelve books of the *City of God* are in a sense the exposition of certain fundamental teachings of Revelation. Indeed, the frequency of the

---

10 22.10.   11 Cf. the author's *Porphyry's Philosophy from Oracles in Augustine* (1959), 63 and 78 below. 12 7.30.   13 19, 23.   14 9.22.   15 2 *Cor.* 3.6.   16 Cf. H.A.Wolfson, *Philo* (1938), 1.103, 142; 2.443.

Scriptural commentary began to be an indication of Christian domination and the Christians' assumption of intellectual responsibility.

The inspiration for the idea of the 'city' of God has been sought in diverse places, from Plato's *Republic*[17] to the writings of the Donatist Tyconius.[18] It is true that there is discussion of political themes in the work-but one must add that this happens from time to time only. There is no suggestion that the city in question, the *civitas*, is to be thought of in terms of walls and houses, government and administration, army and police, internal policy or (in a political sense) external relations. There is no suggestion in fact of anything physical. Neither is there much help to be got from understanding Augustine's use of the term 'city' in an 'ideal' or Platonic sense[19]— as a model city in the truly existing world of intelligibles. Such a city, if the word is to have any meaning, must have the properties in a real sense that we observe in their shadowy participations and imitations here below.

A fresh and careful reading of the *City of God* will confirm the welcome tendency now manifesting itself of taking Augustine at his word. To the explicit testimony of the text from 11.1, already quoted we may add that of 15.1[20] where he with little less clarity indicates that the reference of his title is to the Bible, particularly the *Psalms*, and most particularly *Psalm* 87.3: 'Glorious things are said of thee, O city of God'.

It is not merely that the title comes from the Scriptures: its application is no more precise than it is in Scripture. Augustine apparently saw no inconvenience in this; for the time and number of books devoted by him to his theme afforded him ample opportunity to be as precise as he chose. This is not to say that he allows himself to be inconsistent. His views as expressed in the *City of God* may conflict not only with the teaching adopted by the Church, for example, on the central matter of predestination, but also with his own views expressed elsewhere; but this does not affect the general consistency to be found within the work itself.

His statements, as a matter of fact, are clear enough as far as they go. He speaks, as we have seen, of the 'city' of God, because Scripture has informed us of its existence. When he proceeds to describe what is meant, he usually calls it a 'society' (*societas*): 'these two societies of angels, diverse and contrary to one another';[21] 'societies, as it were cities';[22] 'two divisions of human society, which we can following our Scriptures rightly call cities';[23] 'city, that is society of the impious';[24] 'two divisions which mystically we call two cities, that is societies';[25] 'the city of this world, which indeed is the society of impious angels and men',[26] and so on. Society, however, is not the only equivalent given for *civitas*; there is also 'kind',[27] 'house',[28] 'temple': 'whether it be called the house of God or the temple of God, or the city of God, it is the same'; family[29] and, by implication and in no more precise sense, 'kingdom'.[30]

Augustine defines the term *civitas* as being nothing other than a concordant multitude

17 Cf. E. Barker, *City of God*, Everyman (1947) xvf.   18 Cf. J. Ratzinger, *Revue des Études Augustinien-nes* (1956), 173–85.   19 But see H.J. Marrou, *Augustinus Magister* (1954), 3.200.   20 52 and 53 above.   21 9.34.   22 12.28.   23 15.1.   24 15.9.   25 15.1.   26 18.18.   27 *Genus*, 14.1,   15.1.   28 *Domus*, 15.19.   29 1.35, 29.   30 22.30.

of men (*aliud non sit quam concors hominum multitudo*[31]), or again as being nothing other than a multitude of men bound together by some bond of association (*hominum multitudo aliquo societatis vinculo conligata*[32]).

From these considerations one is led to the conclusion that the essential, if not sole, significance that Augustine wishes us to grasp from his use of the term 'city' is quite simply the idea of association in itself. Other significations may be misleading, and the title has undoubtedly been the cause of much misunderstanding. His justification is that Scripture used the term. In view of the fact that the ancient city with its citadel, tutelary deity, and organized public worship was at least in part a religious entity, the term had also a certain appositeness in the treatment of the subject of religion as it affected, for example, the Roman Empire.

The next point to determine is the nature of the bond that creates the association. Augustine is emphatic and crystal clear: 'so that is the great difference, whereby each of the two cities of which we speak is distinguished: one a society namely of pious men, the other of impious, each of them with the angels attached to them, in which has precedence in one the love of God, in the other the love of self'.[33] One is the society of those who freely serve the true God; the other is the society of those who freely refuse to do so. One is humble, the other proud; one clings to God, the other depends upon itself and does not cling to God. The two associations centre on these two mutually exclusive focuses. The city of God is, reverting to Augustine's definition of the *civitas*, the multitude of men bound in association by the love of God.

Among the misunderstandings that have arisen from attaching undue importance to the term 'city' is that Augustine is speaking, not of two cities—of those predestined to salvation and those predestined to damnation—but of three,[34] that is, the two mentioned, which may be described as the spiritual-heavenly city and the carnal-earthly city, with the addition of a third, the spiritual-earthly city. This is basically an attempt to provide for the apparent good of this world that yet does not and will not belong to the city of God. Must it be relegated to the damned city? With this problem we shall attempt to deal in due course. It must be said straightway, however, that any solution that implies a third city is in direct contradiction with the most explicit statement of Augustine: 'nevertheless there exist no more than a certain two divisions of human society, which according to our Scriptures we may rightly call two cities'.[35] Moreover, it is inconceivable that if Augustine had considered his theme in terms of three cities that he should never have said so, but always spoken of two.

We can now address ourselves to the question of what Augustine more fully means by the 'city' of God. The first thing to grasp, never to relinquish, is that the city of God exists already in heaven and, apart from certain pilgrim men who are on their way to it while they are on this earth, in heaven only. God's unchangeable will is its law. It is composed of the good angels and men who are saved. All these, and those who are yet to join them, were predestined to belong to this city.

On earth this city does not exist, but men, born outside it (and therefore in the earthly

31 1.15.   32 15.8.   33 14.13.   34 Cf. H.I. Marrou, *Studia Patristica*, Berlin (1957), 2.342–50.
35 14.1.

city) can become citizens of it and be on pilgrimage to it while they are here below: 'the city of the saints is above, although it brings forth citizens here, in whom it is on pilgrimage'.[36] Christ is the founder and king of this city in its earthly connection. Entry to the city for men is through regeneration in Christ—by belief in His resurrection: 'as long as the city of God, which is begotten of faith in Christ's resurrection, is on pilgrimage here'.[37] Such of the Hebrews (who as a people prefigured the city of God, but who individually might or might not belong to it) as did belong to this city and such other men of what race soever (including the Erythraean or Cumaean Sibyl[38]) as became its citizens, were enabled to do so through belief in Christ's mediation as revealed in prophecy or other divine means.[39]

Such men as belong to the city of God are saved by grace: 'nevertheless the omnipotent God, the most great and good creator of all natures, who helps and rewards wills that are good, but abandons and condemns those that are bad, while ordering both, was assuredly not without a means by which He might make up a fixed number of citizens, predestined in His wisdom, of His city, even from the condemned race of men'.[40] Without grace one cannot become, what one does not deserve to be, a citizen of this city.[41]

It is to be remarked that Augustine here seems to imply, what elsewhere[42] he states, that the human content of the city of God is intended to make up for the loss of the rebellious angels. In 22.1 he considers the possibility that more men may be saved than angels were lost.

The citizens of the heavenly city, preserving the right order in their love,[43] clinging to God,[44] sacrificing to Him only,[45] and living in the hope of God[46]—and not in earthly expectation—attain through salvation in Christ a state far superior to that which, if Adam had not sinned, would have been man's lot.[47] This gain is stressed by St Paul in his Epistle to the Corinthians:[48] it represented a marvellous elevation of man's nature in Christ's resurrection.[49] It is well to draw attention to this more optimistic aspect of the *City of God*, of which only the pessimism that arises from predestination to damnation is often remembered.

One question of great interest is whether the number of men in the city of God is great or small. Augustine tells us that its citizens are many,[50] but seems to imply, nevertheless, that they are few in comparison with the multitude of the impious.[51] This should mean that the majority of men are predestined to damnation. Moreover, we are informed that those, who do not transfer their allegiance from the devil to Christ while they are alive, are to be presumed to belong to the devil.[52]

The distinguishing mark of the city of God, insofar as it shares with the other city a common mortality, is the worship of the one true God. On this point there cannot but be variance between it and the other city, which is distinguished in refusing to worship the one true God, worshipping false gods instead. The other city, known variously as the city of the Devil, the earthly (*terrena*) city, the city of this world (*huius saeculi*), and

36 15.1.   37 15.18.   38 18.23.   39 18.47.   40 14.26.   41 Cf.15.2, 21.   42 22.1.   43 15.22.
44 12.1.   45 10.1.   46 15.21.   47 Cf. G. Ladner, *The Idea of Reform* (1959), 153ff., 239ff., 242ff.
48 1 *Cor.* 15.21f.   49 Cf. 13.23.   50 17.2.   51 16.21.   52 21.24.

the enemy (*inimica*) city, exists here.[53] It is composed of all those men and angels[54] who are predestined not to belong to the city of God. As we look around us we are looking at, for the most part, the human members of this city—but they are not distinguishable as such: any of them may before death join the city of God. When the end of the world comes and all men are dead, the cities of God and—as it will then be most accurately described—of the Devil will no longer be indistinguishable. Entry for men to this city is simply by birth and is inevitable; we are all born to it,[55] although we may pass out of it through Christ.[56] Our nature, indeed, is good, but it is vitiated by sin.[57] This city has the Devil for its king,[58] draws its human membership from Adam's progeny,[59] and was founded by Cain, in whom it first began to appear.[60] The members of this city refuse through pride to cling to God,[61] turn away from the Creator,[62] and do evil in not observing the proper order in their use of even good created things—in which is their whole interest.[63] They are under the domination of the angels who forsook God.[64] The distinguishing mark of this city is the worship of and sacrifice to idols and false gods.[65] It is deservedly damned in punishment, and that for eternity.[66]

One must be careful, of course, to distinguish between the city of the Devil, which is a mystical city of evil spirits and men who will not worship the true God, and the created nature which they use in common with the citizens of the city of God. This nature, as we have seen, has occasioned the suggestion that Augustine intends that there are three cities, not two. Before, however, we deal with the problem of this nature we should say something about Augustine's idea of what evil is.

It is essential to understand that for Augustine evil is not something positive; it is rather a lack of something. It has, he says,[67] no efficient cause: it may be said to have a deficient one. To use, for example, a created good for any end other than the worship of the Creator is evil: 'The first evil will was indeed a declining from the work of God to its own works rather than any work'.[68] Again: 'to forsake the Creator and live according to the created good, is not good'.[69] It can be seen, immediately, how Augustine, according to this doctrine, can refer to what is merely human or merely humanly considered, as simply evil. This is the *absolute* canon by which all things are judged. If Augustine appears to relent from time to time and speak of goodness apart from this, he is speaking of what is only relatively good. This creates ambiguity and confusion of which the most notorious case is his inclusion of justice in the definition of the State in one instance and exclusion of it in another: but this we shall see later.

Many things have a limited or relative goodness: the flesh itself, female beauty, righteous victory, peace—indeed all created things insofar as they are created are good.[70] Man unaided by any special revelation manifests this goodness in his ability to attain truth concerning the Creator and Providence, to practise virtues such as patriotism and justice, and to attain to friendship and good manners'.[71] Human virtue can even serve as an improving example for the citizens of the city of God.[72]

The reward, however, for this goodness is confined to this life: 'they have received

53 18.1f., 20.14, 21.1. 54 18.18. 55 15.1, 16. 56 21.16. 57 15.2. 58 17.20. 59 15.17.21. 60 15.7, 17. 61 14.13. 62 14.5. 63 4.21; 14.9; 15.22. 64 16.17. 65 18.23, 54. 66 15.21; 21.16. 67 12.6f. 68 14.11. 69 14.5. 70 14.5f.; 15.4, 22. 71 18.41. 72 5.18f.

their reward'.[73] As goodness it is inferior at its best even to the imperfect beginnings of
the virtues of the citizens of the city of God.[74] Indeed a virtue that is without reference
to God is but a seeming virtue and is, rather, *absolutely* vice. It lacks the true justice
which exacts the recognition of the true God.[75] Merely human virtue ultimately involves
the rejection of the true God, which is a disorder arising from pride.[76] The State, for
example, considered from a merely human point of view, aims at dominance and worships
what god or gods will help it thereto: this is a gross perversion of the proper order.[77]

Nevertheless it still remains true that the created nature that is used in common by
both the city of God and the city of the Devil is good in itself.[78] This nature is not only
physical; it also takes the forms of institutions and activities and enters into everything
except the wills of evil men.

But since this nature exists here below—and therefore outside the city of God—it
is natural that it should be confused with the city that exists here: the city of the Devil.
At the same time Augustine more often than not avoids the term 'city of the Devil' and
speaks of the earthly (*terrena*) city, or the city of this world (*huius mundi*), formulas that—
keeping to the actual words themselves—do not necessarily imply any suggestion of
evil, or at worst suggest something less perfect and limited than what is described as
heavenly (*coelestis*). Only the context will show whether Augustine intends by these terms
the mystical city of the Devil or the relative goodness of created nature. When, for
example, he says that the earthly city is not eternal[79] he cannot mean the city of the Devil,
which is eternal.[80]

The things used in common, therefore, by the two great eternal and mystical cities
are good, but limited and temporal. They do not constitute a third city, for the cities in
question have to do with the wills of men and angels. These cities existed before earthly
created nature and will exist when it is no more. In this earthly period, created nature
is used by citizens of both cities who can share most things, with, however, the great
exception of religion and worship: this is the great and significant divide.

It is evident that the two cities were predestined to be constituted as they are and that
God's providence is operative in their realization. Attention must be called to
Augustine's doctrine on these fundamental points.[81]

We have already seen the clear and sombre text from 15.1 where it is stated beyond
doubt that one city is predestined to reign with God and the other to be condemned
with the Devil for all eternity. Another text, for example, is no less clear: 'What shall He
give them whom He has predestined for life, who had given these things even to those
whom He has predestined to death?'[82]

In His providence God has foreseen that those predestined to be damned will be
useful for the saved and will afford a contrast between the two cities: the presence of
evil makes the good more evident.[83] Providence uses temporal disasters, such as wars,
evil demons, and evil of every kind for its purposes.[84] It broods overall, and through it

---

73 15.3; *Matt.* 6.2. 74 5.18f. 75 19.25. 76 14.9, 28; 15.22; 19.24. 77 15.7. 78 15.22. 79 15.4,
17. 80 15.1. 81 Cf. H. Rondet, *Saint Augustin parmi nous* (1954) 201–22, 297–306. 82 22.24.
83 17.11; 22.1. 84 7.30, 33f.; 10.21.

those predestined to salvation are brought not to the perfection that was man's in Paradise, but the higher perfection of God's city.[85]

Ultimately being a citizen of the city of God means salvation. Those who are still on earth are on the 'way' to the fatherland; they are in the harbour whence they may pass to the fatherland itself. Here we recognize the persistence of Augustine's earlier ideas on man's destiny. Plain too is the continuance of his idea of the role of disaster and misfortune in the purposes of Providence. He had discerned this in the pattern of his own life as he had seen it at the time of his conversion. Now he discerned it in the life of mankind.

His picture of that life, presented from one point of view, is gloomy indeed. But we must, for all that, give some of it:

> *Book 22.22* . . . a darksome pool . . . [of] heartaches, troubles, griefs, and fears; such insane joys in discord, strife, and war; such wrath and plots of enemies, deceivers, sycophants; such fraud and theft and robbery; such perfidy and pride, envy and ambition, homicide and murder, cruelty and savagery, lawlessness and lust; all the shameless passions of the impure—fornication and adultery, incest and unnatural sins, rape and countless other uncleannesses too nasty to be mentioned; the sins of religion—sacrilege and heresy, blasphemy and perjury; the iniquities against our neighbours—calumnies and cheating, lies and false witness, violence to persons and property; the injustices of the courts and the innumerable other miseries and maladies that fill the world, yet escape attention.
>
> It is true that it is wicked men who do such things, but the source of all such sins is that radical canker in the mind and will that is innate in every son of Adam. . . . who can describe or even imagine all the later ills that befall mankind? Who can be free from fear or grief in a world of mourning and bereavement, of losses and legal penalties, of liars and deceivers, of the false imputations, violences and other wickednesses of our neighbours . . . of the tragedies of being robbed or reduced to slavery, of bonds and prison walls, of banishment and torture, of limbs cut off and eyes torn out, of bodies made to minister to an oppressor's lusts, and of all other no less dreadful possibilities.
>
> And think of the dread we have of the countless accidents of nature, of the extremes of heat and cold, of winds and rains and floods, of thunder, lightning and winter storms, of earthquakes, landslides . . . of poisoned fruits, and waters, of pestilential air . . . of the bites of wild animals.

The catalogue goes on and on, listing the miseries that befall man in the forests, and the seas, accidents, plagues, floods, assaults from the devils, diseases and their painful remedies, famine (which can lead a mother to devour even her child), frightening dreams, and hallucinations. There is one thing that gives hope and deliverance in the end from all these miseries— the grace of Christ. Such comfort as human philosophy can afford must also ultimately be referred to Him whose gift philosophy is.

Finally comes the question of the role of the Church in the *City of God*.

85 5.1; 22.1.

In a *very general* way Augustine identifies the Church with the city of God on pilgrimage here below. Thus he speaks of the 'city of God, this is His Church';[86] 'the Church, which is the city of God';[87] 'that beloved city which is nothing other than the Church of Christ spread throughout the whole world'.[88] The formula may vary from time to time; he may speak of the Christian religion[89] rather than the Church; or he may allude to the 'city of the great King';[90] or to 'Christ and His Church, that is the King and the city which He founded',[91] or to 'Christ and His Church as the King and Queen of the city'[92]—but the 'identity' is always there.

There were, however, serious reservations to this 'identity'.

First, there were citizens of the city of God on the earth before the Church came into being. They became citizens by the grace of Christ it is true; nevertheless they could not have belonged to the Church as a visible society. The Sibyl, for example, Augustine thought, must have been a citizen, since her verses had not only no tendency towards idolatry, but were all against false gods and their worshippers.[93] The test he applies here is significant. The Hebrews, of course, although their aims were ostensibly purely temporal[94] and they were now the enemies of the Church,[95] had the approval and confirmation of miracles for their Law,[96] and so foreshadowed the city of God, and gave it members.[97]

Second, the Gospel warnings of the cockle among the good seed, the separation of the wheat from the chaff, and the mixed collection of fish in the net led Augustine to conclude that there were members of the Church visible who would not be found in the end to belong to the city of God. He was the more led to this conclusion from the observation that many were becoming Christians in his day for what seemed to be unworthy motives—sometimes merely for political protection or advancement. He believed that many would fall into this class.[98]

Third, it was to be presumed that there were likewise men who did not belong to the Church and might seem not to belong to the city of God, who yet are destined for salvation and do in fact belong to that city.

In connection with this last point arises the question whether a man must now join the Church before death if he is to belong to the city of God. The testimony of the *City of God*, with which alone we are here concerned, is represented by the following text:

'Let him, therefore, who wishes to escape eternal punishment not only be baptized, but also justified in Christ and so truly pass from the devil to Christ'.[99] Or again: 'but if any remain impenitent of heart until death, and are not converted from being enemies to being sons, does the Church then pray for them, that is, for the spirits of such dead people? (No) And why? Because he who has not passed over to Christ, while he was in the body, is already *counted* as belonging to the Devil'.[100] The presumption of their damnation does not seem to be absolute; but there equally seems little room for hope.

Augustine knew that a new era, the *tempora Christiana*, had already come. The persecutions, the martyrdoms, the hostilities of the Jews had not been in vain. Now those

86 13.16.   87 16.2.   88 20.11; cf. 8.   89 17.4.   90 17.4.   91 17.15.   92 17.20.   93 18.23.
94 4.33; 5.18; 10.14f.   95 6.11; 17.17f.   96 10.17.   97 16.3.   98 18.48f.; 20.5, 9.   99 21.16.
100 21.24.

very Jews in their dispersion spread the Christian name. The fulfilment of prophecies and the independent conclusions of the secular philosophers, the confirmation of miracles, the political domination of Christianity, the evident decay of paganism and the overthrow of its idols—all gave assurance that few would remain outside Christianity. In Augustine's words, the whole world was running to Christ. In such a context one can understand that it would have seemed partly unnecessary and partly impolitic to dwell upon any other possibility of salvation than that afforded by the Christian religion.

The author of the *City of God* was, ultimately, no millenarian. He believed that the world was declining and that Christ would gradually withdraw His flock from it;[101] he believed, moreover, that the world in his time was in its last age; but he insisted that we cannot know, and we should not speculate on, how long that age would endure.[102]

In the light of the foregoing analysis of the *City of God*, we might now address ourselves to the consideration of what validity there is in the popular and wide-spread notions that this work contains a 'philosophy of history' or—a view that has spread more recently—a 'theology of history'.

A fair sample, and the likely source of some views on the former notion, is to be found in John Neville Figgis's *The Political Aspects of Saint Augustine's City of God*,[103] in which the whole of the third chapter is devoted to the question whether or not Augustine puts forward a philosophy of history. He quotes the opinions of others to the effect that Augustine was a greater philosopher of history than Hegel or Vico, and was indeed 'the true originator in the field of the philosophy of history'. His general attitude is represented in the following passage:

No one who takes the Incarnation seriously can avoid some kind of philosophy of history. That event—if a fact—testifies at once to the importance of human life on earth, and shows its centre. Doubts of Christianity at this moment are largely due to the difficulty felt by many in making the events in Palestine the pivot of human history. The religion of the Incarnation cannot be mere theology—a system of notions developed from certain metaphysical propositions—nor can it be mere ethics, a code of laws on a theistic basis. It has to do with a life on earth in which Christians hold that in the fullness of time—i.e. at the due moment in history—the eternal reality at the heart of things became self-revealed and self-limited in a living earthly person. The issue of this was the fulfilment of the Jewish theocracy in the Christian Church. Augustine moreover approached Christianity emphatically by way of the Church. No one who did that could ignore the problems which it involved. Take a definite historical fact as your centre, take an actual visible society as the special sphere of God's operation, a society which has a past and must have a future on earth; and then you are compelled to some philosophy of history. You cannot, like a sheer Platonist—and Augustine shows leanings that way—treat as of no account the whole development in time and space, as though this world were the dreams of the Absolute in a fit of absence of mind. . . . On the whole, his belief in the Church and his sense of immediate reality were too great. A man who does not give way to the temptation

101 2.18.   102 22.30.   103 London (1924).

of a doctrinaire's system pure and simple, but has so much regard to the actual as St Augustine, is bound to rest unsatisfied without some philosophy giving history a meaning.[104]

Prescinding for the moment from the rather surprising description of theology as 'a system of notions developed from certain metaphysical propositions', and ethics as 'a code of laws on a theistic basis', we might ask ourselves what Figgis means by philosophy, which he applies to history? Philosophy has at various times meant various things, and its etymology, 'love of wisdom', allows it to be very comprehensive; but on the whole its traditional meaning has been discursive reasoning on the subject matter of logic, physics, and ethics. While one must allow for development in the signification of terms and never bind oneself absolutely to rigidity in their use, one does well to conform to received practice in such matters, to use, in short, technical terms technically.

Does Figgis use the term in this way? Hardly! 'Taking a definite historical fact as your centre and an actual visible society as the special sphere of God's operation' in effect means that you are dealing with history, theology perhaps, but not philosophy. Figgis betrays his position when he remarks that, as compared with Vico's *Nuova Scienzia*, Augustine's *City of God* is primarily concerned not with history but *apologetics*: 'Augustine is mainly concerned with the Church, Vico with the world'.[105] Or again: 'It must be conceded that, to St Augustine, history is the sphere of revelation'. Figgis's whole discussion stresses the importance of the Fall, the doctrine of original sin, the crises of Eden and Calvary, and the necessity to justify the Church, and goes on to speak of the role of predestination and of world history as but an episode in relation to Revelation, and declares that 'the paramount significance of the Church, viewed as the depository and dispenser of grace, is of the essence of this historical philosophy'. Philosophy seems hardly the proper word here.

Indeed, Figgis goes so far as to concede that Augustine did not set out to compose a philosophy of history. 'His purpose was not to comprehend history, but to defend the Catholic Church'. Or again: 'Even if this be not a philosophy of history, strictly so called, it is at least a justification of the Church, historically conceived'.

On the whole it is better to abandon the idea that Augustine in the *City of God* was attempting anything like a philosophy of history in any ordinary sense. Some indeed would hold that a philosophy of history is impossible: this is perhaps going too far, and it is possible that the phrase might legitimately be used of the discovery through reason of a pattern in the course of history. With this question we are not here concerned. Suffice it for us if, from the method and contents of the work as we have seen them, we conclude that at any rate the *City of God* gives no philosophy of history.

V.U. Padovani,[106] while insisting upon the view that there is not a philosophy of history to be found in the *City of God* and that a philosophy of history is in any case impossible, goes on to speak of Augustine as unifying history in the light of Revelation, not reason, and therefore as giving us, not a philosophy, but a theology of history.[107] This idea, first mentioned in 1861 by Cournot, has received notable currency in recent years,

104 34f.   105 49.   106 V.U. Padovani, *S. Agostino*, Milan (1931), 220–63; *Filosofia e teologia della Storia* (1953), 2. 29–75.   107 For a *mise-au-point*, see H.I. Marrou, *Augustinus Magister* (1954) 3.193ff.

not, however, without some questioning even by those who advance it. Nevertheless to anyone who has read the *City of God* as a whole this idea is much nearer the truth about the work than that of a philosophy of history.

One should start, however, with having a clear idea of what is meant by theology. The *Shorter Oxford English Dictionary* describes it as 'the study or science, which treats of God, His nature and attributes, and His relations with man and the universe'. This description would surely be accepted as being nearer the mark than Figgis's 'a system of notions developed from certain metaphysical propositions'. The essential point in the definition is that God is the object of theology.

Now the phrase 'theology of history', properly construed, should mean that history was an object of theology, and so it is; but strictly speaking it can be such an object only inasmuch as it is history as looked at from God's point of view. To describe history as looked at from man's point of view as an object of theology robs the term of its proper meaning. On the other hand, if one spoke of a theological interpretation of history, one's meaning would be perfectly clear, one would use words more accurately, and one would lose but little in foregoing the suggestiveness of the phrase 'theology of history'.

But let us see some of the statements of a distinguished recent commentator on this point, H.I. Marrou:

His [Augustine's] theology of history is a knowledge that has issued from the faith, and as such, *per speculum et in aenigmate*, partial, mixed with darkness, combining certitudes with lack of knowledge. One must search for the deep roots of this mystery of history.

The proper object of his theology, and I think of the theology of history, the historical object properly so called, is the economy of salvation.[108]

Marrou frankly recognizes that our despair, growing as this century proceeds, of ever understanding why and how civilizations rise and fall, or the significance of mortal effort in building them—in brief the problem of what he calls the Meaning of History—cannot only not be relieved at all by purely rational speculation, but is only partly relieved by Revelation: a theology of history is a declaration of the *mystery* of history. This theology of history, moreover, concentrates upon the topic of salvation.

Revelation does indeed give a meaning to history and enlighten us on the problem of salvation. If one accepts that Revelation, one has at least a partial (from man's point of view) guide to the Meaning of History. And if one does not accept that Revelation, one at least has had a view offered that one has had to reject. One in short is dealing not with history, but with a Revelation's account of it; with a theological interpretation of history, not with theology, which tells us of God and history only insofar as God sees it.

A by-product of the interest in a theology of history is the impression occasionally conveyed that Augustine's *City of God* was the first major work to substitute the linear concept of man's destiny (according to which he is born, lives his life, dies, and lives eternally in either heaven or hell) for the cyclic, according to which his soul returns from earth to heaven and from heaven to earth in a succession of lives and bodily unions. It

108 Ibid., 196, 202.

is emphatically true that one of the most important points considered in the *City of God* is this very question; and one of the most important and significant points on which Augustine rejects Platonism in every shape and form is this—and it is well to realize that the implication of his rejection is that he cannot be called a Platonist in any full sense—but one should not forget that Christianity did not wait for Augustine to propound what was essential to it. Moreover, it is assuming too much to suppose that the Platonic and cyclical view of man's destiny was commonly accepted by the ordinary Greeks and Romans, or the majority of them. The evidence of literature does not bear this out. Even of Virgil a recent writer has declared: 'It is evident that for Virgil time is not cyclic, but linear. There is a meaning of history which defines itself at the moment in the foundation in the world of the Roman power.[109]

In brief the position adopted here is that the phrase 'theology of history' is a phrase both unnecessary and misleading: it seems to offer a vague promise that it cannot redeem. The *City of God* most certainly gives a theological interpretation of history: this is enough for us.

109 J. Perret, *Virgile* (1959), 115.

6

Greek Philosophy

So much has been written on Platonism and Neoplatonism in Augustine over the last seventy-five years that the impression has been created that the Platonic influence on Augustine was not only extensive and important, but also in certain ways dominant.

While it is not necessary to describe[1] here the course of the various controversies on Platonism in Augustine since Boissier and von Harnack in 1888 independently formulated the theory that at his conversion in 386 Augustine was a Platonist tainted with Christianity rather than a Christian tainted with Platonism, it is well to draw attention to the unsound results of some of the excesses of this theory. In 1918, for example when this theory was at its strength, one was presented with the following statements by Prosper Alfaric in his *L'évolution intellectuelle de saint Augustin*: 'he considered [the Christian tradition] only as a popular adaptation of Platonic wisdom';[2] morally as well as intellectually he was converted to Neoplatonism rather than the Gospel';[3] '[Augustine's synthesis in 386] perceptibly modified the doctrine of the Master (Plotinus) in order to adapt it to the teachings of the Catholic faith. But its transformation of Catholicism was greater in order to bring it into accord with the philosophy of Plotinus, and it regarded [Catholicism] as but an inferior form of wisdom, good only for weak intelligences or beginners';[4] and, 'In him the Christian disappeared behind the disciple of Plotinus'.[5]

No serious scholar would now make such assertions. In the meantime, however, the general views of an earlier period on this matter persist among non-specialists and to a degree are still current and uncorrected. In 1930 Ernest Barker, in an introduction to a shortened version of the *City of God* that was later printed in the Everyman's library and became for many a common introduction to Augustine's great work, wrote:

> St Augustine, as we have already had occasion to mention, was particularly influenced by Plato. He had read his Dialogues in a Latin translation; he had read the Neoplatonists' interpretations of their master, and he cites Plato again and again in the course of the *City of God*. St Augustine carried the *general* thought of Plato into his own general thought; and through him Plato influenced the subsequent course of Western theology throughout the Middle Ages and down to the Reformation, which was

1 Cf. the author's *Against the Academics* (1950), 19–22 for a summary description; also 32ff. above.
2 Preface viii.   3 399.   4 515.   5 527.

indeed itself, in some of its aspects, a return to Plato and St Augustine. 'The appeal away from the illusion of things seen to the reality that belongs to God alone, the slight store set by him on institutions of time and place, in a word, the philosophic idealism that underlies and colours all Augustine's utterances on doctrinal and even practical questions and forms the real basis of his thought, is Platonic'.[6]

[Barker proceeds]'The history of Church doctrine in the West,' von Harnack has said, 'is a much disguised struggle against Augustinianism.' This is a deep saying, and we must attempt to gloss it. St Augustine, we may say, imbued as he was with Platonic philosophy, always believed in the unchanging perfection of a God who always and everywhere acted by law. Against this clear and pure rigour of an unswerving general order it was natural that those should revolt who wanted a mysterious and emotional world, rich in insoluble riddles, and needing a mediatory and miraculous Church to give a mystical clue. Such a revolt was that of the Nominalists of the later Middle Ages. The trend of their thought turned them towards obscurantism. The individual became an ultimate mystery: God himself became an inscrutably omnipotent individual, acting indeterminately by His individual will. The Nominalists thus came to magnify the authority of the Church as the only escape from 'the burden of the mystery'; they believed in *fides implicita*; and in them may be traced the tendency of the over-subtle intellect to pass through obscurantism to the acceptance of mere authority. It was against the Nominalists that Wyclif and Luther were both in revolt; and they both went back to Augustine for comfort and countenance. It would be too bold to say that St Augustine inspired the Reformation. But it would perhaps be true to say that he took the sixteenth century back to the idea of a general order of the Universe, and back to a conception of righteousness based upon that idea.[7]

It is suggested here that Augustine, 'imbued as he was with Platonic philosophy, always believed in the unchanging perfection of a God who always and everywhere acted by law,' and that if he did not actually inspire the Reformation, he took the sixteenth century back to the idea of that law and away from a mysterious and emotional belief in a miraculous Church. Augustine's Platonism is said to be the basis of his position, against which there has been a disguised struggle in the West. It can be seen immediately that the question of Augustine's Platonism is of great importance and continuing interest.

Before we attempt to describe Augustine's Platonism as seen in the *City of God*, we must first remove from the picture given above by Barker, and retailed by others, certain grave misconceptions.

One cannot overlook that in these pronouncements of Barker he appears to depend without question on the authority of Stewart and, significantly, von Harnack, for the core of his case. The nonspecialist can hardly do otherwise; the inconvenience is that he may generalize more than his source, and at any rate is accurate only to the extent that his source is accurate.

We shall see in the course of this chapter that Barker's main point that Augustine,

6 Quotation from Stewart in the *Cambridge Modern History*, 1.579. 7 Everyman *City of God*, xvf., xxxvi.

'imbued with Platonic philosophy, always believed in the unchanging perfection of a God who always and everywhere acted by law', in contrast with those who accept mere authority, is seriously undermined by the fact that when Augustine quotes Plato in the *City of God*, which is infrequently, he quotes repeatedly the same text from the *Timaeus*, translated by Cicero, to the effect that Plato's God was not unchanging and deliberately contravened the established general order.

When Barker speaks of Augustine carrying the general thought of Plato into his own general thought, he is saying something both true and important. It is true, however, only in the sense that there was a philosophical stock in trade, common to all the schools, seen, for example, in the philosophical works of Cicero, and which was in a general way Platonic. In this sense Augustine—but among many others—might be called, as J. Maritain has called him,[8] a Christian Plato; for he did have this stock in trade and it does underlie his philosophical notions.

It is, however, quite wrong to say that Augustine was so affected by Platonic idealism as to set slight store on institutions of time and place: nothing could be further from the truth, as the content of almost every chapter of the *City of God* proves. Neither is it true to suggest that Augustine had little or no need for a mediatory and miraculous Church.[9] Such assertion can be made only by prescinding from his writings and generalizing from unjustified assumptions both about Platonism as it was known to Augustine and his attitude towards it.

It is of some interest to note that Reinhold Niebuhr, while also connecting Augustine with the Reformation, adopts a position directly opposed to that of Barker.[10] To Niebuhr, Augustine's outlook is Biblical and unsubordinated to Classical thought. St Thomas Aquinas, in his view, was responsible for the subordination in question, and the Reformation was a revolt from St Thomas in favour of the Biblical Augustine. Niebuhr speaks of Christian systems both before and after Augustine as being 'inferior because they subordinate the biblico-dramatic conception of human selfhood too much to the rationalistic scheme, as was the case with medieval Christianity culminating in the thought of Thomas Aquinas . . .'[11] Or again, 'It is in fact something of a mystery how the Christian insights into human nature and history, expressed by Augustine, could have been subordinated to classical thought with so little sense of conflict between them in the formulations of Thomas Aquinas'.[12] Paul Tillich likewise sees in Thomism the dissolution of the Augustinian view.[13]

Before we proceed to examine the question of Platonism in the *City of God*, one at least of the most important evidences on the general question of Augustine's Platonism, we might take warning, against the all too widespread notion, that Platonism, or Neoplatonism, in some way dominated him, from the opinions of two of our recent specialists. J.H. Waszink, for example, has come to the conclusion that Augustine absorbed some fundamental ideas from Platonism, but fewer than is generally thought; although he owed much to Neoplatonism, his method of treating problems from the

8 *A Monument to St Augustine* (1930). 9 Cf. J. Ratzinger, *Volk v. Haus Gottes*, 262–76. 10 *The Nature and Destiny of Man* (1941), I.171. 11 *Christian Realism and Political Problems* (1954), 138. 12 Ibid. 127, 116, 124. 13 Cf. *Union Seminary Quarterly Review*, I. (1946), no. 4.

point of view of the Bible prevents one from believing that his thought is greatly influenced by Neoplatonism.[14] M.F. Sciacca believes that the 'Christian Platonism' of Augustine is a *correction* of, rather than an inheritance from Plotinus; Augustine refused to accept Platonic dualism or Plotinus's teaching on emanation; he insists on the resurrection of the flesh and postulates the faith as the source of truth.[15]

In Platonism, Augustine saw the contribution of Greece to his own life, in the first instance, and to the Christian Era. Philosophy, its schools and disputations, was a Greek thing, or Roman only because Greece became a Roman province. The recognition, therefore, that Greece had its contribution to make to the new era and that that contribution is philosophy is explicit, not only in words, but in the emphasis given to the matter in the whole of Books 6 to 10 inclusive. The matter is introduced as being of more importance than that considered in the first five books; the last book dealing with Greek philosophy, 10, is the last of the negative books and is one of the most important books in the work; and the topic comes up again from time to time in the remainder of the work, especially towards the end.

It is well to make clear at once that when Augustine is speaking of Platonism he is usually speaking of all or any of the following: Plato, died 347 BC; Varro, died 27 BC; Apuleius (a fellow African from Madauros, where Augustine went to school), died after AD 161; but especially the Neoplatonists Plotinus, died AD 270, and Porphyry, died about 305. All of them, except Plato himself, lived in the Roman world, and Varro and Apuleius wrote in Latin. These two are discussed in Books 6–7 and 8–9 respectively. Of all of them Porphyry was both nearest in time and of greatest influence in the world of Augustine, and receives the closest attention in the *City of God*, especially in Book 10. Plato and Plotinus receive only occasional consideration.

In addition to these sources of Platonic doctrine, we must also keep in mind the enormous body of Platonic thought transmitted by the divided inheritors of Plato, the Academics, the Neopythagoreans, and elements in other schools, much of which is to be found in Cicero, an author very well known to Augustine. Nor must we ever overlook the influence of persons of Augustine's acquaintance, especially when he was at Milan, who, such as Mallius Theodorus, were actively interested in Platonism.[16]

His knowledge of Platonism convinced Augustine at the time of his conversion that it had the rational answer to very many things, even if he subordinated it to the authority of Christ. His enthusiasm for it had abated by the time he was in the midst of the composition of the *City of God*. Nevertheless his admiration for it even then and to the end of the work and his life was sincere and generous. This arose, partly no doubt from the recollection of the role Platonism played in his conversion, but perhaps even more because of its agreement with Christianity on many vital issues.

In the *City of God* he indicates precise points of agreement—as he understood it— between Christianity and the Platonists. They taught the existence of an incorporeal Creator, of Providence, the immortality of the soul, the honour of virtue, patriotism,

---

14 Cf. *Entretiens sur l'Antiquité classique* 3 (1955), 139–79.   15 *La possibilité d'une philosophie chrétienne* (1956).   16 Cf. the author's *The Young Augustine* (1954, 1980), 125f.

true friendship, and good morals. Final happiness, moreover, they held to be attainable through participation of the soul in the Creator's unchangeable and incorporeal light.[17] 'They agree with us on many things, both the immortality of the soul, that the true God created the world, and on His providence, by which He rules what He created.[18]

Augustine took some satisfaction in discovering in affirmations of the Platonists their belief in, in effect, the Christian God. Thus Varro, although at one stage he is said to have arrived no further than the idea of the world soul, at another is flattered with the possibility that what he called the world soul might rather be the Creator of the soul. The worship of this Creator he wanted to, but feared to, commend: it was certain that while he had no belief in the Roman pantheon, he had confidence in the existence of some invisible force and all-powerful King.[19]

Porphyry appeared to present less difficulty in this matter: in his *Philosophy from Oracles* he accepted the Hebrew God as the true God.[20] He appeared to Augustine to go almost as far as the Christian Trinity: this is the burden of the very remarkable last nine chapters of Book 10 which link up with the equally remarkable sections, describing his own personal experience, in Book 7 of the *Confessions*,[21] where Augustine sees a correspondence between the Prologue to the Gospel of St John ('in the beginning was the Word . . .') and the Neoplatonic hypostases.

In short it appeared to Augustine that the Platonists came very close indeed—closer than any other thinkers—to the Christian truth. Moreover they brought others to it, even when they themselves refused to follow. Who then was more worthy of earnest and sympathetic consideration?

There were two other reasons why, in Augustine's opinion, the Platonists should be heeded.

That philosophy was, like Revelation, also a gift of God is implicit in his idea of the relation of Faith to Reason.[22] Both derived from the same source, God, and even if their methods differed they both needed God's enlightenment. In general the mass of men were more helped by authority than by reason; but some there were whom reason greatly helped. Augustine was not alone amongst earlier Christians to invest philosophy with a quasi-revelatory character: Justin Martyr and Clement had preceded him in this.[23] To many, indeed, Hebrew Revelation and Greek philosophy seemed to describe the same things. Serious philosophy, therefore, such as was Platonism especially, should be heeded.

The other reason demands greater attention. So lively was Augustine's belief in Providence, arising from the pattern that he saw emerging from the vicissitudes of his own life, that he discovered a good result in everything. He gradually built up, elaborated, and constantly applied what one might call a theory of providential economy, which lies behind his views. The clearest statement of this theory is to be found in an early work *On the Usefulness of Believing*, AD 391, where he discusses three kinds of error, the third of which is beneficial: when, for example, a bad thing is (mis)understood by the reader in a right sense—as if one gathered (wrongly) from a phrase of Epicurus that he

17 1.36; 8.1, 6; 11.5; 18.41. 18 1.36. 19 4.31; 7.6f.; 8.1. 20 19.23. 21 Cf. 7.9ff. 22 Cf. 46 above. 23 Cf. H.A. Wolfson, *Philo*, 1.20, 142.

approved of chastity.[24] Augustine was so enamoured of the irony of such a situation that he declared that if one considered the matter carefully, the whole fruit of reading was attained in this; moreover such an error did credit to the man who was deceived by it.[25] In the paragraph following he distinctly says that the reader may understand usefully *the contrary* of what the writer meant. Of the Platonists he explicitly says in *The Trinity* that 'although they were unaware of it, God acted through them, so that truth might everywhere resound'.[26]

It is difficult not to believe that this theory is related to his own experience with the Platonists at the time of his conversion: we have seen indeed the prominence he gave in the *Happy Life* to those set upon a height at the entrance to the harbour of salvation, who point out the way to safety to others, but who through pride do not possess the truth themselves. The implication of the idea is that Augustine at the time of his conversion may have misunderstood the Platonist position on presumably important points; that in doing so he was brought to the Church; and that later he discovered that the Platonists did not hold what he thought they held. The description of his conversion as it was affected by the Platonists and as it is set out in the *Confessions*[27] makes it plain that at that time he either misunderstood or did not fully understand the Platonist position on, for example, the hypostases, the nature of Christ, and bodily immortality. Both the *Confessions*, however, and the *Against the Academics*[28] tell us that when he read the Scriptures, *after* having read the Platonists, he saw all things *for the first* time with real clarity.

In the light of these considerations one can see that Augustine's attitude towards Platonism seems favourable to the extent even that when he disagrees with it he does so not only without rancour but sees the possibility of good issuing from its very error.

This attitude should not, however, blind us to the true position. *Amicus Plato, sed magis amica veritas* (Plato is a friend, but a greater friend is truth). Augustine's actual position is neatly summed up by himself when, speaking of the Platonists and apropos of the *City of God*, he says: 'With whom or *against* whom we dispute': *cum quibus vel contra quos agimus.*[29] Plato, Augustine thought, was greater than any of the 'gods', but for all that he was not as great as any believer in Christ.[30] Christianity comes first, Platonism second. Near as it is, helpful as it is, great as are its common interests with Christianity against rampant materialism, it has tenets that are at radical variance with Christianity. A Christian must ultimately be an anti-Platonist: *contra quos agimus.*

The Platonist who, in Augustine's view, came nearest to Christianity, but who actually became a most bitter enemy of Christianity, was Porphyry, with whom, therefore, Augustine in the *City of God* is particularly concerned.

Porphyry (232/3–*c*. AD 305) was born in Tyre, studied under Longinus at Athens, and in due course became the faithful follower and disciple of Plotinus, whose biography he wrote and whose works he edited. He was himself a prolific writer, regarding it as his mission to popularize the doctrine of his master. At the same time recent work on Porphyry has tended to portray him as a faithful disciple of Plotinus, it is true, but not

24 10f.   25 10.   26 4.23.   27 7.13ff.   28 2.6.   29 21.7.   30 2.7, 14f.

an uncritical one. In fact the *City of God* itself shows Porphyry in the role of serious critic who is sometimes more in tune with Middle Platonism in certain matters than Plotinus. Moreover the traditional picture of Porphyry as one who was first uncritical, then under the influence of Plotinus became critical, and finally ended his life as an uncritical theurgist is being revised.[31] Be that as it may, by the time Augustine came to write the *City of God* 'the Porphyrian philosophy', in the words of Courcelle, 'was the reigning philosophy': only one philosophy remained, the Neoplatonic: the spiritual master was Porphyry.[32] We must not allow our notion of the relative philosophical merits of Plotinus and Porphyry to affect our judgment of how they impressed Augustine and his contemporaries.

Moreover, Porphyry received most particular attention from Christians. There is a story that Porphyry either was or was about to become a Christian, that he was badly treated by Christians, and that he reacted in violent hostility to Christianity. Certain it is that he wrote fierce anti-Christian tracts of which one has been entitled *Against the Christians*. This, however—if it is a separate work[33]—was not the only work of his to engage the anxious replies of the Christians—his *Philosophy from Oracles*, which I have elsewhere attempted to prove to be identical with the work referred to twice by Augustine (and by him only) as the *Return of the Soul*, was paid the compliment of extensive attention from several Christian apologists. Among these[34] were Eusebius (died 339) in his *Praeparatio Evangelica*, the Africans Arnobius (fl. *c.*300) and Lactantius (fl. *c.*304–317), Theodoret (died *c.*466), Claudianus Mamertus (died 474), Aeneas of Gaza (died *c.*518), Philoponus (died *c.*565), and Augustine in the *City of God*. The chief negative target of this latter book is the work or works which I shall refer to as the *Philosophy from Oracles. It is as an answer to the Philosophy from Oracles that the City of God in the context of its own times can best be understood.*

A reader unfamiliar with the religious and philosophical movements of Augustine's time might at first blush have difficulty in seeing the relevance of a work bearing such a title as *Philosophy from Oracles* to a work commending Christianity and based on the Bible. Since, however, Augustine in the *City of God* explicitly speaks of the Scriptures as oracles, one discovers that in effect the *City of God* is matching the oracles of the Bible against the oracles to which Porphyry relates a philosophy, with which, according to its preface, the *Philosophy from Oracles* is most concerned.

We have already touched upon this matter[35] and need add here but a few instances to illustrate what Augustine had in mind to do. Isaac and Jacob, for example, are said separately to have received oracles;[36] the Lord is said to have spoken in oracles;[37] and verses of the *Psalms* are described as oracles.[38] Among other instances the most important is Augustine's direct comparison of the oracles of Scripture with those of Porphyry in the *Philosophy from Oracles*:

> This God of the Hebrews, whose greatness even Varro attests, gave a Law to his chosen people, a law written in Hebrew, *not an obscure* and *little-known law*, but one

---

31 Cf. the author's *Porphyry's Philosophy from Oracles in Augustine* (1959).   32 Cf. the author's *The Young Augustine*, 134f.   33 Cf. 10 above, n. 2.   34 Loc. cit.   35 58f.   36 *City of God* 16.36, 38.
37 16.21.   38 17.18.

that has long been *common knowledge among all people*. And it is this Law that contains
the words: 'He that sacrificeth to gods shall be put to death, save only to the Lord.'
What point is there in seeking for further proof in His Law and Prophets concerning
this matter? Indeed, there is no need to 'seek' for evidences which are *neither rare nor
recondite*; nor even to collect all those texts that are *so many* and *so manifest*, and to
quote them here. They make it clearer than daylight that the supreme true God
wishes sacrifice to be paid exclusively to Himself. Now, I offer but one statement. It
is *brief, majestic, terrifying*, and *true*. It was spoken by that very God whom the most
distinguished pagan scholars extol so splendidly. Hear it, fear it, heed it, lest death
befall you if you disobey. He said: 'He that sacrificeth to gods shall be put to death,
save only to the Lord,' and that, not because God needs anything, but simply because
it is good for us to belong to God alone. For the Hebrews' Scripture sings: 'I have
said to the Lord, thou art my God,' for thou hast no need of my goods.[39]

We ourselves, who form His City, are His best and most worthy sacrifice. It is this
Mystery we celebrate in our oblations, so familiar to the faithful, as I have explained
already. And it was through the Hebrew Prophets themselves that the divine revelations were given that the symbolic sacrifices of the Jews would one day cease, and
that thereafter all races would offer one sacrifice from sunrise to sunset, just as we
see for ourselves this very day. But I have already quoted enough of such texts
throughout this work.[40]

The contrast between the widely diffused (*omnibus iam gentibus diffamatam*) clear and
frequent (*aperta et crebra*), summary, awesome, fearful, but true *(breviter, granditer,
minaciter, sed veraciter dictum*) and divine dispensation of Scripture with another that is
obscure and unknown (*obscuram et incognitam*), abstruse and rare (*abstrusa vel rara*) is
perfectly clear. It is equally clear, since the oracles of the *Philosophy from Oracles* are
explicitly being contrasted with Scripture throughout the whole of the passage, that
these oracles represent the dispensation that is obscure and unknown, abstruse and rare.

In passing it is convenient to observe that the central point of discussion in the *City
of God*, as indicated here and as the work itself bears out, is the worship of the true God
(as against the worship of false gods). This is more particularly expressed as sacrificing
to Him: *sacrificans diis eradicabitur nisi Domino tantum*,[41] or, to use another scriptural
phrase constantly employed in connection with the two cities: *adhaerere Deo*.[42] Between
them, these two Scriptural phrases sum up the *City of God*.

Augustine maintained that the oracles that were the Scriptures were superior to those
of the pagans in points that should appeal to pagans: their fulfilment, their confirmation
by miracles, and their wholesale acceptance by multitudes. His ideas of divine economy
and providence enabled him to admit that other oracles might help God's revelation of
Himself, but they could not but be worsted by the gradual and ever clearer revelation
set forth in Scripture. Porphyry himself, Augustine contended, was not wholly consistent in his attitude to the oracles he used. It was not clear, for example, if he was a willing
or unwilling believer in these oracles; it was not clear whether he was credulous or critical

39 *Ps.* 15.2 as quoted by Eusebius. Cf. *Ps.* 140.6. **40** *City of God* 19.23. **41** *Exod.* 22.20. **42** *Ps.*
73.28.

in his attitude towards them; and since philosophy, according to its preface, was the main interest of his book, *Philosophy from Oracles*, the interpretation he chose to give to the oracles might be of more importance than the oracles themselves—and philosophy was in that context capable of a very wide understanding: in other words Porphyry's opinions might be of more importance than the declarations of the oracles.

What was clear was that Porphyry had accepted two important, however incomplete, facts from the oracles, which brought him nearer to Christianity than any other Platonist: the excellence of Christ and the fact that the God of the Hebrews was the true God.

To the oracles Christ was 'most worthy', and 'a man of most excellent wisdom'. His soul was immortal in the heaven of the blessed. For them the God of the Hebrews was the one true God, the Generator, King, and Father. Worship of Him should be spiritual in which we should offer the spiritual sacrifice of ourselves, adoring Him everywhere in chastity, justice, and the other virtues, making our life a prayer to Him, imitating Him and seeking Him in all things.

But the *Philosophy from Oracles* went even further than this. Here Porphyry is represented as believing that the knowledge of this God is a 'gift', something suggestive, in fact, of the Christian idea of Grace.

Where Porphyry and Augustine differed was precisely on the nature of Christ, the rejection or acceptance of Him as the universal way of salvation, of His incarnation, and above all His corporeal Resurrection. The description of the help that he, Augustine, got from the Platonists and his final rejection of them in favour of Christ as outlined in the *Confessions*[43] and the highly charged 'oracular' scene of his actual conversion[44] invite one to think that the *Philosophy from Oracles* had a special significance for Augustine. This I have tried to develop in my *Porphyry's Philosophy from Oracles in Augustine*.[45]

To this great difference between Porphyry and Augustine we must now come. Far transcending in importance the abuse by Porphyry's oracles of the Christians (as distinct from Christ) as polluted and impious and the deceived worshippers of demons, was their refusal to accept Christ as more than a man—however elevated He might be after death—or the resurrection of His or any other body and its sharing in immortality with the soul. The painful and shameful nature of the death of Christ's body they took to be evident.

For Porphyry the union of a soul in heaven with a body was an abhorrence: his refrain is constantly found in the tenth book of the *City of God*: *omne corpus fugiendum* (one should shun every kind of body). Porphyry's case was that happiness was possible for the soul only when it would never be joined to a body again. With the strongest commendation from Augustine for having done so, he had departed from the teaching of both Plato and Plotinus that the soul returned in a cycle from heaven to earth and even became joined to nonhuman bodies.[46] Porphyry at least restricted return, if it happened, to human bodies. While this represented progress, in Augustine's view, towards the linear destiny believed in by Christians, it at the same time struck directly at the Christian doctrine of the *resurrected* body.

Augustine confronts Porphyry on this issue with the testimony of Plato:

43 7.13ff. 44 8.29. 45 Cf. 158–68. 46 10.30; 13.19.

Some philosophers, against whose charges I am defending the City of God, that is to say, God's Church, seem to think it right to laugh at our doctrine that the separation of the soul and body is a punishment for the soul, whose beatitude, they think, will be perfect only when it returns to God simple, solitary, and naked, as it were, stripped of every shred of its body.

Now, if I could, in their own writings, find no refutation of this hypothesis, I would have to go to all the trouble of proving that it is not the body as such but only a corruptible body that is burdensome to the soul. That is why, as I quoted in a previous book, our Scripture says: 'For the corruptible body is a load upon the soul.' The additional word 'corruptible' makes it clear that the soul is weighed down not by the body as such, but by the body such as it has become as a consequence of sin and its punishment. And even if 'corruptible' had not been added, this text could have no other meaning.

The fact is, however, that Plato teaches, as plainly as can be, that the supreme God made the lesser gods with immortal bodies and promised to them the great boon of remaining forever in their own bodies, of which death would never deprive them. Why on earth, then, do these philosophers, for the sake of contradicting the Christian faith, pretend not to know what they know full well, except that they would rather squabble and disagree among themselves than agree with us?

Just listen to the very words of Plato, as Cicero has translated them into Latin. Plato is supposing that the Supreme God is addressing the gods whom he has made: 'You who have sprung from seed of the gods, give ear. The works of which I am the parent and maker, these are imperishable as long as I will them to be, even though all else that has been put together can be taken apart. For it can never be good even to think of pulling asunder what reason has joined together. Since you have had a beginning, you cannot be immortal and indestructible; yet, by no means shall you ever suffer dissolution nor shall any decree of death destroy you, nor prevail over my determination which is a stronger pledge of your perpetuity than those bodies with which you were joined when you were brought into being.'[47]

This much . . . I think needed to be said in the face of those who are so proud of being, or of being called, Platonists that they are ashamed to be Christians. . . . Ever on the lookout for something to tilt at in Christian doctrine, they violently assail . . . belief in the immortality of the body, pretending to see a contradiction in our double desire for the happiness of the soul and its permanence in a body to which . . . it is bound by a chain of grief. They forget that their . . . master, Plato, has taught that the supreme God had granted to the lesser gods . . . the favour of never dying, in the sense of never being separated from the bodies which he had united to them.[48]

Porphyry's position, as indicated by Augustine, and that it was affected by Christian teaching are to be seen from this other passage:

I have already remarked . . . that, in Christian times, Porphyry became ashamed of this Platonic theory and proposed not only to free human souls from the bodies of

47 *Timaeus* 41.   48 *City of God* 13.16.

beasts but so to liberate the souls of the wise from every bodily tie, that blessed souls, utterly disembodied, might remain forever with the Father. Not to be outdone by Christ, he denied the resurrection of incorruptible bodies, maintaining that souls will live forever not only without earthly bodies but without any bodies whatsoever.[49]

The importance of the first of these texts in relation to Barker's assertions[50] that Augustine, as opposed to St Thomas, followed Plato in insisting upon an unswerving general order—as against a 'mysterious and emotional world, rich in insoluble riddles, and needing a mediatory and miraculous Church to give a mystical clue'—requires no stressing. Barker's case is based on an illusion. Moreover the frequency of Augustine's citation of Plato to which Barker refers, and which is very unremarkable indeed in itself, arises to a notable extent from Augustine's constant use of this passage from the *Timaeus* because he found it more useful in polemics on the Christian side than the Platonic.

Our main interest, however, in these passages at this point is to show how Augustine thinks of the relations of Christianity and Platonism: the Platonist of immediate importance is Porphyry, and the point of immediate importance with him is the resurrection and immortality of a glorified body. Porphyry had, Augustine says, under the influence of Christianity abandoned what was most characteristic of Platonism (*profecto abstulit quod esse Platonicum maxime*[51]), namely, the doctrine of metempsychosis. On the other hand he did not accept the idea of a glorified body being united to a soul eternally. Augustine agreed with him on the first of these two, but disagreed on the second.

The matter is brought a step further in 22.25ff., where there is lengthy discussion of this problem. Here the argument deals with the Christian doctrine of the resurrected and glorified body being united to the soul for eternity. Augustine appeals to the instance of Christ's resurrection to indicate the fact; he appeals to the Platonists themselves to prove the possibility. From Plato he takes the point that mortal bodies can be made immortal; from Porphyry, that souls will not return to earthly bodies; and from Varro, that bodies dispersed can be reassembled so as to be reunited to their souls: this supplies him with the authority of Platonism for all the elements of the doctrine of Christian immortality.

This eclecticism may seem lighthearted; nevertheless it lent some support to the view that Platonism was fulfilled in Christianity. The fact that, in Augustine's view, Porphyry had been induced to advance from the doctrine of Plato and Plotinus of a cyclical destiny towards a linear one through the influence of Christianity[52] pointed the way in which Platonism should go. Porphyry plays a very particular role in all this: on the one hand he clearly came nearest, in Augustine's view, to Christianity; on the other he in fact was leading the last-ditch battle of the Platonists against the Christians, and was their fiercest enemy. Augustine was disposed to think that Porphyry through pride was misled by the demons from worship of the true God to worship of false gods and that he was but looking for an excuse for his enmity when he refused to accept the doctrine of the resurrected and glorified body.[53] This is, doubtless, wishful thinking; but this is what he

49 13.19.   50 Cf. 81f. above.   51 10.30.   52 13.19.   53 13.16.

says. Despite the general hostility of Greek philosophy towards polytheism; despite his own recognition of the Hebrew God; despite his reverence for Christ and his departure from his masters on the matter of metempsychosis; despite (in Augustine's view[54]) the Platonist recognition of the goodness of the flesh in itself, and above all Plato's words in the *Timaeus*; despite all this and much more, Porphyry's pride delivered him over to the false gods and left him in an insincere disbelief in the cardinal Christian teaching on the immortality of soul and body. Here once again we come to the great division between the two cities: the love of self and the love of God; pride and humility, polytheism and monotheism. In short, Christianity was seen in this to be more philosophical and carrying on the tradition of Greek philosophy; Platonism, on the other hand, was showing itself less philosophical.

It has been said that there is no important doctrine in Augustine that is not founded on an interpretation, erroneous or not, of the Bible.[55] A more conservative view,[56] which would deny that Platonism was a comparable influence on Augustine with the Bible, seems to have much more to commend it. It should be clear from the preceding considerations that, so far as the major work of the *City of God* is concerned, this latter view is an understatement

At the end of his life Augustine, reviewing in his *Retractations* some of his earliest works when Platonism had its greatest influence upon him, expressed regret that he had spoken so favourably of his Platonist friend Mallius Theodorus,[57] and went on to chide himself for using a Porphyrian-sounding expression in the *Soliloquia*.[58] He feared that he might be understood to agree with Porphyry, who is explicitly named, on the impossibility of bodies being eternal. Here he describes Porphyry quite simply as a false philosopher (*falsi philosophi*). These words were written about the time when he was finishing the *City of God*. They reflect accurately his view in the latter work of the *teaching* of Porphyry, the Platonist whom he honoured with special attention.

For Augustine Platonism was, nevertheless, something great, valuable, and good, and Porphyry, the most learned of its recent exponents (*doctissimus philosophorum*,[59]), shared in this admiration. The explanation of such rejection on the one hand and reverence on the other must lie at least partly in Augustine's perhaps nostalgic recollection of what Platonism meant to him just immediately before his conversion, which in fact it had helped. This carries with it the suggestion that the 'acceptance' of Platonic doctrine by him was secondary to the impression that his encounter with the Platonic writings had made. Another instance of this may, perhaps, be seen in the case of his experience with Cicero's *Hortensius*, as described in the *Confessions*;[60] but it is a commonplace that books, if read at a critical juncture, can have an effect far transcending normal expectation.

In some such way must we understand that, although for Augustine the authority of the Scriptures was paramount and decisive, the Platonists both when they approached Christianity in their many and elevated doctrines, and even when they were in error and

54 14.5.   55 G. Quispel, *Eranos-Jahrbuch* (1951), 115–40.   56 E. Hendrikx, *Augustinus Magister* (1954), 285–91.   57 *Retr.* 1.2.   58 1.14, 24.   59 19.22.   60 3.7ff.

in opposition to a basic Christian teaching, received from him a sympathy and consideration that would justify us in believing that he saw in Christianity the fulfilment of Platonism, but not that Platonic doctrine entered into the positive teaching of the *City of God* in any dominant way.

7

Rome

Ernest Barker, in his introduction to the *City of God* in Everyman's Library, says that the 'ultimate effect of the *City of God* is the elimination of the State'.[1] A less radical judgment on this aspect of the *City of God* is represented by the statement that the book combines 'Plato's theory of Ideas and his political blueprints in the Republic'.[2] These two views are erroneous, but they indicate the necessity to consider the *City of God* from this angle.

J.N. Figgis in his *Political Aspects of Saint Augustine's City of God*[3] castigates several such unfounded notions—still, however, repeated in later books—such as that Augustine's purpose in his great work was to develop a theory of Church and State, as of the two swords; or to lay down an industrial and economic programme for the Middle Ages, which was to be discarded in due course in the rise of capitalism; or to condemn the institution of the State in general, and the Roman Empire in particular, as evil. One can only suppose that such misunderstandings persist, partly because of the title of the work, which to those who have not read it may well suggest a book in some way or another in line with Plato's or Cicero's *Republic*, and partly because in the decay of interest in theology more work was done on the political aspects of the *City of God*—at least in the English-speaking world—than on any other. Even so, neither the title nor the fact that there is some discussion of political matters, both directly and by implication, justifies the suggestion that in the work there is any formal and developed political philosophy or theory of an ideal State.

The foregoing and other considerations—such as the question as to whether or not Augustine includes justice in the definition of the State—make it imperative for us to examine the *City of God* in its relation to things political and especially the Empire of Rome.

But first it is important to realize how Roman was the attitude of Augustine and how Rome was the centre of his human interest. There has been so much discussion of Augustine the Platonist that Augustine the Romanist has been neglected, and it has been possible for such as von Harnack to attribute to him the view, surely *a priori* improbable, that the independent state was the kingdom of the Devil.[4]

---

1 xxii; cf., xxxivf.   2 J. Feibleman, *Religious Platonism* (1959), 172.   3 1921.   4 Cf. Welldon's ed. of the *City of God*, 51f.

One must recall very briefly that Augustine grew up in North Africa within a family that supported Rome, was educated according to Roman methods, and embarked on the characteristically Roman career of Rhetor—which often led to high administrative posts within the Empire. Rhetoric marked the very soul of Rome: Rome was pragmatic, eclectic, less interested in metaphysics and eschatology than in ethics and how to achieve happiness. Even the most spiritual of the Romans recoiled from the unambiguous championing of idealism. Virgil for all his wistful mysticism has left us with many doubts on his ultimate philosophical persuasions. Cicero is hardly more clear. And even these two are less typical than, say, Horace with his *aurea mediocritas*, his golden mean.

Great as certainly was the influence of reading something of the Neoplatonists in translation, or even with less ease in Greek, the influence of Roman rhetoric on his mind was all-pervading and is to be seen on almost every paragraph that he wrote, and on many an argument that he used. He is by no means always innocent of the unrealities, exaggerations, and frigidities that characterized the profession he had espoused and practised. 'If one were asked,' he remarks in the *City of God*,[5] 'either to endure death or childhood again, who would not be aghast and choose to die?' Unhappy as his experience of childhood must have been, one would hesitate to conclude that rhetorical exaggeration and unreality had no part in such a terrible declaration. We have already taken note of a remarkable employment of eclecticism in an argument of the gravest import and seriousness: '[the Platonists] agree with us that even blessed souls will return to bodies, as Plato says, but will nevertheless not return to any evils, as Porphyry says, and take this also from Varro, that they will return to the same bodies, in which they were formerly, then their whole difficulty about the resurrection of the flesh for eternity will be solved'.[6]

With regard to this very question of the eternity of the flesh, the Romans, although they might reject it for other reasons, would have had less difficulty than a true follower of Plato, for whom only non-material things could have existence. There was, indeed, a strong materialistic bias in the philosophies that most affected the Romans that would have helped in this. Moreover the Roman, when he was not a materialist was a sceptic. Basically he was a pragmatist, and his attitude towards the doctrine of bodily immortality would be determined less by fine philosophical reasoning than by more practical considerations. Augustine, as a matter of fact, had been a materialist Manichean for the whole of his twenties and had subsequently professed himself to be a sceptic,[7] a follower of the New Academy. It is too much to assume that his acquaintance with the Neoplatonists obliterated the attitudes of earlier and formative years; his eclecticism from Plato, Porphyry, and Varro on the question of bodily immortality is a significant reminder of how thoroughly Roman Augustine continued to be.

The fact that Augustine does not inform the reader from time to time throughout the *City of God* that he is considering his problem not only from the personal point of view but also from the point of view of Rome should not lead us to believe that this is not the case. One of the characteristic traits of Augustine is to assume that the reader will not need to be informed of what, to Augustine, was obvious.[8]

5 21.14. 6 22.28; cf. 91 above. 7 For Stoic ideas in Augustine see G. Verbeke, *Recherches Augustiniennes* (1958), 1.67ff. 8 Cf. R.T. Marshall, *Studies in the Political and Socio-Religious Terminology of the De Civitate Dei* (1952), 6.

A simple and clear instance of this can be seen in his lack of reference to the source books used in the *City of God*.[9] There are hundreds of allusions to Varro's *Antiquitates*, but the title is given only once; there are frequent references to Apuleius's *De Deo Socratis*, but the title is given only once; there are over seventy references to the *Aeneid*, but the title is given only once; and there are over a dozen references to Sallust's *Catilina*, but the title is not given at all. The works of Claudian, Ennius, Lactantius, Livy, Lucan, and Persius are used, but again no title is given. Sometimes he uses a descriptive title, which would not have misled his contemporaries, but may not be even noticed or may be misunderstood by us: a crucial instance of this appears to occur in the tenth book in connection with the *Philosophy from Oracles* a work of Porphyry's of the greatest importance for the argument of the *City of God*.

So it was with Rome. For his contemporaries whose outlook on the world was bounded by the Roman Empire and its institutions, it was unnecessary, and might have been tedious, to have constant reference to what for them was the *praesuppositum* of the argument. Rome was the background and the foreground and the whole context of the work. Even when philosophy leads him to Greece and theology to the Hebrews, his purpose is that Rome should be fulfilled in both.

Nevertheless Augustine does make the point most explicitly. We have already seen Chapter 22 of Book 19, which gives in dramatic and sharpest outline the focuses of the whole work. Here the question is asked: 'Who is that God or how is He proved worthy, whom the *Romans* should obey, so that apart from Him they should worship none of the gods with sacrifices?' The *City of God* is basically concerned with that question, and it is asked in the interest of, not the Greeks or the Jews or any other people, but the Romans. The answer to the question is, as we have seen, that the testimony of the Hebrews, of the Greeks (represented by Porphyry), and of the Romans themselves (represented by Varro) was that the Christian God was that God.

Once again one should not fail to notice in the text just referred to the spirit of eclecticism and reverence for authority. It might be said with some justice that Augustine was aware that there might be difficulty in getting Porphyry and Varro to accept his interpretation of their positions in favour of Christianity and he did not conceal this. Augustine's fondness for a synthesis with firm outline, however, is more evident here than any purely philosophical argument. Some might see in this a basic Roman scepticism allied with a fondness for action, a preference for will as against intelligence, for authority as against reason. It is not surprising, indeed, that, although Platonism was received in Rome, the Bible and the Christian Church became the instruments for her of a new glory and a longer life. That this should be so was the positive purpose of the *City of God*.

It is essential that we should attempt to clarify Augustine's attitude on the question as to whether or not justice should be included in the definition of a State. Some are of the opinion that in his view a State was based on injustice—which of course would make him pessimistic about, if not actually hostile to it.

9 Cf. the author's *Porphyry's Philosophy from Oracles in Augustine*, 16ff.

A *res publica*, he says,[10] according to the definition of Scipio as given in Cicero's *De Re Publica*, is the *res populi*. A populus, or people, Scipio defined as an association of many persons bound together by agreement on right and a common interest (*utilitas*). Scipio explains that by agreement on right is implied for him that a State cannot function without justice. Therefore where there is no true justice (*vera iustitia*) there can be no State. Justice is defined as the virtue that gives to each his own. How can man be just, then, Augustine contends, if he takes himself from God and gives himself over to wicked spirits? For justice demands that men and their sacrifices should be given over to the true God and to Him alone. The Romans failed in this: therefore, if justice is to be included in the definition of a State, the Romans never had a State. 'True justice does not exist except in that State whose Founder and Ruler is Christ',[11] that is, the city of God.

'Pause,' urges Norman Baynes in *The Political Ideas of St Augustine's De Civitate Dei* (1949), 'for a moment and consider the effect of this discussion upon Augustine's view of the character of a State. There was in the early Church a strong tradition that the maintenance of justice was an essential part of the purpose of the State: St Paul had urged obedience to the State upon the ground that the State rewards the good and punishes the evil. Clement of Alexandria had defined a king as one who rules according to law, while Ambrose, Augustine's own master, had contended that justice and beneficence are the essential virtues for any community: justice—*aequitas*— is the strength of the State and injustice spells its dissolution. There have been attempts made to show that Augustine does not really mean to exclude justice from the definition of the State. . . . But as Mr Christopher Dawson has written:[12] "the actual tendency of the passage (4.3: *remota itaque . . .*) appears to be quite the contrary." There cannot be much doubt that Augustine meant what he said. "If he did, I cannot but feel," says Mr Carlyle,[13] "that it was a deplorable error for a great Christian teacher." '[14]

One is reluctant to believe that Augustine was actually in conflict with St Paul and the strong Christian tradition. Appeals to the authority, even of Christopher Dawson, are not decisive. Since this is an important point let us look at the context and see what Augustine did say and mean:

Hence, if the true God is adored, and if He is given the service of true sacrifice and of an upright life, then it is beneficial for good men to extend their empire far and wide and to rule for a long time. This is beneficial, not so much for themselves as for their subjects. . . . But the rule of wicked men brings greater harm to themselves, since they ruin their own souls by the greater ease with which they can do wrong.

As for their subjects, only their own villainy can harm them. . . . Thus, a good man, though a slave, is free, but a wicked man, though a king, is a slave. For he serves, not one man alone, but, what is worse, as many masters as he has vices. For, it is in reference to vice that the Holy Scripture says: 'For by whom a man is overcome, of the same also he is the slave.[15]

---

10 19.21.   11 2.21.   12 *A Monument to St Augustine* (1930), 63.   13 A.J. Carlyle, *History of Mediaeval Political Theory in the West* (1903).   14 7f.   15 2 *Peter* 2.19.

In the absence, therefore, of justice, what is sovereignty but organized brigandage? (*remota itaque iustitia, quid sunt regna nisi magna latrocinia?*)[16]

It is abundantly clear from the *itaque* (omitted, perhaps unconsciously but significantly, by Baynes[17]) that the *iustitia* in question is the justice referred to in II *Peter* 2.19–21:

> For by whom a man is overcome, of the same also he is the slave. For if, flying from the pollutions of the world, through the knowledge of our Lord and Saviour Jesus Christ, they be again entangled in them and overcome: their latter state is become unto them worse than the former. For it had been better for them not to have known the way of *justice* than, after they have known it, to turn back from that holy commandment which was delivered to them.

Whether *remota iustitia* is taken as implying that there *is* no justice in kingdoms, or more probably as a hypothesis ('if there be no justice'), the justice in question is 'the holy commandment': 'the knowledge of our Lord and Saviour Jesus Christ', and 'doing worship and service to the true God in true rites and good morals'. Augustine has gone to the microcosm to discover the truth about a macrocosm: has posited a good man and an evil man as exemplars from which to come to conclusions about 'kingdoms, provinces, nations, or such.' In other words, we are back again to the heavenly and the earthly man, the city of God and the city of this world: 'Well then, even as we have done with these two men, so let us do with two families, two nations, or two kingdoms'.[18]

In brief, the text *remota itaque iustitia . . .* is speaking of justice not in any historical or ordinary sense but in an absolute and theological one. The situation is exactly as is described in the passage already quoted from 19.21, or as indicated in 19.24: 'For in general the city of the unholy, which God does not direct obedient to Himself, so that it does not offer sacrifice but to Him alone, is without the truth of justice (*caret iustitiae veritate*).' Augustine is careful to indicate that he is speaking of *true* justice in all these instances—presumably in contrast to some other justice that is imperfect.

Before we pass on to consider this other justice, we should attend carefully to Augustine's attitude when he faces himself with the inevitable theological conclusion that, since the true God was not worshipped by Rome, if true justice—involving such worship—were to be included in the definition of a State, Rome could not be described as a State. Augustine took no satisfaction in such a conclusion, but rather than accept it for Rome, was willing to go to the extent of defining a State *without reference to justice at all*. He proposed, therefore, to define a people as an association of many rational persons bound together by a concordant and common interest in things it loves.[19] According to this Rome, *pro suo modo quodam*, in her own way, was a State.

It is plain that in 2.21 also, Augustine is driven to this extreme position because of the main thesis of the *City of God*, which centres on the true or ultimate justice that worship and sacrifice be offered to the true God alone:

> . . . I shall endeavour to show that that ancient creation was never a true republic (*res*

16 4.3.   17 7.   18 4.3: Healey's translation.   19 19.24.

publica), because in it *true* justice was never practised. I shall base my position on Cicero's own definitions, in the light of which he briefly determined, through the mouth of Scipio, what was a republic and what was a people. There are many confirmatory opinions expressed in that discussion both by himself and by the interlocutors he introduced.

However, according to some definitions that are nearer the truth, is was a commonwealth of a sort, and it was better governed by the earlier Romans than by those who came later. But true justice (*vera iustitia*) is not to be found save in that commonwealth, if we may so call it, whose Founder and Ruler is Jesus Christ—for no one can deny that this is the weal of the people. This name, with its varied meanings, is perhaps not quite in tune with our language, but this at least is certain: *True* justice reigns in that state of which Holy Scripture says: 'Glorious things are said of thee, O City of God.'[20]

It could not be clearer that the *remota itaque iustitia* that has caused so much difficulty and shocked so many commentators is properly glossed by the phrase above: *vera autem iustitia non est nisi in ea republica, cuius conditor rectorque Christus est.* He is all the time speaking of justice that is *vera.* In the passage just quoted he has used the adjective as many as three times.

But just as we saw that Augustine provided for a *relative* as well as an *absolute* good, so we may presume that beside the *vera iustitia,* so important for the *City of God,* he would be willing to concede the existence of a *iustitia* that was not *vera*; a justice that, if judged absolutely and with reference to our duty to the true God, was not justice at all; but if judged by less absolute standards, could nevertheless be considered in its own way some kind of justice.

It will be seen how important it is to keep in mind the distinction between what is absolute and what relative in relation to arguments involving theological positions in Augustine. His tenaciousness to an absolute view in this matter of justice is an indication at once of his willingness to adopt a position so extreme as to be misleading, and of the importance he attached to the Romans giving the true God the worship that was His due.

Augustine's attitude to Rome itself is, as one might expect, also twofold: theological and historical; she was *absolutely* evil; but *relatively* had a limited goodness.

As the head of the earthly, as opposed to the heavenly, city[21] she stood condemned. In particular her submission to impure demons and false gods[22] marked her corruption and gave her the mystical character by which she is contrasted with the other mystical city. These demons led her astray into evil rites and practices,[23] and in particular debauched her people by the unclean plays of the theatre,[24] in connection with which, therefore, Augustine seems to have almost an obsession. Finally they were responsible for excesses in war—for Mars, Bellona, and Victoria had to have their full measure of cult and honour.[25] The demons, in short, caused pride, vain-glory, and lust to dominate,[26]

20 2.21. 21 15.5. 22 16.17; 19.21. 23 2.6. 24 1.31f. 25 5.17. 26 15.7.

and these were irreconcilable with the heavenly city and the worship of the one true God.

It is difficult for us nowadays to think of these false gods and demons with the same sense of immediacy with which Augustine and his contemporaries thought about them. Yet we must do so, if we are at all to grasp the central argument of the *City of God*. These demons could manifest themselves physically—or at least create the illusion of their physical presence—as they had done in Campania, where they had been seen 'to fight a set battle amongst themselves. At first there were strange and terrible noises heard; and afterwards it was affirmed by many, that for certain days together one might see two armies in continual fight one against the other. And after the fight had ceased, they found the ground all trampled up as with steps of men and horses that had been made in the battle'.[27] Whatever credence Augustine gave to this story of the physical intervention of the demons, he had no doubt whatever about their spiritual interference in the lives of men and States.

It is necessary to know what kind of beings these demons were believed by Augustine to be. They were in fact the fallen angels,[28] led by Satan, who, of course, although the leader of his city, is not an enemy on equality with God. These demons or gods (for they can also be so called) are good by nature but evil by will:[29]

> . . . the false gods . . . were unclean spirits, malignant and lying demons. The truth of this is clear from the fact that these demons go so far as to take delight in their own villainies, to the extent of wanting them exhibited, either as facts or as fictions, in the festivals celebrated in their honour . . . as long as these villainies are exhibited for imitation under divine sanction, so to speak, it is impossible to restrain weak humans from actually reproducing in their own lives the abominable acts committed by the gods.[30]
>
> These demons are spirits ever itching to injure, completely removed from right- eousness, puffed up with pride, livid with jealousy, adroit in artifice. They may inhabit the air, but that is because they were cast down from the sublimity of high heaven, condemned to this place as to a prison in punishment of their irremediable transgression.[31]

The demons had various important fields of activity: as against men of any kind they were far superior in prophecy, the use of dreams, magic, and miracles.[32] Their knowledge of the future was similar to that of the good angels; but, unlike the good angels, they sometimes went wrong.[33] The simplest man, however, could excel them by becoming a citizen of the city of God.

The aim of the demons was to attract worship and sacrifice away from the true God to themselves—to be treated as gods.[34] Their powers were so great that they succeeded in this. The Platonists, however, for example, seemed not to be deceived, but in order not to cause offence gave them some of the honours due to God. Christians, on the other hand, are allowed by Providence to face compulsion to sacrifice to them; and when they refuse they win the crown of martyrdom.[35]

27 2.25.   28 8.22.   29 12.1.   30 4.1.   31 8.22.   32 Cf. 8.16; 9.22.   33 9.22.   34 8.22; cf. 9.7.   35 10.21.

Augustine protests in 19.21 that no one who had read what he had so far written could doubt, unless he were stupid or merely contentious, that the Romans worshipped the evil and impure demons. He was, therefore, attacking, not Rome,[36] as Baynes says, but the service of the gods that she worshipped and to whom she sacrificed. He could not be more explicit than he has been that the *City of God* is concerned with religion,[37] that his target is the cult of the false gods, and that the occasion of his argument is the prohibition of that cult in Christian times.[38]

It has been well remarked by Ladner that for the pagans the cult of the (false) gods was the central focus of the city. Kamlah has suggested that the fundamental idea of the *City of God* is the destruction of the gods, a view in which he is supported by Ziegler. Everything that we have written most strongly confirms and amplifies this.[39]

Speaking of the two cities, Augustine says: 'Both cities observe a peace in such things as are pertinent to this mortal life . . . [but] the two hierarchies could not be combined in one religion, but must needs dissent herein.[40] The Sibyl, even though she preceded Christ and was not a Hebrew, seemed to Augustine to have been a citizen of the city of God *because she spoke against false gods*.[41] Insofar as Rome or any Roman sacrificed to false gods they were absolutely condemned by Augustine.

On Rome's goodness, however limited, it will be best to listen to Augustine himself:

> . . . the earliest and most primitive Romans, like all other peoples with the single exception of the Hebrews, worshipped false gods and offered sacrifices, not to God, but to demons. Yet . . . they were 'avid for praise, liberal with money, pursuers of high glory and hard-won wealth'. Glory was their most ardent love. They lived for honour, and for it they did not hesitate to die. This single measureless ambition crushed their lesser greeds. It was their glory to conquer and control others, and a dishonour for their fatherland not to be free. . . . 'The city grew at an incredible rate, because of their passionate greed for glory.' Thus, passionate greed for praise and glory worked many wonders worthy, according to human standards, of praise and honour. . . . It is well . . . to go to Cato for an opinion on the state of the city. . . . . 'Do not think,' he says, 'that our fathers made our city great by arms. Had this been the case, we would have a far finer city than we have. . . . They had other means to make them great, which we lack: industry at home and justice in their rule abroad, a spirit of freedom in political discussion unstained by wickedness or lust . . . the administration continued to be directed by a small group of relatively good men, through whose foresight the evils of the times were tempered and made sufficiently tolerable for the general welfare to continue to increase.[42]

After all, the pagans subordinated their private property to the common welfare, that is, to the republic and the public treasury. They resisted the temptation to avarice. They gave their counsel freely in the councils of the state. They indulged in neither public crime nor private passion. They thought they were on the right road when they strove, by all these means, for honours, rule, and glory. Honour has come to them from almost all peoples. The rule of their laws has been imposed on many

36 Op. cit., 16.　37 11.5.　38 1.14; 2.2; 6.1; 10.18; 32; 11.1; 14.28; 19.17. Cf. *Retract.* 2.43.　39 *Augustinus Magister* (1954), 3.205f.　40 19.17.　41 18.23.　42 5.12; cf. Sallust, *Cat.* 7, 52.

peoples. And in our day, in literature and in history, glory has been given them by almost everyone. They have no right to complain of the justice of the true and supreme God. 'They have received their reward.'[43]

According to Augustine's thesis, ultimate reward is reserved for the citizens of the city of God, as ultimate punishment is for the citizens of the city of the Devil. There is no harsh judgment, then, in refusing to the pagan Romans, citizens of the earthly city, the greater reward. On the contrary there is a positive recognition here of a virtue that is relative, crowned with a corresponding reward.[44]

If Brutus, Torquatus, Furius Camillus, Scaevola, Curtius, the Decii, Marcus Pulvillus, Regulus, L. Valerius, Q. Cincinnatus, and Fabricius—all of whose names are recited with admiration, if not also pride, by Augustine[45]—are not supposed by Augustine to belong, as did the Sibyl, to the city of God, it is because they did worship idols. Nevertheless Augustine commends their virtues, which were considerable: their love of glory and freedom, their love of honour and honesty, their willingness to make sacrifices for their principles, and their respect for law.

He goes further: God, Augustine says, in His providence gave the Romans help in erecting their city and Empire and let them have sovereignty when and for as long as it was His pleasure.[46] God in fact resolved to erect Rome in the West to be superior to the monarchies of the East in greatness and dignity.[47] As it happened, it was Rome's opposition to evil that brought about so much of Rome's conquest, so that through wars that were honest, upright, and just Rome was providentially compelled to grow.

The fulfilment of the mission of pagan Rome, however, was to be seen in its providing what should be an irresistible stimulus to Christians to be more virtuous for an immeasurably greater reward:

> It was, then, not only to reward the Roman heroes with human glory that the Roman Empire spread. It had a purpose for the citizens of the Eternal City during their pilgrimage on earth. Meditating long and seriously on those great examples, they could understand what love of their Heavenly Fatherland should be inspired by everlasting life, since a fatherland on earth has been so much loved by citizens inspired by human glory.[48]

Even more: Augustine declared that the Romans were found worthy by God to enslave the Hebrews, until recently the very shadow of the city of God on earth, because they had misused their advantages.[49]

Augustine was implacably hostile to Rome's gods; it is impossible to believe that, theology apart, he was other than proud of and favourable to Rome. The measure of his favour for Rome is to be seen in the future destiny he foresaw for her: she was to be at once fulfilled in Christianity and to help, by her own unity and extent, its spread— Rome's Empire was an instrument in man's salvation. Throughout the *City of God* the rigour of the doctrine there set forth on predestination is tempered, partly by consid-

---

43 5.15. 44 Cf. E. von Ivánka, *Augustinus Magister*, 3. 411ff; cf. 203ff. 45 5.18. 46 5.19, 21.
47 4.15. 48 5.16. 49 5.18.

eration of the greater destiny available to man than was available before the Fall, and partly by the optimism engendered by the spectacle of the multitudes—however unworthy and unlikely to persevere some individuals were—running to Christ.

The question naturally arises if Augustine had some vision of a Roman theocratic State or some close union between the Church and the Roman Empire. Although the idea of the union of Church and State is natural to the ancient city, and although later ages attributed such a vision to the *City of God,* and although the relic of such a reality still persists in Established Churches, Augustine did not in fact treat of the problem directly or clearly.

It appears, however, from what seems the sombre teaching that the majority of mankind is damned that, if the Church is not to fail in her mission to save her members, she will not have dominated any one universal State, or a majority of populations organized in States from the beginning to the end of time. This, however, does not preclude the possibility that a State, and in particular the Roman Empire, might have some special union with the Church. Here again this would not preclude the possibility that the Roman Empire for a time might have such a union, and later might not: Augustine was no millenarian.

We must further observe that a union might mean anything from a strict theocracy, which according to the *Shorter Oxford English Dictionary,* is 'a form of government in which God is recognized as the king or immediate ruler, and his laws are taken as the statute-book of the kingdom, these laws being usually administered by a priestly order as his ministers and agents', to something very much less than this.

Augustine does not attempt to define the terms of any union, but it is clear that he intends that the Church should exercise great influence on the Roman State. The chapters at the end of that section of the *City of God* that deals with Rome[50] give a fairly clear impression of what Augustine expects of Christian emperors of Rome: they should 'make their power their trumpeter to divulge the true adoration of God's majesty'; and the repentance of the excommunicated Theodosius is duly approved.

It should be emphasized, just the same, that Augustine did not attempt to determine the sphere of that influence; and the possibility that an emperor, whether Christian or not, might resist such influence could not be discounted at the beginning of the fifth century.

Nevertheless the general position was fairly clear: Rome was fulfilled in Christianity. This idea is set out at length in a letter to Marcellinus, to whom the *City of God* itself is addressed. With an excerpt from it we may conclude:

> In the most opulent and illustrious Empire of Rome, God has shown how great is the influence of even civil virtues without true religion, in order that it might be understood that, when this is added to such virtues, men are made citizens of another commonwealth, of which the King is truth, the law is love, and the duration is eternity.[51]

Rome's natural virtues are an ideal base on which religion builds the citizen of the city of God.

50 5.24ff. 51 *Ep.* 138.17 (translation of McCracken in Loeb series of the *City of God,* vol. 1. Introduction lxvi.

Epilogue

The approach throughout this study has been to present the *City of God* as a vision of man's destiny springing from Augustine's reflection upon his own life and in particular his conversion.

Augustine's absolute position was that only those who gave due worship to the Christian God were truly virtuous and could hope for salvation. Those, therefore, such as the worthies of Rome, who gave worship to many gods, were *absolutely* vicious, and the State they served, in not recognizing the true God, lacked *true* justice. Similarly Greek philosophy, as represented in Porphyry, who came so very near (as it seemed to Augustine) the Christian truth, was *absolutely* to be rejected because it refused to accept the possibility of a body that was eternal.

But divine Providence as it had led Augustine himself through errors and disorders to Christianity, likewise permitted good to arise from what, theologically, must be condemned. One must recall that for Augustine *merely not to serve* God was evil.

Speaking, however, non-theologically, in a *relative* and indeed normal way, Rome, polytheism apart, was not only good but was chosen to prepare, but differently from the Hebrews, for the coming of Christianity in which it was to be fulfilled and prolonged. Platonism, likewise, could be viewed as leading inevitably to Christianity in which its problems, Augustine suggested, were finally resolved. Augustine, of course, was not unaware that neither the polytheistic Roman nor follower of Porphyry would agree with him.

The *City of God* is, therefore, directly more concerned with justifying the Christian prohibition of polytheism than with defending the Christians against the charge of being responsible for the decline of Rome and its sack in AD 410. Its approach is not philosophical in any strict sense; it does not give a theology of history unless by this phrase is meant a view of history in the light of theology. It is not, using the word in its ordinary sense, hostile to the State, which is not founded, in its view, on injustice, as we normally speak of injustice. Neither does the *City of God* rely on a Platonic teaching of an unchangeable law as contrasted with the notion of an unpredictable authority, against which the Reformation is regarded as being a protest.

Although, doubtless under the stress of the Pelagian controversy, the work shows too little optimism in its expectation on the number of men destined for salvation, it reflects the growing confidence of a Church that at once promised to men a beatitude greater than that possible before the Fall, and witnessed the thronging of multitudes to submit to its authority. The fulfilment of the prophecies of the Old Testament, the truth contained in the secular oracles and philosophy of Greece and Rome, and the confirmation of Christianity by miracles all strengthened the Christian's faith and hope.

Augustine was not among those who believed that the end of the world was at hand. He left the future to God on whose providence all must depend. In the meantime he would seek to find in all merely human things the good that, as created, they must possess.

If the radical division between the two cities is in the will; if love is the final determinant between their citizens, love is also the dominating quality of Augustine's book. Failure to serve the true God apart, all else he loves; all else he cherishes; all else he freely embraces.

It is this calm confidence for the future and love of the created good that the Christian believer, if he is to follow the lesson of the *City of God,* must show.

PART III

GENESIS UNDERSTOOD LITERALLY

8

Augustine, Literal and Scientific:
His Interpretation of *Genesis*[1] on Creation

One of the great preoccupations of the Fathers of the Church, eastern and western, was the interpretation of the account of the creation given in the *Book of Genesis*. From them we have derived a number of works, some bearing the title *Hexameron*—the story of the six days of creation—in which at different levels of learning they sought to relate *Genesis*, which they accepted as necessarily true, to the received knowledge of their day. These *Hexamera* had a profound influence on the course of human knowledge. They confronted the cosmologies of the Graeco-Roman world with an arsenal of arguments made available, it has been suggested, to Greek and Roman Father alike in manuals in the vernaculars. The end result may be given in the words of Pierre Duhem:[2]

All the Hellenic Cosmologies are in the final analysis Theologies; at the heart of each of them we find religious dogmas-dogmas either admitted as axiomatic, discovered by intuition, as Platonism and Neo-Platonism have them, or the result of an analysis, using experience as a starting-point, when it has been conducted as far as it can go, as is the case with the analysis of the Peripatetics. These dogmas in fact in their essentials are the same in all the Greek philosophies— they are those taught by the Pythagorean schools of Magna Graecia: the heavenly bodies are divine, they are the only true Gods. Eternal and incorruptible, they know no change other than perfect movement, movement that is circular and uniform. By this movement they regulate in accord with the most rigorous determinism the progress of all the changes that happen in the theatre of the sublunar world.

Modern Science was born, one can say, on the day when this truth was proclaimed: the same Mechanism, the same laws, rule the heavenly movements and the sublunar movements, the circling of the Sun, the ebb and flow of the sea, the fall of gravity. Before it became possible to conceive such a thought, the stars had to be demoted from the divine order where Antiquity had placed them. A theological revolution had to take place.

This revolution was the work of Christian Theology.

Modern-Science was lit by a spark that sprang from the clash of the Theology of Hellenic Paganism and the Theology of Christianity.[3]

1 Cf. 18 above.   2 Translations into English, except where indicated, are by the author.   3 *Le Système du Monde*, Paris (1954), tome 2.453.

Of all the Fathers of the Church the one who took the pagan cosmologists most seriously and did not suppress their views was St Augustine—'le seul Père', to quote Duhem again, 'qui n'ait point dédaigné et passé sous silence les doctrines de la Science profane'.[4] His basic physical position was Neoplatonic and ultimately derived from the *Timaeus* of Plato. He departed, however, from Neoplatonism in a number of radical ways.

If Duhem's claim that Modern Science was lit by a spark from the clash of the Theology of Hellenic Paganism and the Theology of Christianity is true, then Augustine is cast in a role of some importance in relation to at least the preparation for modern science. It is clear, of course, that the purpose of the Church Fathers, including Augustine, was concerned, not with science, but with theology. In the case of Augustine, however, one can see clearly an interest in and respect for science which has not been sufficiently appreciated.

Augustine did not write a work entitled *Hexameron,* but he did write a book bearing the title *de Genesi ad litteram (Genesis Understood Literally)* which was frequently referred to by the title of *Hexameron:* by Johannes Scottus Eriugena in the ninth century, for example. To Eriugena and others of the early Medieval period this book was of greater interest and use than even Augustine's *Confessions* or *City of God.* Yet it is curious that, although there were and are numerous manuscripts of the *de Genesi ad litteram,* some of them very early, the work was not printed *separately,* either when printing was introduced, or until relatively recently. It was first printed, but in a collection of the works of Augustine, by Amerbach in Basel in 1506. There was no edition or translation of the work available in English until 1982.[5] An edition and translation into French with very useful introduction and notes appeared in Paris in 1972 in the *Bibliothèque Augustinienne* series, volumes 48 and 49. To its authors, P. Agaësse and A. Solignac, contemporary scholars, and I hasten to add myself in particular, are necessarily heavily in debt.

The *de Genesi ad litteram,* unlike much of the work of Augustine, is mainly non-controversial. Indeed it makes quite a point of considering various solutions to many a problem and insisting on few as definitive. At the beginning of the twelfth and final book Augustine writes: 'I have set down in writing as far as I could my exposition of the first part of holy scripture, which is called *Genesis,* up to the point when the first man was expelled from Paradise. I have asserted and defended what I hold as established. I have investigated, given my opinion, and expressed doubts on what I do not hold as established. I do not seek so much to prescribe what each one should believe in relation to things that are obscure, as to show that I myself need instruction in matters on which I have been in doubt; and to restrain the reader from the rashness of coming to firm conclusions where we have been unable to provide knowledge that is certain.[6]

The prevailing mood, then, in the *de Genesi ad litteram* is, in fact, one of prudent and comprehensive investigation issuing only sometimes in very tentative conclusions. The approach is leisurely, understanding and serene. Since the topics treated—the origin

4 Ibid., 411.   5 Cf. John Hammond Taylor, *Ancient Christian Writers* series vols. 41, 42.   6 *de Gen. ad litt.* 12.1, 1.

and earliest history of man—cannot but be of great interest to any man, and the treatment is generally rational, highly intelligent, well-informed for the time—or indeed, on basic matters, for any time—and compassionate, the book is well worth our attention.

But Augustine's book has a challenging title: *Genesis Understood Literally.* How can one understand *Genesis literally?* Or how does Augustine understand the word literal? Since, also, the first chapters of *Genesis* give an account of creation and, if they are to be understood literally, must raise precise physical questions, one cannot but be curious about Augustine's capacity to handle things scientific. What kind of information had he? Could he be said to have a scientific attitude or at least an appreciation of the scientific method as it would now be understood? It will be my purpose here to attempt some answers to these questions, to give a few instances in which we can observe Augustine being Literal and Scientific.

Augustine accepted the account of creation in *Genesis* as true. He made four attempts to expound this truth and had no final confidence in any of them. His first effort, the *de Genesi contra Manichaeos*, was written about AD 388–89, shortly after his conversion and return to Africa. He felt at the time that the literal interpretation he could make neither avoided what he considered blasphemy, nor could be reconciled with Catholic faith. He therefore often had recourse in this work to an allegorical approach. Subsequently he wrote of this attempt as a failure. Four or five years later he tried the literal approach a second time in the *de Genesi liber imperfectus.* As the title suggests he abandoned the task —and that quickly.

When he was writing the last two books of his *Confessions* about the year 400 he found himself using *Genesis* again—but this time he did not attempt a literal interpretation. He deliberately sought out an allegorical one. 'Different meanings can be understood in these words (of Scripture) which nevertheless can (all) be true. . . . While, therefore, each one tries to understand the holy scriptures as *he* understood them who wrote them, what harm is there if each of us understands them as You, light of all minds that speak true, show to be true—even if the author did not so understand? The author understood a truth but not *this* truth.'[7] Augustine says, therefore, that he considers the Bible was intended to be interpreted allegorically and not literally: *crescite et multiplicamini;—si autem figurate posita ista tractemus—quod potius arbitror intendisse scripturam.*[8] The Bible injunction 'increase and multiply,' he says, allows and enables him to interpret in many ways what he read formulated in one obscure way. Hence he allegorically interprets the firmament of *Genesis* as the Church, the fishes and whales as sacraments and miracles, the fruits of the earth as the works of mercy, and so on. His purpose in doing this was to bring together Creation and the new dispensation of the Church in one hymn of recognition of the Creator.

Although he had legitimately excused himself from it in the *Confessions*, the challenge of a literal understanding of *Genesis* remained. He soon embarked on what we now know as the *de Genesi ad litteram, Genesis Understood Literally*, which occupied him for some

7 *Conf.* 12.18, 27.   8 Ibid. 13.24, 37.

fifteen years, from about 401 to 416, from his forty-seventh to his sixty-second year. It is, therefore, a mature and pondered work. He specifically states in his *Retractationes* that he did not employ the allegorical method here, but rather treated the scriptural account as fact: *non secundum allegoricas significationes, sed secundum rerum gestarum proprietatem.*[9]

One hastens to say immediately that one must not take Augustine's 'literally' in his title *Genesis Understood Literally* quite 'literally'. To begin with he declares that some things recounted as, and taken by him to be, facts, can have an allegorical interpretation *as well*. This applies particularly to events described in the old dispensation as figures and prophecies of the new: *res ipsas quae ita narrantur et esse, et aliquid etiam figurare.*[10] Secondly, and more importantly, the human words used in *Genesis* of God's creating cannot, without imputing human limitations to God, be understood literally. While using all that the letter can tell us, we must deny all 'literal' implications and seek an understanding worthy of God who is outside of time. In this way Augustine is as apophatic as the Greek Fathers, and like them has recourse to the highest speculations of Neoplatonic philosophy to help him attempt to comprehend what cannot literally be understood. When *Genesis* reports: *God said*, it reports, according to Augustine, something real, not that God enunciated successive syllables in time, which until time existed was not possible, but rather that God said what he had to say in his Word. What is reported is real, actually true that is, but not 'literal'. Similarly when God is reported to have said: *Let there be Light*, what is reported is real and true. But the sun and moon, from which we know light, were said to have been created subsequently on the *fourth* day. Hence *Let there be Light* cannot refer to the sun or moon. Augustine consequently considers various hypotheses—and he puts them forward as hypotheses only, and decides that this injunction of God might best be referred to the creation of the first beings, spiritual beings, the angels. They are light in the sense that they see—which implies illumination—in God a further creation to be; they *see* that further creation in itself; and finally they see in their knowledge of that creature the praise of its creator. These perceptions by the angels he calls day-knowledge, evening knowledge and morning knowledge respectively, and the angels 'correspond', from that point of view, to the light we experience in our whole day.[11]

Augustine is aware that a reader may not follow in believing with him that the hypothesis he has proposed to explain *Let there be Light* is 'literal' and not allegorical. He would wish him to do better himself and with God's help to succeed: *quaerat et divinitus adiutus inveniat.*[12] Indeed Augustine might do better himself some day.

One has to take account of the fact, too, that the report on creation in the first three chapters of *Genesis* is in reality two reports succeeding and in part seemingly in conflict with one another.[13] The dividing point between these two reports, now known as the 'Priestly' and 'Yahwist', is at 2.4. Augustine, although believing that there was but one reporter, saw clearly the division and inconsistencies. He therefore understood the two

9 *Retract.* 2.24,1.   10 8.7,13.   11 Cf. *Bibliothèque Augustinienne* 48, 646ff. As this is a good commentary on the text and provides recent bibliography on most topics, reference, for the sake of convenience, will normally be made to it in the first instance.   12 4.28, 45.   13 Cf. 118 and 121ff. below.

accounts not as being independent one from the other, but as referring to two 'moments' or aspects of creation. The first of these referred to was what he calls the *prima conditio*, the first stage 'when all things were made', as *Ecclesiasticus* says,[14] 'at the same time'. This was God's unique act of creation of all creatures, which was outside time but was already the beginning of time. Creatures, including man, then began to exist in their *causal reasons*. The second 'moment' of creation refers to the development in time, not without God's help, of the creatures already existing in their causal reasons. This second moment or aspect, as distinct from the first 'when all things were made at the same time', is fully temporal. Consequently what is said in *Genesis* about Paradise is fact, although it is also full of mystical significations. In general, therefore, though Augustine purports to interpret the account of both moments of creation in a literal sense, he attempts to be more purely literal for the second.

Even in the account of the second creation, however, not everything can be taken strictly to the letter. This applies particularly, once again, where God's intervention is indicated. Thus when *Genesis says* that 'God formed man from the dust of the earth', these words are not to be understood as implying that God with bodily hands modelled man from dust. This, Augustine says plainly, is too puerile a notion: *quod enim manibus corporalibus Deus de limo finxerit hominem, nimium puerilis cogitatio est.*[15] Indeed he adds, lest there should be any doubt about it, that if the scripture *had* said that God with bodily hands had modelled man, we ought rather believe that the scriptural author had used a metaphor than that God was limited by the outlines of such limbs as we see in our own bodies. No one, Augustine declares, would be so silly as to say such a thing: *quis usque adeo desipit?*[16]

We have, then, to bear in mind that the literal interpretation of *Genesis* attempted here is literal in the sense that it is historical and refers to facts, things that happened. In the very nature of things what is said of God in creation cannot be, in our sense, literal, but it is historical. Here Augustine, in following *Genesis* literally, sharply departs from the Neoplatonists: creation for him was an historical fact, not as for them a metaphysical necessity. What is said of man and creation is also historical: thus the first sin was not the sin of a soul before time, resulting in its fall into the temporal; it was an historical event, which took place in time, brought about by a creature who was not soul only, but a composite of soul and body. Here again Augustine followed *Genesis* literally and again differed sharply from the Neoplatonists.

Augustine's approach, therefore, in the *de Genesi ad litteram* is only as literal as it can be. It assumes the historicity—or, in the case of God's action 'prehistoricity'—of the account of *Genesis*. This account establishes certain definite points of reference and provides an underpinning to the interpretation at every juncture. What happened before time cannot be literally understood. What happened in time is to be literally understood when it can be. In all cases the historical facts may, as well as being facts, be allegories.

I have just used a phrase which needs explanation: 'what happened in time is to be literally understood *when it can be.*' We have just seen that Augustine ridiculed the notion that the scripture should ask us to believe that God with bodily hands modelled man.

14 18.1.   15 6.12, 20.   16 Ibid.

In this case clearly Augustine assumes that we follow our reason, and do not believe the words themselves of scripture. But this is not just an isolated case. Augustine goes to some pains to give guidance for general application where the kind of difficulty indicated by this case arises.

There has been an opinion abroad that Augustine puts faith before reason and when the two conflict that reason must yield. Byron has promoted this notion:

> But Saint Augustine has the great priority,
> Who bids all men believe the impossible
> *Because 't is so.* Who nibble, scribble, quibble he
> Quiets at once with 'quia impossibile'.[17]

What matter if it was Tertullian,[18] not Augustine, who was responsible for the *quia impossibile!*

This is totally and most damagingly to misrepresent Augustine. On the contrary in the *de Genesi ad litteram* he assumes that when a fact has been established—established, mind you—by reason, it is to be accepted: the Bible is not a Science book.

At this point we may perhaps address ourselves to the other questions we have asked: had Augustine an appreciation of what we would now call the scientific method? What was his attitude to science? How informed was he in the science of his day?

We might begin to answer those questions by quoting one of his declarations from the *de Genesi ad litteram.* 'It happens often,' he writes, 'that a non-Christian too has a view about the earth, the heaven, the other elements of this world, the movement and revolution or even the size and distances of the stars . . . the natures of animals, plants, stones and such things which he derives from ineluctable reason and experience. It is too shameful and damaging and greatly to be avoided that such a one should hear a Christian talk such utter nonsense (*delirare*) about such things, purporting to speak in accordance with Christian writings. He has difficulty in keeping from laughing, seeing as he does the Christian wandering, so to speak, a million miles away from the truth. It is not so troublesome that a man in error should be laughed at; but rather that our writers should be believed by those who are outside our fold to hold such views, and are castigated and condemned as ignorant to the great injury of those for whom we labour. When these men see a Christian in error appealing to our writings in support of his wrong opinion on a point which they know perfectly, how are they to believe the same writings on the resurrection of the dead and the hope of eternal life and the kingdom of heaven? They think that those writings contain false teaching on matters which they have been able to test by experience or know through calculations that it is impossible to doubt.'[19]

Pierre Duhem's comment is useful: 'Saint Augustine was never among those who block their ears. Even when a teaching seems to contradict Holy Scripture, he listens with attention, in order to discover whether the contradiction is apparent or real. In all things he is careful not to come to a precipitate conclusion without understanding fully.

17 *Don Juan* 16.5–8.   18 *de carne Christi P.L.* 2,806: *resurrexit; certum est, quia imposibile est.*   19 1.19, 39.

The assurance with which a Basil, a Gregory of Nyssa, an Ambrose, a John Chrysostom put forward the naive assertions of their puerile 'science' against the teachings of secular Physics greatly saddened the Bishop of Hippo. He was pained to see the Doctors of the Church of Christ expose themselves to the same lively ridicule as that to which he himself had treated Mani. With a delicacy of wisdom he admonished them.'[20]

Duhem may have gone too far in so closely identifying the objects of Augustine's remarks. Even so it is well to be reminded with some emphasis that Augustine did have a regard and respect for the claims of science which was, among the Fathers of the Church, unusual. Doubtless an explanation for this is to be sought in the impression science had made on him in comparison with the absurdities of the followers of Mani. His account is found in the *Confessions*: 'and since I had read many teachings of the philosophers and retained what I had committed to my memory, I compared some of these with the long-winded fables of the Manicheans. The teachings of the philosophers seemed more probable to me. They were competent to give an account of the world, although its Lord they had been altogether unable to discover.'[21]

It is a useful thing to compare science with the fables of the Manicheans; it is useful also to castigate his fellow-theologians who talked nonsense; but is Augustine willing himself to confront Christian Theology with science? The answer is, yes and here from the *de Genesi ad litteram* are his views on the matter: 'whatever the [scientists] themselves can demonstrate by true proofs about the nature of things, we can show not to be contrary to our scriptures. But whatever they advance in any of their books that is [clearly] contrary to our scriptures, that is to the Catholic faith, we should either indicate by some argument that it is false [or according to another reading, 'indicate a solution'] or believe without hesitation that it is false. . . . Thus we shall not be led astray by the eloquence of false philosophy or the superstition of false religion.[22]

This passage accepts the fact *scientifically established* as primary. If there appears to be a conflict between it and scripture, the onus is on the theologian to show that there is no conflict. If there is not question of a fact scientifically established, but of a scientific *hypothesis* which appears to be in conflict with scripture, the onus is still on the theologian to show that the hypothesis is false [or, according to the alternative reading, that there is no true conflict]; if he cannot do this he must continue to maintain scripture against what is an hypothesis, not a fact scientifically established. It is to be noted that according to Augustine the theologian must respect the established fact above all else; must be on his guard against the superstition of false religion; must demonstrate the falseness of that which he believes to be false; but must also maintain the scriptural position against the unproved hypotheses of philosophy. In this way Augustine takes what might not unjustly be called scientific precautions against error. There is danger, he says, of getting ourselves into a situation where we find ourselves defending not the truth embraced by Scripture but our own 'truth' which subsequently may be found to be error.

Galileo commended this 'circumspection', as he called it, of Augustine as admirable and to be imitated. He wrote out and examined in his 'Letter to Madama Cristina di Lorena' of 1615[23] the passage just quoted and analyzed. In this letter he appealed

20 Op. cit. 2.491. 21 5.3, 3. 22 1.21, 41. 23 *Le Opere di Galileo Galilei*, vol. 5, Firenze (1895), 327f.

constantly to Augustine and especially to the *de Genesi ad litteram* as justification for his own reserve in relation to conclusions that were obscure, or where human resources were insufficient to yield a clear solution. It is significant that at so crucial a stage in the development of modern science its practical originator should have so strongly commended Augustine.

The assessments of Duhem and Galileo of Augustine's scientific attitude, so to speak, lead us to advert, however briefly it must be here, to what we know of Augustine's information on the science that was available to his contemporaries. We can safely assume that of this he had at least a gentleman's knowledge—at least that imparted by the school manuals of his day. At sixty-six years of age he boasted, perhaps humorously and ironically, that if he wished to reveal how many things about human nature he could discuss knowledgeably, he would fill volumes: *quam multa possim de hominis natura scientissime disputare . . . si explicare velim, volumina implebo.*[24] In the main, however, he must have been limited, as were his contemporaries, to such scientific information as could be found in the philosophies, especially the Neoplatonic, and in Varro, Pliny, Posidonius and Apuleius. This would have included mathematics (he seems to have studied the *Introductio arithmetica* of Nicomachus[25]), physics and some biology.

He would appear, however, to have some special knowledge of medicine and astronomy, the latter of which would be of special use for the interpretation of *Genesis.*[26]

In the *de Genesi ad litteram*, for example, he shows acquaintance not only with the medical teachings of Erasistratus and Herophilus but also significantly, it would appear, of Galen. He is at pains to insist upon the need to justify views on medicine by clear evidence and demonstration. Outside of the *de Genesi ad litteram* he shows evidence of even close acquaintance with the *Gynaecia* of Vindicianus[27] who, we know from the *Confessions,*[28] was a friend of Augustine at Carthage, and who may have been the source for such special knowledge of medicine as he manifests.

With regard to Augustine's acquaintance with astronomy, we have the evidence of his *Confessions* how profoundly he was impressed by the precision and certainty of its calculations: '[the astronomers] have discovered many things, and predicted many years before, eclipses of the sun and moon, what day, what hour, the degree of these eclipses to come—and their calculation proved correct. What they predicted happened exactly as they had predicted. They committed to writing the rules they had discovered and these we read to-day. From these rules we now predict in what year, in what month of the year, on what day of the month, on what hour of the day, and to what degree will the sun or moon be eclipsed: and so it shall happen, as we predict'.[29] Augustine attributes

24 *de anima et eius origine, P.L.* 44.526. 25 Cf. *B.A.* 48. 634. 26 For bibliography on Augustine's scientific knowledge cf. T. van Bavel, *Répertoire Bibliographique de saint Augustin* (1950–60) (it takes account of earlier work), The Hague (1963), 424–40. *B.A.* 48, 49 (1972), have considerable information in their *notes complémentaires*, to which there are useful indexes: cf. *Table Analytique* (49, 619ff.) under *astres, éléments, médecine* for example. Cf. also A. Solignac 'Doxographies et manuels,' *Recherches Augustiniennes,* I (1958), 120–37, and (for manuals dealing with the physical questions arising from the account of creation in Genesis) J.P. Bouhot, 'Pentateuque chez les Pères,' *Dict. de la Bible, Suppl.,* 7.708. 27 Cf. *B.A.* 48.711. 28 4.3, 5; 7.6, 8. 29 5.3, 4.

his knowledge of these things to what he calls 'secular philosophers'. Nevertheless it seems likely that he was also acquainted with manuals of astronomy, and that some of these at least incorporated teachings from the *Megistē Syntaxis*—later known as the *Almagest* of Ptolemy—which are discerned in Augustine's references to astronomy. Another source would seem to be the *de architectura* of Vitruvius.[30] What is to be noted is the impression the exactitude of secular science made upon him: its certain findings had to be accepted. Thus he says that one may believe that the stars are equal, in spite of St Paul's statement apparently to the contrary in 1 *Cor.* 15.41: 'The sun has a splendour of its own, the moon another splendour, and the stars another, for star differs from star in brightness.' One may concede to St Paul that he agrees with what our eyes seem to tell us—the sun and moon shed more light than the other stars *upon the earth*. But one doesn't go to St Paul for *scientific* instruction.

Since the matter is of some importance in relation to a modem audience—which inevitably is profoundly impressed by the scientific discoveries of the last hundred years—one might illustrate both Augustine's approach and knowledge in some detail on at least one issue: that of the existence of water not only under but also above the firmament. *Genesis* says plainly: *and God divided the water that was under the firmament from the water that was above the firmament. And God called the firmament 'heaven'.* If the doctrine on the location of the elements according to weight, prevailing when Augustine wrote, were to be respected, this text could not be true; water could not be found above air and fire. Origen interpreted the text figuratively and avoided trouble.

Ambrose gives some grounds for reconciling science with scripture, but in the main asserts that there is question in scripture here of a miracle—like the separation of the waters of the Jordan to let the Hebrews pass—which God could perform. Augustine makes no reference to Ambrose, but does appear to refer to the solution put forward by Basil, known to him doubtless through the translation of Eustathius, according to which, since the 'air' is sometimes in scripture called 'heaven', that is firmament, it is a matter of observation to those who climb to mountain tops that water is suspended as vapour in clouds above the air beneath: the air or firmament thus divides waters, as scripture says. Augustine describes this attempt at reconciliation as 'laudable'.

He is, however, clearly not satisfied with this approach to the question. Once again he fears that secular scholars will at best not be impressed. He reviews the problem and, perhaps thinking of Ambrose's 'miraculous' solution, declares that one must not 'refute' sound scholars by appeal to God's omnipotence, to whom all things are possible: 'Our business it is to discover how, taking account of his scriptures, God arranged the natures of things, not what he might wish to do in or with them to show his miraculous powers.'[31] This observation is very significant for it clearly implies that Augustine accepted that there is a rational order in nature and that it is the philosopher's and Augustine's business to discover it as far as he can.

Augustine refers to two other considerations which might be taken into account in the problem of the super-celestial waters. The first is based on a scientific view of his

30 Cf. *B.A.* 48.604–9.   31 2.1, 2.

day that every body was infinitely divisible. Although water was heavier than air, water, divided and refined to the condition of vapour, was observed to be suspended above air, as has just been reported. If the particles of water were divided and refined to a degree we do not observe, could they not be suspended above even the firmament, even if this is lighter than air? The second arises from the then known phenomenon that Saturn, which should, because of its obvious properties, be extremely hot was, in fact, extremely cold. Fellow-Christians, Augustine says, put forward the hypothesis that Saturn was cooled by the super-celestial waters, of which the scripture speaks, which would be in the vicinity of Saturn, not in the form of vapour, but of solid ice.

In the end Augustine advances none of these arguments as acceptable: *the matter is still open even if what scripture says is to be taken as true—quoquo modo autem et qualeslibet aquae ibi sunt, esse ibi eas minime dubitemus.*[32] The words of Scripture involved—as in the case of the words of *Psalm* 136.6 'he established the earth upon the waters'—could legitimately be interpreted in a figurative manner, or even in a 'literal' sense, but not one, however, that would conflict with the then established scientific truth that the waters were supported by the earth. What was proved *certis rationibus vel experimentis manifestissimis*[33] was the *datum* in relation to which scripture had to be interpreted and which it could not contradict.

A question that must arise in connection with any consideration of Augustine's understanding of *Genesis* on creation from the point of view of science is as to whether or not he could be described as an Evolutionist in any modern scientific meaning of that word? There has, naturally, been a good deal of controversy on this point, much of it, understandably, centring on the *de Genesi ad litteram*.[34] Some would hold that he was not an evolutionist, that all the *genera* that ever were to be, were created in the first stage of creation, when all things were created at the same time: there could not, therefore, be any evolution, there could be no new *genera*. In fact, however, Augustine's very doctrine that all things were created at the same time in their *causal reasons*[35] (which are described as woven into the existing elements) precisely allows new, or to then unappearing, *genera* to *manifest* themselves at the second stage of creation, when all things come into being differently and at different times according to their original causal reasons or possible causal reasons. He makes two separate references in fact to spontaneous generation of which here is one: 'for it has been observed that certain things are born from the waters and the earth. These have no sex. Their seed, therefore, is not in themselves but rather in the elements, from which they have their origin.'[36] These creatures also were created at the first stage of creation; they appeared later. To this extent, therefore, Augustine is an evolutionist.

Augustine is not an evolutionist, however, inasmuch as he denies that things develop *differently* from the rationality of their causal reasons: a given cause, according to him, does not produce *simply any effect at all*: it produces an effect corresponding to the potentiality of its cause. Nor does he admit that anything new can come to be which was not created as a causal reason at the first stage of creation.

32 Ibid. 2.5, 9.   33 Ibid., 2.1,4.   34 Cf.   B.A.   48.665ff.   35 See 112 above and 121ff. below. 36 3.12, 19.

In general it might be said that Augustine's theory of the causal reasons provides a rather favourable context for a scientific theory of the evolution of living species and the evolutionary transformation of the universe. He uses the term 'evolve' very freely and naturally, but of course he is not using it in a strict modern scientific sense. He insists, moreover, that God created the causal reasons and that under Providence what evolves from them does so rationally. Everything must be susceptible of a rational explanation.

The reverent search for rationality in the world which Augustine thus displays has an echo in the words of perhaps the most famous scientist of our century. Albert Einstein wrote in 1930: 'What a deep conviction of the rationality of the universe and what a yearning to understand, were it but a feeble reflection of the mind revealed in this world, Kepler and Newton must have had to enable them to spend years of solitary labor in disentangling the principles of celestial mechanics. Only one who has devoted his life to similar ends can have a vivid realization of what has inspired these men and given them the strength to remain true to their purpose in spite of countless failures. It is cosmic religious feeling that gives a man such strength. A contemporary has said, not unjustly, that in this materialistic age of ours the serious scientific workers are the only profoundly religious people.'[37]

Einstein speaks here of 'cosmic religious feeling'. He describes it as strongly emotional and the searcher for knowledge as having been inspired by Spinoza's *Amor Dei Intellectualis*. Augustine was convinced in early life that true reason and true faith could not conflict, since the source of the affirmation of both was the same Truth Itself. This same attitude is to be seen in the *de Genesi ad litteram*. To this extent Augustine might have featured among Einstein's 'Kindred spirits scattered wide through the world and the centuries'. Augustine's attitude to science, I believe, deserves to be better known and better appreciated.

37 *Ideas and Opinions*, New York (1954), 39f.

9

The Creation of Man and Woman

It would, I think, not misrepresent many people's notions of the account of the creation in *Genesis* to say, that they think that God is there described as creating first Adam, the male, in his image, and later, taking a rib from Adam, making Eve, the female. If this impression represents the account in *Genesis* fairly, then the Jewish-Christian tradition would appear to start off with an acceptance of what looks like the inferior status of the female. Does it appear that the female, unlike the male, was not made in God's image? If that were so, then she would indeed according to *Genesis* be altogether inferior. And does not the fact that she was made from a rib of Adam necessarily make her 'dependent' on him? As we probe into the history of the domination of the male over the female in western society we cannot ignore the problem as it is posed by this impression of the creation account in *Genesis*. This after all is the basic context of the question in the West, which should help to put into perspective and to some extent even explain subsequent events and attitudes.

I propose, therefore, to give here St Augustine's reading of the *Genesis* account of creation and, since this is normally neglected, to draw out from time to time its implications in relation to woman in particular. It is important to do this latter especially. For Augustine has been represented to women as *the* Father of the Christian church who held firmly that procreation was the only end of marriage, who inculcated a Puritan attitude to sexuality—whether in or out of marriage—and who authoritatively opposed contraception of any kind. Did not Augustine re-act from a life of sexual excess, and represent sexuality as sinful and necessarily degrading? Did he not cast his mistress, the mother of his son, aside when she was no longer of any use towards his career? Although such notions are scarcely founded, they are current, and one can understand that some women feel much hostility towards Augustine. Other women, of course, have praised him for the very matters mentioned. They have admired the story of his conversion as set out in the *Confessions* and the attitude he there represents himself as having towards his mother, Monica.

I hope to show here, however, that Augustine took what one might call an unusually, for his time, enlightened and sympathetic view of woman and her special problems. He accepted without question with his contemporaries, pagan and Christian, layman and Church Father, eastern and western, the existence of biological and social inequalities in life—including submission of a woman to her husband—which are not acceptable to our generation. But if in the context of his times he helped and favoured women notably and in important issues, it is hardly fair to seize on him for doing no more in other instances than reporting views that he inherited and were prevalent among all types of people among his contemporaries.

Augustine's analysis of the account of creation in *Genesis* is in fact an instance, and obviously an important and significant instance, of a favourable attitude to woman. His approach is rational, informed, mature and scrupulous. I feel also that it is sympathetic to woman.

Here is what *Genesis* (I. 26f.) says, in the Septuagint version used by Augustine, of the creation of man and woman: *Et dixit Deus: faciamus hominem ad imaginem et similitudinem nostram; et dominetur piscium maris, et volatilium caeli, et omnium pecorum et omnis terrae et omnium reptilium repentium super terram. Et fecit Deus hominem, ad imaginem Dei fecit eum: masculum et feminam fecit eos.* This text on the face of it, contrary to the ordinary impression to which I referred earlier, clearly implies that male and female, *distinct from one another, were made 'at the same time'* by God and *were given equally domination* over the fishes of the sea, the birds of the air, the beasts, the whole earth, and every creeping thing creeping over the earth. It also appears to say that male and female were created in God's image and likeness—again *equally*, without any limitation on either. The scripture uses the term *homo* in preference to *vir*, which could only refer to the male, and makes the point quite unquestionable by spelling out explicitly that *homo* meant male and female, not just as within the concept of *homo*, but separately (*eos*).[1] But what about woman made from man's rib? Is not this too in *Genesis*, and can it be reconciled with the text just given?

The explanation is sought in the fact, discerned by Augustine, that in the first three chapters of *Genesis* there are *two* accounts of creation.[2] The verses referring to Adam being made from dust and Eve from his rib, coming in the seventh and twenty-second verses respectively of the second chapter, fall clearly and wholly into the second or Yahwist account. The text I have quoted earlier on the creation of the male and female in the image of God comes from the first chapter of *Genesis* and so from the first or Priestly account.

Basil of Caesarea, whose homily *In Verba Faciamus* Augustine follows closely at this point in the *de Genesi ad litteram,* interprets the two accounts of the creation of man and woman as referring to the 'inner' man or woman and the 'outer' man or woman.[3] St Paul had spoken of the inner and the outer man.[4] Basil takes the inner man to be the real one, and the outer man to refer only to the things that he possesses: My hand is not me: it merely belongs to me. The rational part of my soul, which is invisible, is me. The first account of the creation of man and woman Basil takes as referring to the *mens* of man and woman only—the inner man and woman—and the second—involving the dust and the rib—to the body, the outer man and woman. This way of reconciling the two accounts seemed plausible and had good authority.

---

1 *de Gen. ad litt.* 3.19, 29 to 22, 34. Cf. *B.A.* 48, 622–8.   2 Cf. 101 and 107 above.   3 *Sur l'origine de l'homme,* Sources Chrétiennes 160, Paris (1970), 170.   4 2 *Cor.* 4,16.

But Augustine will not accept it at any price. He insists that the first account involves the *bodies* of man and woman equally with their souls: *masculum et feminam fecit eos.* The first account emphasizes sexual differentiation which, Augustine says, necessarily implies bodies.

Augustine has recourse to a much more subtle explanation of the two accounts in *Genesis.*[5] He posits, as we have seen,[6] two 'aspects' of creation which he refers to as the *prima conditio* and the *administratio* respectively. I shall refer to them henceforth as the first and second 'aspects' of the creation. These aspects correspond respectively to the first and second accounts of the creation of *Genesis.*

What are these two aspects? Augustine evolved a theory of what are sometimes called 'seminal reasons'. The nomenclature is helpful to the extent that it suggests the notion of an inchoative stage of a being which later is developed. Thus in relation to humans the *semen* is inchoative and the grown man is developed. But Augustine rarely uses the term 'seminal' in this connection, and when he does he refers to *animalia* who are generated by *semina*. He more usually uses the term *rationes causales,* 'causal reasons,' from which all things—and not merely animals—develop. He also uses the term *rationes primordiales,* primordial or original reasons. I shall, however, use only the term *rationes causales* or 'causal reasons' here. In brief the first account in *Genesis,* Augustine suggests, describes the creation of the 'causal reasons' of man and woman (including their separate but invisible bodies), and the second their development into visible humans. The two aspects, though to some extent separated by the second aspect being in time, are to be considered together: one creation only, two moments or aspects. In this way he attempts a reconciliation of the two accounts in *Genesis.*

Let us look first at his treatment of the first aspect of creation, the creation of the causal reasons: we shall then see how he employed the term 'literal' and in fact how rational he is.

Augustine's theory of causal reasons is not wholly original. It derives ultimately from Stoic doctrine, but more immediately from Plotinus's theory of *logoi* or 'reasons'. Plotinus sought to account for the existence of things in their emanation from the One, the First Principle. 'Logos' or 'reason' is at once 'thinking' and 'thought', and the *logos* of the One—the first emanation from it—is *Nous,* that is Intelligence. *Nous* is the rich actualization of the One, of its simple potentiality. *Nous* in its turn communicates, without disturbance or alteration in itself, other *logoi,* the intelligibles, to the Soul, which is the third Plotinian hypostasis. Soul is the great point of mediation between the immaterial and the sensible. The Soul as contemplative communicates *logoi* to the Soul as active; the Soul as Universal communicates *logoi* to particular souls. Particular souls in this way make it possible for the sensible things of the material world to participate in *logos* or reason. The Soul, that is, the Universal Soul, plays a vital mediative part in all of this: it produces in the sensible world that we know the intelligibles that it contemplates in the *Nous.* In this way 'the *Nous* is the model of which the universe is the image'.[7] But sometimes it is also said to be the true maker.[8] Likewise the *logoi* or

---

5 Cf. *B.A.* 48, 653–68; 685–9. 6 Cf. 19, 112 and 121 above. 7 *Enneads,* 3.2.1. 8 Ibid., 5.9, 3.

'reasons', though fragmented and diminished in all existing things and their parts, are immanent in them and properly constitute substances as we know them.'[9]

It will be necessary to look somewhat closer at Plotinus's *Nous*. The One, the first hypostasis, produces in *Nous* the radiance from itself—a *perilampsis*. This radiance or light looked towards the One, recognized that it was separated from the One, saw reflected in itself the potentiality of the One, and moved in love towards its origin.[10]

Augustine adapted these Neoplatonic ideas on the *logoi* or 'reasons', and the *logos* or 'reason' of the One, which was *Nous*. *Genesis* also reports that the first creature was light, which Augustine sees as corresponding in some way to the *perilampsis* of Plotinus. This light Augustine takes to be the intellectual being *par excellence*, the angel. The creation of this *logos* or reason, the angel, follows, therefore, fairly closely Plotinus's description of the coming into being of the *Nous*. God wills the creation of the intellectual creature: the intellectual creature, existing as formable, turns towards and knows the illuminating and creating Word, of which it is an image; knows itself as separate from the Word; and turns again to its Creator to praise him: 'immediately on the word of God, light (the angel) was made, and the light created clung to the creating light, seeing it and itself in it, that is the reason by which it was made. It saw itself in itself, that is as being separate, because it was made from him who made it.'[11]

It must be stated clearly *en passant* that apart from the possibility that Augustine's understanding of the Neoplatonic position on the *logoi* and *Nous* may be somewhat forced, Augustine was also quite clear in his mind that there were radical differences between the Neoplatonists and himself on creation. For Augustine the Trinity— explicitly Father, Word and Spirit—was the Creator. Moreover the creature needed the continuing support of its Creator to develop: 'the *Principle* of the intellectual creature is eternal wisdom: this *Principle,* remaining in itself without change, never ceases to speak, secretly inspiring and calling to the creature, whose *Principle* it is, to turn towards that from which it has its being. Otherwise it cannot be formed and become perfect.'[12] It is in the possibility that the creature, here the angel, may turn away from God that sin may arise.

But to return to the first creature, the intellectual creature, the light, the angel: as we have seen the angel has, according to Augustine who follows in this Plotinus, and perhaps Porphyry also, three phases of knowledge—it knows the illuminating Word; it knows itself as separate from that Word; and it turns back again in recognition of its Creator. Since God called the light or angel 'day,' these three phases of the angel's knowledge are called by Augustine respectively 'day' knowledge, 'evening' knowledge and morning 'knowledge'.[13] The first 'day' of creation in *Genesis*, therefore, is the completion of the three phases of the angel's knowledge and is the creation of the angel.

The remaining five 'days' of creation are, of course, not days in our sense at all. They also are the creation of all things that ever are to be in an order[14] or logical succession

---

9 Cf. ibid., 3.2,1; 5,16; 5.1, 6; 9.3 30–6. *B.A.* 48, 654ff. adds other references to primary and secondary sources for these points.　10 *Enneads*, 5.1, 6, 28; 2.1; 3.8,19–23.　11 *de Gen. ad litt.* 4.32, 50; cf. *B.A.* 48, 629f; 659.　12 Ibid. 1.5, 10.　13 Ibid., 4.24, 41. For Porphyry's angelology, which was well-known to Augustine, cf. F. Cumont, 'Les Anges du Paganisme,' *Rev. de l'Hist. des Rel.* 12 (1915), 169.　14 Ibid., 12; *B.A.* 48, 659.

according as they are diffracted in the angel's intellect as he sees and knows them as eternal reasons in the Word.[15] In the Word they exist, so to speak, simultaneously. But although the angel, being an intellectual creature, can see them simultaneously, he contemplates them in an ordered or logical succession, according to the three phases of his knowledge, and with his contemplation of them as eternal reasons they come to be in a corresponding order. Some of them become full sensible realities—these are the elements fire, earth, air, and water, from which other realities develop; and others become 'causal reasons' interwoven in these elements.[16]

Although Augustine insists that the angels do not create—only the Trinity does that—he assigns them an important role, partly similar to the Plotinian *Nous* and partly similar to the Plotinian *Soul,* in the creation of the other creatures. These creations Augustine calls a certain sixfold representation: *sexies quodamodo praesentatus.*[17] The angel's three-phased knowledge of eternal reasons in the Word signalled the creation of these as a succession of 'causal reasons' inhering in the elements.

That the number of days of creation is six is merely symbolical. Six is the first perfect number, that is to say the first number which is the sum ($1+2+3$) of its divisors (1, 2 and 3).[18] There were no days at all in our sense of day, never mind six days: it was merely appropriate that the number of 'days' of creation should be the first perfect number. The act of creation, of angels and all other creatures, was one, and in its first aspect simultaneous for all: it started with a bang: *in ictu condendi.* With it time began.[19]

It will not be necessary to describe the creation of man and woman in their causal reasons since it is modelled on that of the creation of the angel: '[our] nature itself, which is intellectual is like that light (namely the angel), and therefore its creation is its knowing the Word of God by which it is made.'[20] What Augustine insists upon, however, is that in the first aspect of creation man and woman were created in the image of God in their *mentes* and were sexually differentiated and so possessed bodies, even if these were invisible.

But a number of difficulties arise in connection with Augustine's view of the first stage of creation, of which the first is this: if God created all things at once in their causal reasons, and if they will develop according to natural processes in due time, how can God intervene, *miraculously*, later? How, for example, could he make Adam from dust, or Eve from his rib? These were not natural processes taking place in due time. Augustine considered this problem from many angles. God's transcendent will must be saved; but likewise the rationality of miracles. His final solution, given precisely in connection with the formation of Eve from Adam's rib, is as follows. One must distinguish between the usual course of nature and the Creator's power which transcends it. This latter can do something *else* than what is included in the causal reasons of things: this other thing, of course, will have been included in the causal reasons as a possibility. These possibilities are hidden to us, but seen by God. They are not in contradiction with the causal reasons of things. Though they may seem miraculous to us, they were provided for from the beginning. Adam or Eve might have developed slowly in time.

15 Cf. *B.A.* 48, 650.   16 Cf. ibid., 660, 677.   17 *de Gen. ad litt.* 5.5, 15; cf. 4.35, 56.   18 Ibid., 4.2, 2.   19 Ibid., 4.33, 51.   20 Ibid., 3.20, 31f.

But God had included in their causal reasons the possibility that the one might be made from dust, probably as a fully grown adult, and the other, likewise an adult, from his rib. And so it happened.[21]

It is necessary to emphasize that the causal reasons of men, women and all other things are, though invisible to us, fully existing. They explain the rationality of the universe of which they are the origin. No new creations are required. The universe has begun. One should note too that related as Augustine's causal reasons are to Plotinus's 'reasons', the creation in Augustine is the immediate work of the Trinity, without any intermediaries and without any separately existing order of Intelligibles.

The account of the first aspect of creation in *Genesis* proceeds: *Et benedixit eos Deus dicens: crescite et multiplicamini et inplete terram et dominamini eius et principamini piscium maris . . . ecce dedi vobis omne pabulum . . .* God enjoined the man and woman to increase, multiply, fill the earth and he proffered them food to eat. Here a second difficulty arises. According to Augustine's interpretation of the creation account so far, the bodies of male and female, though existing, were invisible, and could need no food. The injunction to propagate did not necessarily involve physical union: there could, Augustine suggests as an hypothesis, have been another mode of propagation. Offspring, daughters as well as sons, could have been born to these bodies from the loving bond alone (*solo pietatis effectu*) without any corrupting concupiscence. Neither parents nor offspring would die. Then when the earth was filled with men, and a people that was holy and just had been established—as we believe will be the case after the future resurrection—there would be an end to propagation. This, Augustine admits, would be an hypothesis difficult to sustain. In the case of the food, however, it could hardly be claimed that invisible bodies could use it. The explanation he gives is that man's action in relation to the offer of food and injunction to propagate was simply noted by man. The words of scripture deliberately omit any reference to his proceeding to action—to eat or propagate. To confirm this—it is clear, Augustine contends, from scripture itself that Adam and Eve did not propagate until after the second stage of creation. It can be assumed the case was similar in relation to the proffered food: whether they could eat it or not, they did not.

Augustine reports what appears to be Origen's way of dealing with the problem created by the injunction to propagate and the provision of food before the second stage of man's creation (when he would have a visible body).

This supposes that the references to propagation and food, although coming in the earlier account, apply to the second stage only. This so de-emphasizes the body at the first aspect of creation that it becomes necessary to find some way of differentiating the male from the female in the first aspect of creation that was not bodily. Origen suggests that the male contemplates eternal verity, while the female administers temporal things; the one commanding, the other obeying, both related in a quasi-marriage.

Augustine sets aside such an interpretation very firmly, even if it seems possible and has the authority of Origen. He insists that male and female, images of God, with sexually differentiated though invisible bodies, were there from the first instant of man's

21 Cf. *B.A.* 48, 688ff.

first stage of creation. He will not have images of Mary and Martha, much less conventional stereotypes of man's and woman's roles, imported back into the discussion of this crucial problem.

The greatest difficulty about his theory, however, is a text of St Paul which seems to be in radical opposition to his whole doctrine: *vir . . . imago et gloria Dei est, mulier autem gloria viri.*[22] Man is the image and glory of God; but woman is the glory of man. This on the face of it denies that woman is the image of God and it is commonly taken that way. Moreover, since Augustine quotes it—to interpret it in his own sense—careless readers believe that he too denied that woman was the image of God. But Augustine constantly and confidently appeals to the words of *Genesis* which are explicit on the point that *both* male and female were created in God's image. St Paul, he explains, is using allegory. The external differentiation of man and woman is a figure (as Origen had suggested) of the internal differentiation in the soul of man or woman between the contemplation of truth on the one hand and the administration of temporal things on the other. St Paul is referring not to man and woman in this text, but to the figurative man (contemplation of truth) and figurative woman (administration of temporal things). In this understanding of the terms only the man is the image of God: *in cuius rei figura Paulus . . . virum tantum dicit imaginem . . . Dei.*[23] This is not the obvious meaning of St Paul's text but, as Augustine maintains in general, scripture can be figuratively as well as literally understood.

Augustine is unmoved by St Paul. He reaffirms positively that in the first condition of man, taking account that woman too is man in that sense, she certainly had her *mens,* and it was rational, and according to it she herself also was made according to the image of God. *Genesis* deliberately added the words male and female precisely to prevent any possibility—as later could arise from an exclusively literal understanding of St Paul— that woman's being in God's image might be questioned, and also lest there should be any doubt that the bodies of both man and woman were created at the same time, and that male and female were quite separate—unlike androgynes who contained within the one person both male and female.

Having dealt with difficulties that arise from his 'literal' understanding of the account of the *first aspect* of creation in *Genesis,* Augustine turns to the *second*: this is described in the second account in *Genesis.* Although God created all things in their rational causes in the first stage he did, as we have seen, provide for the possibility of his later intervention—in the case of a miracle, for example. God not only may intervene in this way, but he is also the immediate cause of all things that come into existence. The world of the causal reasons is not something like a machine made to function on its own. The scripture says 'my Father works until now'.[24] The existing thing, as distinct from its causal reasons, is not a phenomenon, a manifestation of a possibility. It is a reality, brought forward to perfection implied in its causal reasons by God's transcendent causality.

22 1 *Cor.* 11.7.   23 *de Gen. ad litt.* 3.22,34.   24 *John* 5.17.

God, therefore, in this sense created man from dust and woman from his rib by this transcendent causality. The potential man, the potential woman, *mens* and body, became the visible historic Adam and Eve. The long natural process of their maturing to the age when they are made in Paradise was by-passed by God's creative causality. Here we shall have to consider the second stage of their creation, taking them, man and woman, separately.

Formavit Deus hominem pulverem terrae, vel limum terrae—hoc est de pulvere vel limo terrae. Augustine understands this text as saying that God formed man from the dust of the earth. He discusses immediately a physical meaning. To think that God modelled man's body from dust is simply too puerile. He insists that here scripture is using a metaphor: *translato verbo usum credere deberemus*,[25] even if some respected commentators could also understand it at its word. Nor would Augustine accept the more refined interpretations that in saying that man was modelled by God, the scripture was emphasizing that the creation of man was special and man was superior: other creatures came into being on God's *word, or* on his *order,* but in man's case God intervened with his own hands. Basil of Caesarea, for example, whose comment at this point seems to have been known to Augustine, interprets the scripture here as showing God's special love for man: 'with his own hand, lovingly he made us'.[26] The dust, Basil says, indicates our nothingness; but our being made thus indicates surpassing honour.

Augustine, keeping to his insistence that man's (and woman's) greatness is in being in the image of God, does not discover in the method of the formation of man's (or woman's) body a sign of man's true excellence. He does, however, make use of the old theme that the fact of man's being of erect stature was an indication of the harmony of his body with his soul. He looks upwards to contemplate the heavens for his fulfilment, not downwards as do the beasts: *ut quae sursum sunt sapiat, non quae sunt super terram.*[27]

Was Adam formed fully grown or as all other infants, but without parents? Augustine raises the question formally. He does not take it for granted, even if others do, that Adam was made fully grown. 'Did God make him, suddenly at full age or, did he make him as men are made now in the wombs of their mothers?'[28] It is clear, Augustine adds, that Adam had no parents and so could not have been begotten and gestated in the ordinary way-but otherwise God could have made him as men are now made, and the normal lapse of time could have been necessary to bring him to full adulthood. What is of special interest here is that Augustine is careful not to skip over or dismiss the more developmental or evolutionary hypothesis of the second aspect of Adam's—and likewise Eve's—making. He leaves the matter open saying simply that we do not have to concern ourselves with it. What prevailed was God's will: *eius voluntas super omnia.*

It is to be noted that in this, Augustine's interpretation of the account of the second aspect of the creation of Adam, not only is the description explicitly considered as being metaphorical, but it is not, even as metaphorical, sufficiently precise: Adam could have

---

25 *de Gen. ad litt.* 6.12, 20. **26** *Sur l'origine de l'homme*, S.C. 160, 230. **27** *de Gen. ad litt.* 6.12, 22.
28 Ibid. 6.13, 23.

been made at a stage so early in human life that with or without special intervention of God he would survive and develop. Furthermore, Augustine denies that there is significance in the metaphor of God's forming Adam—such as Adam's superiority to beasts, who came into being simply on God's word or command. Even the erect posture of man is something that might have escaped notice at Adam's earliest possible stage. Altogether Augustine can see no special significance in the *Genesis* account of God's forming man from dust. There is nothing here additional to what was implied in the first aspect of creation, except the possibility that Adam was 'miraculously' made as an adult.

Augustine raises the question if Adam's body—and the question equally affects Eve's—was animal or spiritual (that is, of the nature of spirit, not spiritual=pious), mortal or immortal. He canvasses various opinions, into which we need not go, and takes account of the relevance of what we know from scripture, including its report on the qualities of resurrected bodies. His view finally is that Adam's body (as Eve's) at this point before the Fall was both animal and mortal: animal inasmuch as Adam *could* engage in the processes of, for example, taking nourishment and reproduction; and mortal— but potentially immortal but for the Fall. Adam's body would in due course, if he had not sinned, have become spirital, and this is the kind of glorified body that man shall attain in the resurrection.

An animal body should, Augustine knows, be mortal. But God had provided a remedy against death in the fruit of the tree of life, and in due course if man had not sinned the animal body would become spiritual and thus immortal. Adam's body was mortal because it could (and in fact after the Fall did) die, and immortal because it had the possibility of not dying: *mortale, quia poterat mori, inmortale, quia poterat non mori.*[29] Adam was thus clearly in a state of probation.

Augustine's insistence on man's animality in the beginning is reassuring, one imagines, to our contemporaries. He could easily have followed those who thought that Adam and Eve were invested with their animal bodies *after* the Fall, when God put on them tunics of skin: Jerome attributed such a view to Origen, who certainly taught that Paradise was no material place but was purely allegorical. One cannot think that Augustine was incapable of the elevation, subtleties and refinement of thought of an Origen, a Gregory of Nyssa or a Philo, or was unaware of their theories on man's first state.[30] But Augustine was clearly at pains to respect not only God's immaterial, but also his material creation; not only the spirit but also the body. This is fundamentally what is hinted in the title of his book, *Genesis Understood Literally.* Adam's and Eve's bodies in Paradise were as ours are now.

The question of Adam's soul is one which Augustine discusses at very considerable length from this point on in the later books of the *de Genesi ad litteram*, but one which we cannot go into here. It is of transcending importance, nevertheless, belonging more to the first aspect of man's creation, when man's *mens* was made in the image of God: did the soul pre-exist? Was it made from something? Are souls transmitted along with

29 Ibid., 6, 25, 36.   30 Cf. *B.A.* 48, 690ff.

bodies and if so, how? Augustine admits that he is undecided on many questions affecting the soul.

He is certain only that the soul is no part of God's substance; it is immortal but does not exist from eternity; and it is incorporeal at least in some sense.[31] He is not certain that Adam's soul was created in the first aspect of creation in *the form of a causal reason*. He favours at one point the possibility that it was fully created *in its proper reality then*—but if so he has difficulty in answering the questions as to the mode of its separate existence until it was insufflated into Adam's body, or indeed why it should be joined to such a body at all? In this last connection he approaches the view of Plotinus that the soul, in such circumstances, would join with body through a voluntary inclination.[32] Augustine even considers the possibility (but he rejects it) of the soul's being created only at the time of union with the earthly body. In sum though Augustine's discussion of the soul takes up a great deal of the *de Genesi ad litteram*, as it took up the whole of his long life, and though his discussion is subtle and illuminating, he left most questions on the soul either wholly open or having only provisional answers: others he said, or even himself might do better later.

We come to the *second aspect* of the creation of Eve. Augustine considers this creation side by side with the Incarnation. Both events he pronounces to be incredible to those outside the faith. But to those within—why should they believe literally in the event of the Incarnation, but regard the account of the creation of Eve as only figurative?: *tantum ad figuratam significationem?* His assertion is that he believes that in the case of Eve she was made from a man without physical union: *fideliter credimus factam feminam ex viro nullo interveniente concubitu.*[33] If he is willing to believe that the detail, for example, of the rib is not figurative, it is perhaps *because* he is instituting a comparison between the creation of Eve and the Incarnation. So intent is he on the comparison that just as an angel played a role in the Annunciation, so he suggests the angels played a role in Eve's making too. Since she was not, and could not be, born of physical union, God made her miraculously, the angels, Augustine says, playing a role which we cannot determine.[34]

But there was another comparison which was also occupying Augustine's mind at this point—that of the opening of Christ's side in the crucifixion, and the flowing of the sacraments therefrom in the Church. Eve's making was, he says, prophetic of this— a symbol. As the Church sprang from Christ's opened side, so did Eve from Adam's. As Christ is 'weakened', so to speak, in that opening, while the Church draws strength from it, so Adam is 'weakened' and Eve strengthened. The bond of Adam with Eve is of flesh with its own flesh; as intimate as the bond of Christ with his Church.[35]

Augustine delights here in these comparisons and prophecies; but his net assertion adds only one thing to what was asserted of Adam's making—which was without physical union and therefore 'miraculous'—namely that Eve was made from Adam.

Here at last we seem to get the first suggestion that *Genesis* understood literally by Augustine indicated an inferiority of the female to the male. But this is no more implicit in the account than would Christ's inferiority to his mother be implicit in the account

---

31 *de Gen. ad litt.* 8.2, 1; 28,43.   32 Cf. *B.A.* 48, 714ff.   33 *de Gen. ad litt.* 9.16, 30.   34 Ibid. 9.15, 28; 16, 29; cf. *B.A.* 49, 527.   35 Ibid., 9.18,34.

of his being born of her. Insofar as Augustine, who examines his words and thoughts carefully and alertly, actually institutes a comparison of the birth, so to speak, of Eve with the birth of Christ, the implication, one could argue, might be quite the reverse.

What Augustine above all emphasizes in all this is that Eve's being made in a 'miraculous' way from Adam signifies the intimacy of the union of male and female. Whereas elsewhere he uses the reading *inmisit Deus soporem in Adam*, 'God sent a sleep on Adam', and even earlier in the *de Genesi ad litteram: iniecit Deus mentis alienationem,* 'God threw a loss of consciousness', on him, here he follows the Septuagint and reads: *inmisit Deus extasim*: God enveloped him in 'ecstasy'.[36] Augustine writes in this connection that one could legitimately think that in that ecstasy Adam's *mens* joined the assembly of angels and, entering God's sanctuary, understood the great mysteries of life. Waking then in a spirit of prophecy, and beholding Eve, he spoke with inspiration 'this now is bone from my bones, and flesh from my flesh. She will be called woman, for she has been taken from her man. And on this account a man will leave his father and mother and stick to his wife, and they will be two in one flesh.'

The point of Eve's being made from Adam is that their intimacy in sharing the one same flesh should be emphasized.

The story of the creation of man and woman as interpreted by Augustine in the *de Genesi ad litteram* insists on male and female having been created in the image of God in the first aspect of creation. In the second aspect they were both produced by God's creative causality (which had from the beginning provided for this as a possibility), the one from dust, the other from the other. Though two separate beings, they are modelled on the same God and are the same flesh.

When we turn our eyes to the life of Adam and Eve in their earthly Paradise, as seen by Augustine, we shall have occasion to note again his respect for reality, including the reality of our nature. Was there physical love, as we experience it, in Paradise? Augustine is remarkably understanding, as we shall see presently, on this and other matters, as he serenely scrutinizes the words of scripture. But then the serpent comes and sets a trap, not for Adam, but for Eve. Why Eve?

---

36 Ibid. 9.1,1. The other references are to *de Gen c. Man.*2.1,1; *c. Adim.*3; *civ. Dei* 22.17 and *de Gen. ad litt.* 6.5,7 respectively.

10

Man and Woman in Paradise

With the building of Eve's body from Adam's rib we have the constitution of man and woman in the earthly Paradise. Their being images of God in their rational causes is clear, even if Augustine is not at all clear on how future souls were to be transmitted to future bodies. Were souls to be begotten of one another? This is the theory of traducianism, which Augustine wishes fully to refute (even if it would simplify certain of his problems concerning original sin) but cannot. Were they created? This is the solution to which he leans, but he has serious difficulties about it. We should note, however, that the creation of souls of which he speaks goes back, as does that of Eve's soul, to the first aspect of creation,[1] not to the time of the becoming of the body of which they are the souls.

To appreciate Augustine's views on the life of man and woman, *qua* man and woman, in Paradise one must be aware of the teachings of those Church Fathers, notably Gregory of Nyssa and John Chrysostom, which he appears to controvert. According to Gregory the human race was to be propagated in Paradise without any physical union. Men would live and multiply in some other way. If man and woman were physically differentiated, this was not related to any need or use at the time of creation, but solely to God's foreknowledge that man would sin and, if he were to escape extinction through death, would need another mode of propagation. Sexual differentiation was, therefore, not related to creation in itself but in anticipation of the Fall.

Augustine absolutely rejects such views. Even if the description of Paradise in *Genesis* has overtones of spiritual significance, Paradise was a corporal place, with real trees, and with Adam and Eve experiencing real bodies. Their sexual differentiation had nothing to do with the Fall: it was present when man and woman were created in God's image. There was, he contended, no valid reason to deny that the propagation of mankind in Paradise was to be by sexual union. But the union would, probably, take place without *libido*, as birth would be without discomfort. One should add that at a later stage in his life Augustine was willing to concede that Adam and Eve before the Fall might allow *libido* to make itself felt when a chaste prudence indicated the need for sexual union. Such views, and especially such a concession, must surely make Augustine seem, as in so many other ways, distinctly modern. But we shall return to this point later.[2]

1 *de Gen. ad litt.* 7.24,35. Cf. *B.A.* 48, 715.   2 134ff. below.

Augustine asks himself if there was any reason why man was made male and female other than for procreation? *Genesis,* describing the second aspect of man's creation, says that God made an aid for man, like himself: *faciamus ei adiutorium secundum ipsum.* What kind of aid was woman to be? It is necessary to quote Augustine's attempt to face this problem, for it marks a stage of special interest to us in his interpretation of the account in *Genesis* of the creation of man and woman.

If woman was not made for the specific aid of begetting children for man, for what aid was she made? Was it to work the land with him? There was no toil then and he had no need of aid. If he were to need it, a male would have been a better aid. One might relate this aid even to companionship in the case where man began to get tired of being alone. But for living and speaking together would not two men who were friends live with one another more harmoniously (*congruentius*) than a man and a woman? And if they had to live together on the basis of one giving orders and the other obeying, lest opposing wills should trouble the peace of those living together, provision had been made for achieving this, since one was created before, the other after—and especially since the second was created from the first, as woman was created. No one would claim that God could have made a woman only and not also, if he so willed, a male from the rib of the man. And so I can discover no aid for man for which woman was made, if child-bearing is eliminated.[3]

Put concisely, Augustine implies that woman's end is child-bearing, that she is subject to man's orders and that she is inferior as a companion.

Here it becomes necessary to attempt to put Augustine's attitude to women into its proper perspective. He was the inheritor of particular traditions—Greek, Roman and Jewish-Christian.[4] These traditions continued to have influence long after his time, even indeed to our own days.

Prominent in the mythology of the Greeks was the story of Pandora, the Greek Eve. Until her coming men lived without having to work and without any sorrow. With her came innumerable woes and troubles. Hippocrates the physician held that, while men and women produced male and female seed, male seed was the stronger.[5] Aristotle declared that 'woman is an infertile male; the female, in fact, is female on account of inability of a sort, viz., it lacks the power to concoct semen out of the final state of the nourishment . . . because of the coldness of its nature.'[6]

In a speech attributed to Demosthenes the general pragmatic attitude resulting from such theories is succinctly stated: men keep mistresses for the sake of pleasure, concubines for routine attendance on them, and wives to bear legitimate children and look after the house carefully.[7] The influence of Plato and Platonism strongly supported such practical attitudes: it was not only that woman was weaker, inferior and dangerous. She was also for a large part irrelevant. The male dominated philosophical society of Greece

3 Ibid., 9.5,9.   4 Cf. the author's 'Pagan Attitudes in Christian Love', *Theology,* London (October (1972), 520–5.   5 *On Generation,* Oeuvres Completes, E. Littré, vol. 7, Paris (1851), 478.   6 *Generation of Animals,* 1.20,15.   7 *Against Neaera,* 122.

looked rather to the love of males for companionship in the pursuit of Truth and Beauty. These attitudes of the Greeks, especially the medical and philosophical, were known to Augustine. In particular his *Confessions* show clearly how his own conversion was affected by Plotinus's *Ennead On Beauty,* which is indebted to Plato's *Symposium.*

The Roman world was more indulgent and respectful to women in certain ways— even in its legal prescriptions—but nevertheless it radically favoured for the most part the male. In earlier days a woman might be punished with death for drinking wine or adultery, whereas a man guilty of adultery might not have a finger laid on him. In marriage a woman passed to 'the hand' of her husband to whom she became subordinate. The assumption of the law was that woman had a levity of disposition which made her the prey of deception. Consequently she needed the protection of menfolk. The unequivocal purpose of marriage was procreation, so much so that wives who proved barren could be legally penalized. Much of the prejudice of Greek literature and philosophy against women and the love of women inevitably passed into the Greek dominated literature and philosophy of Rome. Lucretius's hatred of the love of women was pathological. Rome's great epic, the *Aeneid* of Virgil, elevates the choice of duty over love, of obeying Jupiter rather than succumbing to Dido, in a remarkable way and, it may be said, in a way that profoundly affected Augustine: constantly he returns in his *City of God* (which is a kind of Christian epic in prose) to the line of Virgil that describes Aeneas's painful choice: *mens immota manet; lacrimae volvuntur inanes,* 'his mind is unmoved: tears roll down his cheeks unavailing.' On the other hand Roman matrons were held in the highest regard, especially when they reared numerous good citizens for the state and showed an utter devotion to their husbands. In general, however, women were objects of danger and indeed some of the women of Imperial Rome, even making allowances for Juvenal's exaggeration in his description of some of them, were true horrors. Women simply had to be kept down. We have eloquent testimony to this view from Livy in a speech, which he puts into the mouth of Marcus Porcius Cato, going back nearly two hundred years before Christ: 'Give loose rein to women's uncontrollable nature and to this untamed creature, and expect that they themselves set bounds to their licence! . . . It is complete liberty or, rather, if we wish to speak the truth, complete licence that they desire. If they win this, what will they not attempt? . . . Even with all these bonds you can scarcely control them. . . . If you suffer them to seize these bonds one by one and wrench themselves free and finally to be placed on a parity with their husbands, do you think that you will be able to endure them? The moment they begin to be your equals, they will be your superiors.[8]

It was the world of the Old and New Testaments, however, that most directly influenced Augustine in his thinking on these matters—for he took guidance from the Scriptures. The account of the creation of man and woman in *Genesis* is, of course, the centre of our enquiry: for the proper understanding of Augustine's interpretation of this account we are momentarily engaged in examining his perspective. In general the position of woman in the earlier world of the Hebrews depended on her fertility, her being able to provide for the maintenance of property and clan. Women remained under

8 34 ch. 2 (Loeb translation).

the authority of their fathers and husbands, the latter of whom could repudiate them but might not be repudiated by them. Men and women were not equal in worship before God either: men might cancel vows made to God by women. Women were valued as mothers and housekeepers. A glance at *Proverbs* 31 will indicate what activity was expected of the ideal woman: for this she was to be praised: 'Give her of the fruit of her hands, and let her works praise her in the gates.' The New Testament has more pronouncements on women from St Paul than from Jesus who showed evident sympathy for them. In the *First Epistle to the Corinthians* Paul tells us that as the head of every man is Christ, the head of every woman is her husband; man is the image and glory of God, but woman is the glory of man—for the man was not made from the woman, but woman from man. Man was not created for woman, but woman was for man. Women should be subordinate, as even the law says.[9] *The First Epistle to Timothy* stresses again that Adam was formed first, then Eve; and that Adam was not deceived, but the woman was, and transgressed.[10]

This brief survey of the context within which Augustine formulated his views on women may help us in due course gradually to appreciate how *moderate and relatively 'enlightened'* his views actually were, and to what extent he in practice *sought to be as favourable as possible to women*. The emphasis upon the biological deficiency of women, their alleged immaturity and irresponsibility, the menace they represent to man, the necessity to keep them subordinate and tightly under control, and to look to them only for frivolous amusement or serious procreation—all presented eloquently and persistently over many centuries in literature, philosophy, law and Scripture left Augustine little choice but to take it that woman's end was childbearing, that she was subordinate to her husband, and that men were more suitable companions. Augustine's fellow Christian theologians were of little help. Indeed *he controverted many of their views unfavourable to women*. But these ideas frequently persisted, where Augustine's did not. Even Aquinas in the thirteenth century could still use phrases reminiscent of Aristotle about woman being biologically defective. And as for definitive phrases such as Tertullian's reference to woman as the 'door-way to the devil', *ianua diaboli* [11]—they continued to be used and improved. The Islamic religion which bordered the Christian was no more favourable to women: indeed the birth of female children was considered to be a disaster and disgrace, so much so that female infanticide had to be forbidden formally.

Augustine, having decided that the aid for man intended by God in his creation of woman was child-bearing, discusses briefly at this juncture certain general aspects of marriage and not merely marriage as seen in the union of the first couple for the begetting of children. Marriage was a topic on which he had written an interesting and for its earlier part too little appreciated work—the *de bono coniugali*, *The Good of Marriage*. To this book he formally refers at this point of the *de Genesi ad litteram*[12] for a more developed account of his present views on marriage. We must, therefore, glance briefly at aspects of this work that are relevant to us here.

It opens with a scene on which many films end—a man and woman walking side by side towards a beckoning future. Adam and Eve are described as walking side by side,

9 11.3ff.   10 2.12.   11 *de cult. fem. P.L.* 1.1419A.   12 9.7, 12.

looking to the way before them. Augustine presents the pair romantically. He puts an extraordinary emphasis on the bonding and intimate union of their flesh. That union, he says, need not have been of the flesh: it might have been simply *amicalis et germana*, 'loving and true'. But God chose rather a union that involved lying together and mingling of their flesh: *non coniunctionis maris et feminae sed concubitus . . . commixtio.*[13] And these mingling bodies shared even beforehand the intimacy of being the same flesh, the flesh of Adam. From so intimate a union Augustine derives the unity and intimacy of the whole human race, a unity which has many consequences, and an intimacy that has its obligations.

He goes on to give a view on the good achieved by marriage (and here he is speaking of marriage after the Fall): marriage 'seems to me to be a good not exclusively on account of the procreation of children, but on account also of the natural bonding of the two sexes in itself: [*coniugium esse bonum*] *mihi non videtur propter solam filiorum procreationem sed propter ipsam naturalem in diverso sexu societatem.*'[14] One should notice that this is given as a personal opinion: *mihi videtur*. Moreover the form in which the opinion is couched not only denied that procreation was the exclusive good attained by marriage, but suggests that the natural bonding of the two sexes is not something marginal. Indeed it is so important that without it one could not speak of marriage at all as existing between those who were too old to procreate: *Alioquin non iam diceretur coniugium in senibus.* He says that to use marriage without intending to beget children, if one can beget them, is a 'venial' sin. But he asks if anyone ever heard any person, who was married, aver in private conversation that he or she never had relations except in the hope of conception?[15]

Augustine compares sexuality to food. As man needs food, mankind needs generation. The use of both involves concomitant pleasure. Such pleasure is not *libido*.[16] In his *Retractationes* he glosses this last remark with a striking phrase: *libido non est bonus et rectus usus libidinis*, 'the good and correct use of *libido* is not *libido*.[17] This is not just a paradoxical or clever phrase. It exempts *libido itself* from fault—after all it is a creature of God's and therefore a good, as even the Devil is in himself a good. Just as food, however, should not be taken gluttonously, so sexuality should not be without control. Control or, as Augustine puts it, obedience is critical. A virgin who was disobedient was not superior in virtue to a married woman who was obedient. Not only is marriage not a pit of sin, as some think, in comparison with virginity: it can be a better thing and is a hill of only lesser eminence than virginity.[18]

One needs to appreciate in all of this a persuasion about disorder and evil which Augustine inherited from the Neoplatonists, probably Plotinus, and which is quite foreign to those who think in terms of black and white, of absolute right and absolute wrong. Augustine is ready to admit the existence of absolutes of this kind, and he was himself responsible for the formulation of more than a few of them. But such formulations by him did not prevent him from taking—as did God in the Redemption and Jesus in his earthly life—a compassionate and practical view of the imperfections of life. Plotinus, speaking of Providence, pointed out that in a well-ordered state there was place

13 de bono coniugali 1.1. 14 Ibid., 3.3. 15 Ibid., 8.15. 16 Ibid., 16.18. 17 2.22, 2. 18 *de sancta virginitate* 18.18.

for the hang-man whose office in itself was an ugly thing. Beauty and order, however, was in the *whole*, in the harmony (*congruentia*) of the beautiful and the ugly.[19]

Proceeding from this characteristic way of looking at humanity, Augustine is able to contemplate incontinence in marriage, although in itself it is, though venial, a sin. The whole act of marriage is good: *neque enim quia incontinentia malum est, ideo connubium vel quo incontinentes copulantur, non est bonum*: 'even if incontinence is an evil (sin), that does not mean that marriage, or however otherwise the incontinent copulate, is not good.'[20] He goes on: 'this good does not become faulty because of that evil, but rather that evil becomes venial because of this good.' The word 'venial', even if to us now it suggests sin (though a lesser one) suggests in itself actually 'Pardon'. It is the word used even by St Paul. Augustine uses graphic phrases in the *de bono coniugali*: referring to the use of marriage *without any intention whatever of procreating—provided incontinence in marriage is not overdone (si tamen non nimius) and does not go against nature—Marriage pleads and implores that such a sin be forgiven.*[21]

Augustine, following Plotinus, may seem to go beyond the pardon authorized by St Paul. He has this remarkable passage in the *de Genesi ad litteram* to which we now return: 'who is so mentally blocked as not to see what an ornament mankind is to the world, even if those who live rightly and laudably are few? And is not order in a state of great value, that brings even sinners within the bonds of some earthly peace. For no matter how depraved men are, even they are superior to beasts and birds. Yet who is not delighted to contemplate this small part of the universe ornamented according to its position with all kinds of beasts and birds?'[22] This passage refers primarily to the positive value he attributes to the possibility of procreation *before* the Fall: it was not simply a provision for propagation *after* it. The companionship of fellow humans was of better value in itself than the mere replacement of those who, after the Fall, must die. But the passage also accepts the existence of disorder within order and harmony, of ugliness within beauty, of imperfection within perfection, of evil within good.

It is not difficult to discern in all of this a considerable understanding and compassion in Augustine for the role of *libido* in marriage. He speaks of carnal concupiscence as burning, yet being modest, and of a flaming passion that had, nevertheless, a certain gravity. In a passage which must refer to the mother of his son and their life together before his conversion, he says that he does not dare lightly to condemn her—and here he is not writing of marriage—though he does condemn himself.[23]

Augustine's sympathy for the problems of sexuality is the more remarkable in view of his persuasion that in his day the population of the world had almost reached its limit and should be controlled. This influenced him strongly not only to practise, but to commend virginity, and to preach abstinence as far as might be possible to those who were married. Marriage was related to the propagation of the human race. For the achieving of such an end the Patriarchs, for example, acted virtuously in having many wives, whereas now a man would act virtuously in having none. This was connected with the great mystery of time—a mystery that never failed to cause Augustine wonder. In

19 Cf. Augustine, *de ord.* 2.4, 12. Cf. Plotinus, *Enneads*, 3.2, 17; 2.3, 16, 45–54; 3.2, 18, 20–21; 3.1, 7. **20** *de Gen. ad litt.* 9.7, 12. **21** 10.2. **22** *de Gen. ad litt.* 9.9, 14. **23** *de bono coniugali*, 3.3.

the earthly Paradise Adam and Eve were meant to propagate a certain number of children who would never die, and who with Adam and Eve at the end of a certain time would have their animal bodies, potentially mortal, become spirital, and so immortal, and thus join the angels.

Augustine accepted that man was created to fill the places left empty by the angels who fell with Lucifer. Whether man, after his own creation, fell or did not fall, only a certain number, therefore, of men were destined to join the angels. The actual number could not be indicated. Nevertheless it was fixed: *donec certo numero inpleto, certa numerositate inpleretur.*[24] It was limited in another way also. God's command in *Genesis* was to 'fill the earth'. When the earth was filled, the injunction to increase and multiply had been fulfilled. While one might be in doubt as to when one might consider the earth 'filled' with mankind, Augustine felt that this stage was imminent when he was writing: *largissima subpetat copia.* Hence procreation was no longer a duty, it was a remedy for incontinence: *quod sanis esse posset officium, sit aegrotis remedium.* Now was the time for abstaining from propagation: *isto nam tempore continendi ab amplexu.*[25] Men should now be exhorted to choose continence. If anyone objects that if all choose continence the human race would not subsist, Augustine answers that he would wish them so to choose, and thus the City of God would the sooner be filled (that is, the required number of men to replace the fallen angels would have been achieved) and the world would the sooner end.[26] Had not St Paul said that others should imitate him in not marrying, and that the time was short and that those who had wives should act as if they did not have them? At the same time, even if the earth seemed now overcrowded, the certain number of men who were destined to fill the places of the angels in the City of God had, evidently, not yet been born and died. There was still need for marriage and the physical differentiation on which it was based.

Adam and Eve were so constituted in Paradise, according to Augustine, that they could in due course, in order to carry out the duty of propagation of man for which Eve was given as an aid to Adam, have physical relations. Augustine is not certain that they did not have the appetite for carnal pleasure. He asks, however, if it is not more honourable and better to believe that they had not? Why would we not believe that this was so?[27] At the same time, as we have mentioned, he actually concedes to the Pelagians that one could hold that Adam and Eve could have felt *libido* which, however, would be subject to their wills and their decision that it was necessary to procreate.[28]

Genesis, however, is understood by Augustine to say that Adam and Eve did not feel *libido* and did not have intercourse before their Fall. They were awaiting God's order to procreate. It was only after the Fall that they became aware of *libido* and of the need to procreate in order to replace those, including themselves, who must now suffer death.[29]

Was the forbidden fruit a symbol of sexual relations 'stolen' prematurely? Some modern commentators rather incline to this opinion. Clement of Alexandria, of whose views Augustine seems aware, held it in earlier times. But Augustine dismisses it peremptorily: Adam and Eve were, presumably, fully adult and would not have had to

24 *de Gen. ad litt.* 9.3,6; 6.10. **25** 9.7.12. **26** 10.10. **27** *de Gen. ad litt.* 9.10, 16, 18. **28** *c, duas epist. Pel.,* 1.17, 34f. **29** *de Gen. ad litt.* 9.4, 8.

wait until puberty for sexual relations; to have such relations when they could, he thought, would be entirely legitimate.[30]

Another idea, however, receives more attention from him although he does not advance it as more than possible. In this interpretation the forbidden fruit symbolized knowledge which Adam and Eve pursued prematurely. A difficulty, however, arises for Augustine in any such interpretation: how could Adam, who was endowed with spiritual intelligence, believe the devil's representation that God was jealous of the knowledge he would have, if he ate the forbidden fruit? Someone else less spiritual and intelligent had to be found to succumb to such a temptation. *Genesis* reports that the person found was Eve. Was this why Eve was given to Adam in the first instance, to *influence* him, who could not himself be deceived by so patent a ruse? Was this why Eve, not Adam, was approached by the serpent? Adam, Augustine speculates, could not be and was not misled by Eve's words, but, like Solomon later, he was undone by love.[31]

> Can one believe that Solomon, a man of remarkable wisdom, thought that there was any use in the cult of idols? No, he was unable to resist the love of women which brought him to this evil, doing what he knew should not be done, lest he should disappoint the mistresses whom he loved to destruction and who destroyed him. Likewise Adam, after the woman had been seduced and eaten of the forbidden tree and had given to him to eat with her, could not bring himself to disappoint her. He felt sure that she could waste away if she did not have his support and were alienated from his mind. The disagreement would be the end of her. He was not overcome, however, by any feeling having to do with the sexual appetite (which he did not feel as yet) . . . but rather by a certain loving benevolence (*amicali quadam benevolentia*) through which it usually happens that, for fear of turning a friend into an enemy, we offend God.[32]

Augustine does *no more than report* this hypothesis now associated with the name of Theophilus of Antioch. His final words are: 'but why say more? They were induced to commit that sin in the way in which it was possible to induce such as they were. The account, however, is given as it is to be read by all, even if few understood these things as they are to be understood.'[33] He does not profess to be among the few. He does not know what the temptation really was or how it could happen.

While *reporting* (but no more) *the hypothesis* which centres on Eve's having a lesser intelligence and being too influenced by the things of sense, Augustine takes care to observe that she would eventually have emulated her partner in living according to the spirit. He makes no personal comment on her intelligence. What is remarkable, however, is the loyalty and affection which, in the recounting of this theory, he ascribes to Adam. Augustine notes that Adam avoids accusing her of deceiving or seducing him: he reports merely the fact that it was she that gave the fruit to him (whereas Eve accuses the serpent of seducing her). Adam, as Augustine sees him, is not only loyal to her but, such is his love for her, he consciously chooses to become God's enemy rather than cause her any

30 Ibid., 11.12, 57; cf. *B.A.* 49, 556f.   31 *de Gen. ad litt.* 11.12, 56   32 Ibid., 11.42, 59.   33 Ibid., 11.42, 60.

sorrow.[34] Augustine, who had been deeply affected by the story of Aeneas choosing to follow Jupiter's will as against his love of Dido, could not approve of Adam, but understood only too well the power of love:

Love, never conquered in battle
Love the plunderer laying waste the rich!
not even the deathless gods can flee your onset,
nothing human born for a day—
whoever feels your grip is driven mad.[35]

The consequences of the Fall in general do not concern us here. But for Eve it bore the penalty that whereas before it her 'subjection' to Adam was not by nature, but by love, now it became one of status and arose from her fault. If women led men as Eve led Adam, the world would be even worse than it is. Augustine endorses St Paul's view—that woman should not be man's master.[36]

In the course of the treatment of the temptation and Fall Augustine refers again to St Paul's statement that 'man is the image and glory of God, but woman is the glory of man.' It will be remembered that on an earlier occasion in the *de Genesi ad litteram* Augustine understood St Paul to speak figuratively and to indicate merely that the male symbolized the contemplation and image of God and the female the administration of temporal things: but in reality man and woman were equally images of God.[37] Here he again interprets the same words of St Paul in the same sense. Eve succumbed to the serpent's temptation because, perhaps, being 'created' later, in the second 'aspect', than Adam, she was *still* and for the moment less concentrated on spiritual things and more on things temporal. That is, although her *mens* was, as much as was Adam's, the image of God, she acted not according to its spiritual or masculine part but according to its temporal or female part. In so acting—according to the allegory—she was not the image of God. In reality, however, she was. But she would *in due course* and in emulation of her husband cease to act according to the temporal or female part of her *mens* and act according to the contemplative or masculine part.[38]

Notions such as that woman was created 'exclusively' to aid man to procreate have led to the easy, if unjustified, association of sexuality more with woman than with man. Inasmuch too as the writers and artists treating of love and sexual themes were in the past for the most part men, and so fixed on woman as the sexual object and also as representing man's fear of the involvements and restrictions that can arise from love, woman has sometimes been thought of as almost alone typifying sexuality. The consequence of this was that woman and sexuality tended to a considerable extent—but of course not altogether—to be identified in the mind of the writer or artist. Hence attitudes to sexuality tended to represent attitudes towards woman and *vice versa*.

Augustine to some extent necessarily shared this outlook, as he almost inevitably shared also the assumptions of the Greek, Roman and Jewish traditions of woman's

34 Ibid., 11.42, 59. 35 Sophocles, *Antigone*, 879ff. Translation (uninspired) by R. Fagles. 36 *de Gen. ad litt.* 11.37, 50. 37 Cf. 126f. above. 38 *de Gen. ad litt.* 11.42, 58.

subordinate role. Moreover he had to avoid contradicting St Paul when he echoed similar views.

Nevertheless within the restrictions of dominating traditions and theological *data* Augustine shows a profound and sympathetic understanding of sexuality and women that is in no way condescending. Anyone who has read his *Confessions* must know how intensely he experienced sexuality. Anyone who has observed the memory of Virgil's Dido in his *Confessions* and the *City of God* will know that he could see life intensely from a woman's point of view. His life has been dramatized in terms of indulgence of the flesh followed by reaction against it. But psychological theories are not necessarily truths. I at any rate do not view his life in this way, nor do I read his most fundamental work on the anthropology of woman, the *de Genesi ad litteram*, as being unappreciative towards women or sexuality. His ideas on women and sexuality are in fact surprisingly 'modern'—and, unfortunately, not sufficiently known.

In the *de Genesi ad litteram* he insists in the face of opposition and with clear deliberateness on the equality of man and woman as images of God. This, in the world that looks back to the Jewish-Christian scriptures for its fundamental truths, should be considered an absolute. Augustine equally insists that woman's body and man's body, sexually differentiated as they now are, were created at the same time in their causal reasons—as possibles that later would become their developed realities. This again is a significant recognition of woman's honour and the honour of sexuality. And when in the second aspect of creation, Adam and Eve are alive in what Augustine regards as a *real earthly* Paradise, he does not share the embarrassment of other Fathers that Adam and Eve could *feel libido before the Fall*, or their feeling that the temptation to which Adam and Eve succumbed was sexual. In his view their use of their sexual differentiation, presumably in their case before the Fall, under the control of their will, would have been proper and would tend to make life, even in Paradise, more enjoyable with the addition of more fellow humans.

Augustine goes further to praise the special intimacy of the flesh. Procreation could have been arranged without the mingling of the flesh. But God chose precisely that mingling—sed *concubitus . . . commixtio. Even when the flesh errs in marriage*—but not when it errs against nature—*indulgence is to be shown: beauty is in the final harmony.* There is something here that reminds one of the toleration involved in Heisenberg's uncertainty principle. It should not, however, escape our attention that Augustine greatly elevates and romanticizes the Fall of Adam and Eve. Whether Eve was easily deceived or allowed herself to be deceived easily, Adam, as Augustine interprets the event, offers no recrimination. He does not blame her. He chooses to offend God, not because he was afraid of Eve, but because he could not bring himself to hurt her. Here Augustine is explicitly not talking of sexual passion: he is talking of an attitude of mind and heart and will. In Augustine's words, 'Adam did not wish to sadden her. He was afraid that without his comfort, and estranged from his mind, she would pine away and even die because of their disagreement.'[39] Adam followed the love that disposed him to help her rather than to obey God's command.

39 11.42, 59

Here Augustine, perhaps unconsciously, has in his mind the picture of Orpheus and Eurydice in Virgil's fourth book of the *Georgics*: there Orpheus yields to the impulse of love, thereby disobeying a clear command, and involves his wife and himself in calamity. But perhaps he *was* conscious of another picture from Virgil's *Aeneid* where the hero Aeneas rejects the love of Dido in order precisely to carry out faithfully a clear command. The very words he uses in this part of his discussion of the Fall are reminiscent of Virgil. Augustine could not but approve of Aeneas, who went on to found an Empire and lay down laws for the world. This in a way Augustine did too.[40] But his heart remained with Dido.

40 Cf. the author's 'Augustine the Artist and the *Aeneid*,' *Mélanges Christine Mohrmann*, Utrecht (1963), 252–61, reproduced in *Studies in Augustine and Eriugena*, ed. T. Halton, the Catholic University of America Press (1992), 59–68.

Appendices

I

The *Confession* of St Patrick and the *Confessions* of St Augustine

Although St Patrick is very emphatic on his own lack of learning, scholars have attempted to discover from his writings proof of an acquaintance with books which would reduce to some extent the reality of his professed ignorance. Thus Dr Bieler, to whom we are indebted for his achievements within the field of Patrician studies, in a learned article in a Dutch periodical,[1] has attempted to determine the range, so to speak, of Patrick's reading. He puts forward the suggestions made by himself and others before him that Patrick may have read in Latin, not merely the Bible and liturgical texts, but also Cyprian, Sulpicius Severus, Pope Innocent I, Secundinus and St Augustine. Dr Bieler was careful not to advance his findings with any show of confidence, and I believe that he was well advised not to do so.

Here I confine myself rigorously to the question of Patrick's possible *use* of the *Confessions* of Augustine when he was writing his own *Confession*. That Patrick could have read Augustine's famous work there can be no doubt, no matter what date we give to Patrick's birth. St Augustine's story of his own life must have been known in the monastic settlements in Gaul and Britain when Patrick was being trained. The campaign of the great African Father against Pelagianism must also have made his name and works famous amongst the missionaries fighting Pelagianism in northern parts in the second quarter of the fifth century. It has also been suggested that the form of the hymn *Audite Omnes*, said by some to have been written about the same time as Patrick's *Confession* and to come from a source close to Patrick, is based on Augustine's *Psalmus contra partem Donati*. When, therefore, Patrick calls his *apologia* a *confession*, it must immediately occur to one that he may have been imitating the *Confessions* of Augustine. We read through the *Confession* of Patrick to see if there are clear conscious or unconscious echoes of Augustine's work, from which we might argue not only that he had heard of that book, but had read at least part of it and modelled, in however limited a way, his own confession on the earlier one.

A number of scholars have indicated phrases which in their opinion might be echoes of Augustine's *Confession*. G. Misch, in a book written many years ago, but only since 1950 available in English, under the title *A History of Autobiography in Antiquity*, gives

[1] *Vigiliae Christianae*, April (1952), 66ff.

143

1950 available in English, under the title *A History of Autobiography in Antiquity*, gives some instances.[2] G.F. Hamilton, in a pamphlet *St Patrick and his Age*, published in Dublin in 1932, treats of the question in a manner too general to be of any use. Père Grosjean in *Analecta Bollandiana* for 1945[3] quotes Hamilton's opinion in favour of Patrick's having read Augustine's *Confessions* without expressing any dissent from it. Finally, Dr Bieler in 1952, in the article already referred to,[4] resumes the evidence quoted by Misch and adds some phrases of his own. I think it possible to add still a few others at least as strong as any suggested.

It may be well, however, at this stage to describe very briefly the two books in question. We shall then be able to compare and contrast them: to see what they have in common and in what they differ, and so assess the value of some details.

Patrick's *Confession* runs to less than 5,000 words—about four full columns in a newspaper. It tells most of the facts we know about his life but in no clear or orderly fashion. It is in part a humble confession of praise to God, who had exalted him, sinner and ignorant as he was. It is also in part a defence and explanation of his life and conduct for both his enemies and his friends.

Augustine's *Confessions* is more than twelve times longer. It, too, gives us facts about his life and it is likewise a confession of praise to God for His goodness, and at the same time is meant to let his friends know what kind of man he was.

There are odd coincidences both in the lives of these two saints and in their confessions.

Both men were born into approximately the same social condition: the father of each held the office of *decurio*—something like a member of the municipal council, implying then some standing. Both were separated from their parents in their early teens. Both confess to certain excesses in their youth. Both were 'converted', although Patrick's conversion was much earlier in his life and his transgressions would seem to have been less serious and less frequent. Both became bishops and the leaders of their people in ecclesiastical matters. Both had a special interest in monasticism, and both—but Augustine obviously in a more important way—were engaged in the combat against Pelagius.

Their confessions, too, have certain points in common. Both are at once letters of explanation and confessions of sin and faith and praise—especially of praise. Neither is intended to be an autobiography, and each has great defects on the point of ordering and arrangement of material. On this question I may be permitted to remark that not enough attention seems to have been paid to the structure of Patrick's *Confession* and the possibility of excisions, interpolations and re-arrangement in the text. Both books illustrate a theme, propounded by Augustine and exemplified in both: that Providence leads us through many admonitions and adversities to salvation. Accordingly the incidents related in both documents are selected with reference to this theme, and other facts, which might be of extraordinary interest to us, are omitted as not being useful for the theme. In both confessions dreams and voices are said to have intervened at critical

2 See vol. 2.357, 360, 367, 370.   3 Tome 63, 107.   4 69f.

junctures in the saints' lives, and in both the truth of what is being said is guaranteed by the appeal to God as a witness—and God is not mocked.

But the points of contrast between the lives of both saints and their confessions are far more numerous and, I think, more significant.

Patrick's educational career was interrupted at a very early age. This made for a radical difference in outlook between the two. Apart from some slight traces of introspection in his *Confession*, Patrick is the man of action who is only too conscious of the limitations of his intellectual equipment. His conversion, as he calls it, was but the awakening in youth (which had not been altogether blameless) to the reality of the faith that was in him. Augustine's case was far otherwise: his was an intellectual pursuit of truth away from the religion in which he was born, through many discoveries, all of them becoming in the end disappointments, until in mature manhood, he yielded to Christ. Augustine had a paramount influence in the theology of the West: he was a creative intellectual leader, a true Father of the Church, who planned, for example, the campaign against Pelagius in which Patrick, however devoted and successful, was but an executant.

This contrast in their lives is borne out in their confessions. The works are totally different in tone. Patrick's, if sometimes perhaps, ironic, is diffident, halting, clumsy in style, and fragmentary to the point of obscurity. Augustine's has the confidence of a man who had given his life to Rhetoric—his humility is before God and not before literary men, the equal of any of whom, when it came to writing, he knew himself to be. His periods are developed with a sonorous smoothness which show up only too plainly the awkwardness of Patrick's occasional efforts in the tricks of Rhetoric; and the over-all length of Augustine's book gives the impression of padding rather than the opposite : there are more facts, relatively that is, found in Patrick's work. Augustine's book is far more sophisticated. When he discusses the intervention of dreams and voices in the crises of his own life, he does so with far greater subtlety than Patrick. Augustine reduces the supernatural element in these interventions to the extent that the reader is hard put to it to judge whether the intervention is meant to appear as truly supernatural or merely allegorical and human. Patrick, on the other hand, imitates the directness and usually the very phrasing of the Gospels, and in his case one is faced with the stark challenge to accept his words literally as describing actual wonders or to regard these episodes as pure inventions: much of the value of his *Confession* depends on this crucial point. Patrick's book is more direct, even naive, with a greater air of simplicity and sincerity, as befitted the work of one whose main pre-occupation in life was action in the missionary and pastoral fields. Augustine's is more complicated, speculative, and invested with a universal reference—the book of one who, although hardly yielding to Patrick in either humanity or sincerity and playing no insignificant part in the exterior world of his day, was yet much concerned with moralizing, memory, and introspection. Both Patrick and Augustine confess to God and explain themselves to their friends ; but Patrick is particularly anxious to defend himself on specific points against his calumniators within the fold, while Augustine has no need to defend himself except against the charges of the Manicheans outside of the Church of Christ. There is, therefore, a striking contrast in execution and tone between these two documents, accounted for partly by the difference in intention and scope, but also by the great remove of Patrick from Augustine in education, interests and circumstances.

One may now turn to the vital point of assessing the alleged and possible echoes, conscious or unconscious, of Augustine's *Confessions* in Patrick's *Confessio*. As it would be excessively pedantic to mention phrases which occur to one as possible echoes, only to dismiss them immediately, I shall confine myself to the suggestions of others. These are all brought together in Dr Bieler's article in *Vigiliae Christianae*[5] in the following quotation:

> Some connection between the two works (Patrick's *Confessio* and Augustine's *Confessiones*) was first assumed by G. Misch. It is not clear whether Misch thinks of actual borrowing. Some of the parallels which he lists are certainly suggestive of literary dependence, esp. Aug. Conf. 1. 10. 16: *non enim meliora eligens inoboediens eram*—C. I: *sacerdotibus nostris inoboedientes fuimus qui (nos) nostram salutem admonebant;* IV. I. I: *sed inrideant nos fortes et potentes, nos autem infirmi et inopes confiteamur tibi*—C 45: *rideat autem et insultet qui voluerit, ego non silebo neque abscondo signa et mirabilia quae mihi a Domino monstrata sunt;* IV. 16, 31: *sed sic eram nec erubesco, Deus meus, confiteri tibi in me misericordias tuas*—C 44: *sed confiteor Domino meo et non erubesco in conspectu ipsius;* VII. 20. 26: *quid interesset inter praesumptionem et confessionem*—C 10: *sed quid prodest excusatio iuxta veritatem, praesertim cum praesumptione?* A similar idea is expressed in III. II. 19: *et misisti manum tuam ex alto et de hac profunda caligine eruisti animam meam* and C 12: *ego eram velut lapis qui iacit in luto profundo et venit qui potens est et in sua misericordia sustulit me;* a phrase is borrowed from a different context in C 42: *avidissime arripuit* (Conf. VII.21.27: *avidissime arripui*).

The mere repetition of *inoboediens*[6] in the first instance given proves nothing. Dr Bieler, by the way, reads *non oboedientes* in his own edidon of the *Confessio*.[7] For the same reason, the occurrence of *inrideant* and *rideat* in the two texts of the second instance is of no account. These sentences have pronounced biblical overtones.[8] The third instance is again in both cases a tissue of biblical phrases. The fourth has only the use of the word *praesumptio* in common: the *quid* in one case introduces an indirect and in the other a direct question. The fifth again is in both cases a tissue of biblical phrases. Only the last merits some consideration. These texts show one important thing, however, namely, that both Patrick and Augustine echoed the Bible in its words, phrases, and even sentence structure, to a degree which is only nowadays duly appreciated, even in relation to Augustine.[9]

---

5 69f.   6 The word *oboediens*, of course, occurs frequently in the Scriptures; e.g., 2 *Cor.* 2.9.   7 Cf. *Classica et Mediaevalia*, vol. 11, Fasc., 1–2 (1950).   8 A mere consultation of a Latin Concordance of the Bible under the significant words will reveal the extent of this. This applies also to the texts of the third and fifth instances. The verb *confiteor*, e.g., occurs over 160 times in the Bible as a whole, 62 times in the *Psalms* alone, and 30 times in the New Testament. The noun *confessio* likewise is found 26 times in the Bible as a whole, 9 times in the *Psalms*, and 7 times in the New Testament. The verb *erubesco* also occurs 52 times in the Bible as a whole, 10 times in the *Psalms*, 10 times in the New Testament, 6 times in St Paul and 3 times in St Luke. The idea of (not) blushing and confessing naturally go together.   9 Cf. G.N. Knauer, *Psalmenzitate in Augustins Konfessionen*, Göttingen (1955).

Coming to the last instance: Patrick in the course of his narration says of a young girl 'she told us that she had received a message from a messenger of God, and he admonished her to be a virgin of Christ . . . on the sixth day after this she most laudably and eagerly chose what all virgins of Christ do.' The full phrase is *optime et avidissime arripuit.* Augustine's phrase is *itaque avidissime arripui*: 'and therefore I most eagerly seized.' But, although the words are undoubtedly the same, the situation is totally different—the girl *chooses* (I use Dr Bieler's own translation) virginity; Augustine *seizes* (Pusey's translation) a book. If Patrick is echoing any source and not merely using the ordinary words to describe a given set of circumstances, it is more likely that he is echoing the scene in the Gospel where the Saviour says: 'Mary hath chosen the best part' *Maria optimam partem elegit,*[10] a phrase which Patrick partly reproduces in his *optime arripuit.* If the words *avidissime arripuit* are to be judged apart from their context (which is hardly permissible), one might argue that Patrick was echoing Cicero's *De Senectute,* where the phrase *avide arripui* occurs,[11] or a number of other texts be they from Pliny[12] or the Bible.[13]

The Bible, in fact, and especially the *Psalms* and New Testament, but particularly the Gospels and St Paul's *Epistle to the Corinthians,*[14] is the true inspiration behind St Patrick's *Confession.* In short, it seems to me that even if Patrick had heard of, or even read, Augustine's *Confessions,* his own document reveals no *sure*[15] echo of it, not even in the title, *Confession,* a word found several times in the Scriptures in a sense similar to that in which Patrick uses it—as for example 'I will confess against myself my injustice to the Lord';[16] or again 'Whosoever shall confess me before men him shall the Son of man also confess before the angels of God.'[17] Here, indeed, is the true inspiration of St Patrick.[18]

10 *Luke* 10, 42.   11 26.   12 *Nat. Hist.* 5, 4; 14, 148.   13 Various uses of forms of *arripere* and *avidus* are found there.   14 Cf. D. Nerney, S.J., *I.E. Record* (June–September, 1949).   15 For the voice summoning Patrick to Ireland (C.23.11ff.), not discussed above, cf. 148–51 below.   16 *Ps.* 32, 5.   17 *Luke* 12, 8.   18 For a sequel to this paper see the author's Patrick's *Confessio* and Augustine's *Confessions* in *Studies in Augustine and Eriugena,* ed. T. Halton (1992), 31–8.

2

The Voice Bidding George Moore

Readers of George Moore's *Vale*[1] will recall that he claimed to have heard on three different occasions a voice bidding him pack his portmanteau and return to Ireland. The voice had to be obeyed. Hence Moore's return to Ireland and participation in the literary movement of the time.

Hone in his *Life of George Moore*[2] refers to the episode with some scepticism: 'It is no wonder that in *Ave* he could give "no reasonable account" of his condition at this time, and that he fell back on a *story* (my italics) of mysterious voices in the Chelsea Road bidding him go to Ireland.' At the same time he asserts that Moore, while he might place events where they 'composed' best, nowhere invents out of nothing. 'Half imagination, half reality' was Moore's brother's comment on his *Memoirs,* and he added that the details must certainly be often accepted with reserve. From all of which we might conclude that the episode of the voice was not total invention.

Some scholars, as for example Weferling,[3] have discerned in Moore certain mystical proclivities. He himself is, I think, to be trusted more: 'to be ridiculous has always been *ma petite luxe*,' but immediately he goes on to ask if anyone can 'be said to be ridiculous if he knows that he is ridiculous?'[4] The answer clearly is at least, 'not quite'. Moore declared of himself: 'I am feminine, perverse'.[5] We need not accept his implied equation; but we can, perhaps, agree with him that he liked to *épater les bourgeois*. One might sum the matter up in Moore's own words: 'A man can only have one sort of conscience, and mine is a *literary* (my italics) one.'[6] This seems just: Moore bent truth to his all-dominating literary purpose.

This brings us to the difference he perceived between his confessions and the *Confessions* of St Augustine: 'St Augustine's *Confessions* are the story of a God-tortured, mine of an *art*-tortured soul. Which subject is the most living ? The first ! for man is stupid and still loves his conscience as a child loves a toy.' [7] Here Moore at once suggests a comparison between his life and Augustine's (Moore is rarely over-modest) and emphasizes a radical difference: Augustine's conscience concerned itself with God, his with art.

1 References to *Ave, Salve, Vale* are to Heinemann's 1947 ed. Here, *Vale*, 208. 2 1936, 223. Subsequently 273f., and 267. 3 *Das Religiöse Gefühl bei George Moore.* 4 *Vale*, 40. 5 Hone, 268. 6 *Vale*, 309. 7 *Confessions of a Young Man*, Heinemann (1928), 185.

Let us, however, pursue a little further his conscious acquaintance with and imitation of Augustine—for Augustine, too, reports that he heard a voice bidding him at a most critical juncture in his life, and it is my brief purpose here to indicate the similarity of Moore's report to his.

In *Salve*[8] Moore reveals his attitude to the *Confessions of* Augustine: '[Christian Literature] began well, I said, with the *Confessions* of that most sympathetic of saints, Augustine, who was not all theology, but began his life, and began it well, in free thought and free love; his mistress and his illegitimate child endear him to us, and the music of his prose.' What Moore found of interest in the *Confessions* of Augustine were his sin and his style. Hence it is not surprising that he should have thought of depicting his own life after Augustine's model :

Conscience: I do not hope to find a Saint Augustine in you.

I: An idea; one of these days I will write my confessions! Again I tell you that nothing really matters to me but art.[9]

There is, in fact, some common ground between the two *Confessions*, even if the one is concerned with God, and the other with art. Both were written by men in their early thirties. Both disclaim any pretence of being real autobiographies: rather are they meant to be (in Moore's words) records of their mental digestions. Both emphasize with gratitude the great boon of many friendships in their lives. Both especially speak excitedly of their author's sins; but whereas Augustine regrets and repents, Moore seeks occasion for self-congratulation:

. . . subtle selfishness with dash of unscrupulousness pulls more plums out of life's pie than the seven deadly virtues. If you are a good man you want a bad man to convert . . . admit that you feel just a little interested in my wickedness . . . admit that your mouth waters when you think of rich and various pleasures that fell to my share.[10]

Moore takes pleasure in Conscience's condemnation of him as rotten to the root. When Conscience speaks of the women 'he had held to his bosom in the perfumed darkness of the chamber',[11] Moore objects on grounds of taste only: 'it is very *common*.' Augustine addresses his *Confessions* to God; Moore to the 'exquisitely hypocritical reader'.[12] Moore once again is primarily concerned with art.

That Moore was acquainted with the *Confessions* of Augustine and had entertained the thought of imitating them in some way there can be no doubt. When, therefore, we come upon the 'voice' passages in Moore we may have little difficulty in indicating one source whence they may well have been consciously or unconsciously derived:

When I entered the Hospital Road I did not dare to look behind me . . . and walking in a devout collectedness, I heard a voice speaking within me: no whispering thought it was, but a resolute voice, saying, Go to Ireland! The words were so distinct and clear that I could not but turn to look. Nobody was within many yards of me. I walked

8 Ibid., 135. 9 Ibid., 207. 10 Ibid., 210. 11 Ibid., 200. 12 Ibid., 209.

on, but had not taken many steps before I heard the voice again . . . Of this I am sure—that the words 'Go to Ireland' did not come from within, but from without . . . So the summons has come, I said—. . . and I walked, greatly shaken in my mind . . . 'Go to Ireland!' . . . this time it was close by me, speaking in my ear . . . forced to my knees, [I] prayed, but to whom I prayed I do not know. Doubt was no longer possible.[13]

My thoughts melted away and I dreamed a long while, or a moment, I know not which, on the pure wisdom of the East and our own grossness. But of course, I said, waking up suddenly—and I asked myself what manner of man I was . . . but that day sitting under my apple-tree, it seemed to me that I had suddenly come upon the secret lair in which the soul hides itself. An extraordinary clear and inflexible moral sense rose up and confronted me, and, looking down my past life, I was astounded . . . I rose from the seat, and looked round . . . and on the road to Chelsea, thinking of this great and merciful Providence, I heard a voice bidding me back to Ireland.[14]

Here is an excerpt from Augustine's description of the climax of his conversion:

So was I speaking, and weeping in the most bitter contrition of my heart, when lo! I heard from a neighbouring house a voice, as of boy or girl, I know not, chanting, and oft repeating, 'Take up and read; Take up and read.' Instantly, my countenance altered, I began to think most intently, whether children were wont in any kind of play to sing such words : nor could I remember ever to have heard the like. So checking the torrent of my tears, I arose: interpreting it to be no other than a command from God, to open the book . . . I seized, opened, and in silence read that section, on which my eyes first fell . . . No further would I read; nor needed I; for instantly at the end of this sentence, by a light as it were of serenity infused into my heart, all the darkness of doubt vanished away.[15]

Readers familiar with the *Confessions* of Augustine will know that the episode there is described at very great length and as having taken place under a fig tree. Although the order of events in the accounts of Augustine and Moore differs, there is much in common, as can be seen even from the short extracts just given: the solemnity of the situation; the emotional intensity but ultimate serenity of the actors; their isolation; the voices; the certainty after testing and in spite of some indefiniteness on other details that the voices were from outside the actor; the peremptory bidding; the force of morality personified; the instantaneous effect; the disappearance of doubt.

It is, of course, not intended here to maintain that Moore did consciously imitate Augustine in his description of the voice. Elsewhere I have examined briefly similar problems in relation to Rousseau and Newman and the question of the historicity of all such episodes, including Augustine's.[16] Moore, at any rate, was fully capable, following

13 *Ave*, 281ff.   14 *Salve*, 23ff.   15 *Conf.* 8.12.29f. (Pusey's translation).   16 *The Young Augustine*, Longmans, London (1954), 166ff., 180ff. In his *Confessions*, for example, Rousseau describes how while walking to Vincennes one day he read in the *Mercure de France* the title of the topic proposed by the Academy of Dijon for a prize: 'Has the progress of the sciences and arts done more to corrupt morals or improve them?' 'The moment I read this,' he says, 'I beheld another universe and became another man.

his own artistic impulses, of creating episodes where visions (as in *The Lake,* chapter 12) or voices play a part. But it is difficult in view of his declared desire artistically to imitate Augustine's *Confessions* to exclude some element of derivation of his heightened account of an historical event (his return to Ireland) from Augustine's similar treatment of a similar situation (his conversion).

It is impossible, finally, not to recall in connection with the voice of Moore the bidding also that came to Patrick the Apostle of Ireland:

> For there I saw in a vision of the night a man coming as it were from Ireland—His name was Victoricus—bringing very many letters. He gave me one of them and I read its beginning . . . As I read it out I felt that at that very moment I was hearing their voice . . . "We ask you . . . to come and continue to walk among us." I was much stricken in my heart and could read no further and so I woke . . . And another night—I do not know, God knows, whether in me or beside me—."[17]

Even if there is no compelling evidence that Patrick actually had read Augustine's *Confessions* or its conversion scene, the idea that he may have is difficult to ignore: Patrick was not bound to supply us with compelling evidence that he *had*. Then again, the experience of being profoundly moved by a book and expressing this in emotional and quasi-ecstatic terms is not so uncommon as to have it related necessarily to Augustine's *Confessions.*[18]

George Moore may have been thinking, appropriately enough in the context of his own self-imposed mission to Ireland, of the call heard by St Patrick. We shall never know if Patrick or Augustine or both did inspire his account of the voice that he heard. But this short *exposé* may help to determine more exactly to what extent the account employs a literary convention and to what extent it is historical. The context in which I have placed it at least helps to underline its seriousness, while raising, perhaps, the question of the historicity of all such accounts.

Although I have a lively recollection of the effect they produced on me, the details have escaped me . . . I was in a state of agitation bordering on delirium. Diderot noticed it; I told him the cause and read him Fabricius' soliloquy which I had written in pencil under an oak tree . . . All the rest of my life . . . followed inevitably as a result of that moment's madness' (Book Eight. Translation by J.M. Cohen). Likewise Newman in his *Apologia* speaks of reading an article in the *Dublin Review* in which Augustine's saying: *securus iudicat orbis terrarum* was quoted. These words kept ringing in Newman's ears: 'they were like the "Turn again Whittington" of the chime, or . . . "Tolle lege,—Tolle lege", of the child, which converted St Augustine himself. *Securus iudicat orbis terrarum!* By those great words of the ancient Father the theory of the *Via Media* was absolutely pulverized.' (116ff.). While all of these descriptions of 'conversion' (of one kind or another) might be consciously or unconsciously related, the element of the historical in all, the common experience, could be sufficient in itself to explain the similarity in the treatment. **17** *Conf.* 23.11f. One must keep in mind when dealing with St Patrick the many Biblical instances of Voices of various kinds. **18** Cf. the case of Toynbee 153 below.

3

Toynbee and St Augustine

Arnold J. Toynbee's *A Study of History* and Aurelius Augustinus's *City of God,* both great and lengthy books, have much in common. This correspondence has been remarked upon at length by critics of Toynbee's work,[1] and it is not surprising, since the modern historian himself proclaimed his debt to the Father of the Church.[2] The extent of the likeness between these two works has, nevertheless, not been fully realized, largely because the problem has not been approached by scholars sufficiently familiar with Augustine's *City of God.* It is important, however, to stress also the profound and ultimate differences between these two visions of the destiny of mankind.

But rather than compare immediately and contrast these two great books let us go behind the books to the men themselves. For the similarity and dissimilarity of their work reflect their likeness and unlikeness. There is nothing cold or impersonal in the message of the one or the other. Each book bears the strong imprint of its author's character and experiences, his prejudices and weaknesses, his nobility and courage. Here we shall attempt to indicate, very briefly, some of their more significant correspondences and differences.

Toynbee, with that mock modesty to which we must become accustomed, spoke of the comparison between himself and Augustine as being one between a pigmy and a giant,[3] in which, of course, the pigmy comes off always second best:

> *Sic canibus catulos similes, sic matribus haedos*
> *noram, sic parvis componere magna solebam* [Virgil, *Eclog.* 1.22].

Yet, although the comparison, ironical as it may be, is inevitably flattering to the pigmy, the pup, or the kid, it can be instructive for both terms in the comparison, and be of use even in relation to the giant, Augustine, in drawing attention to the relevance of his great work for Toynbee's contemporaries.

One should take note at the outset of the special regard each of these men had for his mother. As Monica had given Christ to Augustine with—as he says—her mother's milk, so Toynbee's mother, who had written *True Stories from Scottish History* to pay for his nurse, told the young Toynbee, night by night while she was putting him to bed, the

---

1 *A Study of History,* 12, 650f. 2 Op. cit. 4, 6f; 10, 236; 12, 2. Cf. Ved Mehta, *New Yorker* (8 December 1962), 92. 3 Op. cit. 12, 650, n. 5.

history of Britain from Caesar's landing to Waterloo. When he was nine or ten years old, in 1898, the arrival of four historical volumes in his parents' house, therefore, had a significant effect. I give Toynbee's own words: 'Yet that morning in AD 1898 in which those mighty suns the Egyptiac, Babylonic, and Syriac civilizations swam into his ken in all their overwhelming grandeur *was the decisive* moment in the intellectual experience of this young watcher of the skies of History. . . . The child flung himself upon the Ocean.' With a frankness characteristic of him Toynbee notes at this point that, whereas at Abersoch in Wales his nurse had rescued him at two years of age on his deliberate venturing into the sea to discover what would happen to him, no one pulled him back 'from the intellectual plunge that he made . . . into the ocean of History'. More briefly in another place he says that if his mother had not given his mind and heart this early bent he was sure that he would never have written his great work.[4]

Popular artists and writers have elaborated on the mother-complex of Augustine, and drawn various and varying conclusions, of probability little and great, from the intimate relationship of mother and son. The Plotinian scholar Henry seems to account for the mystical element in Augustine by saying that his mother was a mystic before him. This may or may not be true. What is true is that both Augustine and Toynbee share a very remarkable poetic and visionary approach to life, which proves disconcerting to those of us more accustomed to judging things by the world's coarse thumb.

Many people consider that Augustine had been a great sinner and, taking the words of his *Confessions* at their face value, one must come to such a conclusion. Yet it is clear to scholars that Augustine is induced, in part by his use of rhetoric and in part by his desire to glorify the Grace of God, which had delivered him, to use expressions of what seems to us greatly exaggerated self-depreciation. A harsh and inexact term for this in the case of Augustine would be masochism; it would not be harsh with reference to Toynbee. Listen to this: 'If I am convicted of being one of the offenders (in thinking my contribution to scholarship unique), I hope I shall lean over backwards, in revulsion from myself, till my head touches my heels.'[5] More significantly he stresses that the creative spiritual effect of suffering for the sake of love is the distinctive and significant feature of human nature—whether one approaches the matter as a Christian, a Jew, a classical scholar, the Buddha, or whom you will.[6] This desire to suffer, in almost welcome acceptance of being in the wrong, more particularly of being at variance with one's own environment, contemporaries, and, as Toynbee would say, parochial community, manifests itself as an impassioned detachment—an ostentation, as Geyl calls it[7]—which is one of the most revealing and important features of Toynbee's work.

It reveals itself in speaking ill of many things he loves, of England, of Rome, of Athens, and in particular of classical education. 'The feel of the barbarian blood in my veins has made me shudder. . . . If it were possible to change one's lineage, I might find myself tempted to barter my Anglo-Danish birthright for a Jewish, Arab, Greek, Italian, Dravidian or Chinese one'.[8] He is mortified by the discovery of a critic that Egypt receives only six times more space in the Index to volumes 7–10 of his work than

---

4 Op. cit., 10, 19.2.10, 213.　5 Ibid., 10.634.　6 12.617.　7 Cf. 12, 584.　8 12, 631.

England, when it, he declares, should be sixty times more. He happily accepts Barker's judgment that he does not know English history and does not love it.[9]

It is the same for Rome. Toynbee's dislike of Rome is so great that the Roman Empire, when considered in its most beneficial manifestations, is called a late Hellenic rally; the Roman Empire was but a Hellenic universal state; Rome should not be treated as a separate historical entity in its own right; it was but an element in the history of Hellenic civilization; 'the outstanding event in Rome's history is Rome's absorption by Hellenism'.[10]

Lest, however, we be led to believe that if not Rome, at least Athens receives Toynbee's enthusiasm, we are told that he is anti-Athenian: 'I look askance at Attica'.[11] In this connection Toynbee writes a most revealing paragraph:

> In reacting against Athens in particular and against Hellenism in general, I am also exercising my human right of self-defence. Considering that my formal education has been an Hellenic one deriving from the renaissance of Hellenism in fifteenth-century Italy, I should be a lost soul if I allowed myself to be completely captivated by the double spell of Hellenism and Hellenism's Italian renaissance. I must react against this if I am not to succumb to it. But in thus fighting for my intellectual independence, I am at the same time showing black ingratitude. I am remorsefully aware that my debt to the Italian renaissance and to Hellenism is immeasurable. The only extenuating circumstance that I can plead is that, after I have seen thoroughly through them both, and have thought and written the worst about them, I find myself still loving and admiring them as much as ever.[12]

There you have it: the admission of the charge I am making, the explanation and the remorse: in short the paradox of Arnold Toynbee.

Before we turn to Augustine and his problems of detachment, I may be permitted here to dwell a little longer on Toynbee's attitude towards the classical education of which he is so proud. He considers this matter more formally in Annex II *Ad hominem,* 575ff. in Volume 12. He recalls that 'classical' education is being driven out by science, which regards piety towards the past as a vice intellectually and ethically, which has the obligatory ambition of striving to supersede even its own past achievements, and which makes it a point of honour to discard ruthlessly everything so superseded.

Toynbee claims to have been one of the last to profit and to suffer from an education in the Greek and Latin languages and the literature that remained faithful to the strictest fifteenth-century Italian standards. He commends it for teaching one to appreciate and revere a culture that is not one's own. Here, however, he can mean little more than that it gives historical perspective. He has more precise points to make against it. He claims that in his own case, it has not only supplied him with a limited range of knowledge, but also had a bad effect upon his writing of English. He writes English, says Ernest Barker, 'in a Ciceronian style, as if it were a foreign language'.[13] This, to my mind, is to slander Cicero. Notice this fairly normal item:

9 21, 630.   10 12, 377, 392.   11 12, 636.   12 12, 636.   13 Cf. 12, 588.

After having been intimidated by an ever more sensitive 'awareness of the possible pitfalls' in a mental landscape in which a once solid Earth was melting into a dreamlike kaleidoscope of 'total reconstructions', these distracted latter-day Western historians were appalled by a nightmare in which they saw this Protean chaos solidifying again, only to confront the tormented observer with a novel universe of an incomprehensible complexity.[14]

Or what about this for a title: 'The Human Spirit's Educational Use of a Physical Generation Cycle as a Psychological Regulator of Social Change'?[15]

The *Times Literary Supplement*'s critic wrote, justly I think, of Toynbee's mastery over words and of his style, as being encumbered like a man who loads himself with souvenirs from every resort he ever visited.[16] His pages are spattered with unlovely epithets, notable among them being 'latter-day' and '*ci-devant*', which seem to exercise an irresistible fascination for him. One feels that he cultivates clumsiness and flaunts it in our faces.

Toynbee does not agree with those who form a favourable estimate of his style—but is he repentant and anxious to mend his ways? Not at all. And why? He is inhibited, he says, from correction by a 'distaste for the vernacular languages of the Western World, which is also the result of a classical education':[17] 'I have been educated into seeing in French a vulgar deformation of Latin, and in English a barbarous substitution for it. But I also have a rational ground for finding these Western vernaculars inferior to Latin and Attic Greek, and also to Pre-Atatürk Ottoman Turkish (of which I have a smattering)'.[18]

Toynbee is full of surprises and, one has the impression, of too many smatterings. Who can really accept his plea that Greek and Latin are to blame for his being more in tune with them than with his mother-tongue? Can we really believe him when he claims that he would feel more at home if Greek and Latin were the media of communication between him and his public? If a Newman and the writers of his century, a Gilbert Murray or a Maurice Bowra nearer our own day—although they were professionally and for a longer time involved in the use of Greek and Latin, suffer though they might from some inevitable deformations in their writing of English—could still write naturally and admirably in their mother tongues, must we not conclude that here again Toynbee has succumbed to the temptation of adopting an exaggerated, indeed slightly ridiculous, and unusual view?

Toynbee reminds this writer of no one so much as Newman's bad candidate in classics, as described in the chapter on 'Elementary Studies' in the *Idea of a University*. The fond father of the bad candidate explained that he had never met a faster reader. Newman, however, construed this kind of reading as 'little more than the result of mental restlessness and curiosity'. Once again Toynbee can be quoted against himself:

In December 1906, he had been staying with a pair of distinguished scholars in the persons of his uncle Paget Toynbee ... and his aunt Helen Toynbee. ... At the close of an agreeable and stimulating visit, in which the boy had unselfconsciously

14 9, 209. 15 9, 319. 16 Cf. 12, 588. 17 12, 589. 18 Loc. cit.

disclosed historical interests embracing the Assyrians, the Fourth Crusade, and what not, he was chilled by a piece of parting advice which his uncle gave him out of the kindness of his heart. 'Your Aunt Nellie and I . . . have come to the conclusion that you have been dispersing your interests too widely, and our advice to you is to make your choice of some single subject and to concentrate hereafter on that'. In AD 1952 the writer had a still freshly vivid recollection of his *own instantaneous conviction* that this advice was bad, and of his likewise instantaneous decision not to follow it. Few will dissent from Toynbee's own judgment on himself: 'I am by nature intellectually rash.'[19]

By now one is, perhaps, weary of Toynbee's championing of the untenable and luxuriating in self-accusation. One may well ask if any of this can be true of Augustine? Can he share this masochism, this restless exhibitionism? Gone are the days when hagiographers felt that they did a service to their subject in treating his human limitations lightly, if at all—perhaps we have gone too far, nowadays, in the other direction. For our part let us give a short and simple report of what Augustine, like Toynbee, says of himself.

One should recall that the volume of Toynbee's *Study of History* in which he indulges in such merciless self-criticism is called *Reconsiderations* and would, he says, have been called *Retractations* after St Augustine's *Retractationes* if his reading audience would permit it. This volume, however, whatever its title, is more obviously inspired, where it gives personal reminiscence, by Augustine's *Confessions*. In both volumes there is, of course, autobiographical content, much self-castigation, moralization, prayers to God, professions of faith and praise. Each work—the *Study of History* and the *Confessions*—tells of conversion and the intrusion of the influence of some book at a critical juncture, and of 'visions' and the extension of preoccupation with the author's own life to the salvation of mankind.

Enough has here been said of the autobiographical content and the self-castigation. Any reader of the *Confessions* of St Augustine will know, however, that even without making allowance (as should be made) for the rhetorical conventions of Augustine's time and the genre in which he was writing, and the important fact that Augustine was formally addressing God and confessing his sin before Him, there is very much more restraint in the Father of the Church. If he dilates upon the sinfulness of an infant's temper, of an adolescent's wanton stealing of pears, or of a youth's sinfulness in the flesh, he is obeying the conventions of rhetoric and conforming to his own image as a pastoral bishop as well as, of course, recounting truths. But even then the emphasis and tone are less personal and more controlled.

Whereas Toynbee's prayers and profession of faith and praise are syncretic, indeed exotic, Augustine's are confined within the terms of Christian theology. It is not to be thought that Augustine was insensitive to the claims and, as at times it seemed to him, the true claims of other systems, philosophical or theological. No one at all familiar with the study of Augustine's developing attitude—from his *Dialogues* to the *City of God* (to

19 10, 28f. 2.12.

the philosophy of Neoplatonism and particularly Porphyry with his theurgic background)—will be unaware of the broadness of Augustine's sympathy and tolerance: the Sibyl earned her place in the City of God; Porphyry was credited with belief in the Hebrew Father, in something like the Christian Trinity and even Grace; the religious aspirations of the Egyptians, Phoenicians, people of India, Assyrians, Lydians, Chaldaeans, and Jews were recognised as pointing to one universal way of salvation for all mankind. But broad as was his sympathy and generous his tolerance, for Augustine the one universal way was Christ, the Christian Saviour. How different the 'theology' of Toynbee, as expressed, for example, in this prayer:

Christe, audi nos.
Christ Tammuz, Christ Adonis, Christ Osiris, Christ Balder, hear us, by whatsoever name we bless Thee for suffering death for our salvation.

Christe Jesu, exaudi nos.
Buddha Gautama, show us the path that will lead us out of our afflictions.

Sancta Dei Genetrix, intercede pro nobis.
Mother Mary, Mother Isis, Mother Cybele, Mother Ishtar, Mother Kwanyin, have compassion on us, by whatsoever name we bless thee for bringing Our Saviour into the World.

Sancte Michael, intercede pro nobis.
Mithras, fight at our side in our battle of Light against Darkness.

Omnes Sancti Angeli et Archangeli, intercedite pro nobis.
All ye devoted bodhisattvas, who for us your fellow living beings and for our release have forborne, aeon after aeon, to enter into your rest, tarry with us, we beseech you, yet a little while longer.

Sancte Joannes Baptista, intercede pro nobis.
Noble Lucretius, who, in spite of thyself, art also a forerunner of the Saviour, instil thy poetry into our hearts and thy sincerity into our understandings.

Sancte Augustine, intercede pro nobis.
Jalāl-ad-Dïn Mawlänä, singing reed, make heavenly music for us as the breath of God's spirit pours through thee . . .[20]

Here, doing, one presumes, violence to his own Christian heritage, Toynbee confines himself to a 50 per cent representation of Christian theology, which, for all that, will seem too much to the exponents of the other systems mentioned. This is the kind of pantechnicon theology which has earned from the incisive A.J.P. Taylor the derisive description of a religion of mish-mash.[21]

On this point are revealed the fundamental differences in the characters and attitudes of Toynbee and Augustine. Toynbee will be loyal to nothing, will be confined by nothing. Having a love for Christianity, recognizing it as not only his birthright (conquered for him by Augustine) but the source of greatness in *Homo Occidentalis*, believing that it is

20 10.143f. **21** *Encounter* (June 1957), 20.

at least on a par with all other higher religions and to that extent an essential aspect of life (inasmuch as it transfigures and elevates the earthly city so that it becomes a heavenly one)—Toynbee yet proclaims himself, following Gilbert Murray, to be an agnostic, although having something like conviction in a realm beyond knowledge, where there are but imperfect intimations, guesses or hopes. In this sense he describes himself as a 'trans-rationalist'. And for him all the higher religions have relative truth and relative saving-power.[22] But:

> I reject the pretension of Christianity to be a unique revelation of the truth about Reality and a unique means of grace and salvation. I reject the Christian Church's argument that it is unique in virtue of the uniqueness of Christ and of His incarnation . . . . We have to consider whether it seems to us credible that a God . . . will have done this self-sacrificing deed of 'emptying Himself' at one time and one time only.[23]

So spoke Porphyry also in the works controverted by Augustine in his *City of God!* The constant refrain throughout Augustine's book is that worship should be paid to the Christian (Hebrew) Father and Him *alone*. Christ was the one and only way of salvation for all: He came in the time judged good by God. Like Augustine, Toynbee insists on the necessity for one Father to bring about one brotherhood amongst mankind—but unlike Augustine he believes that there are *many* ways to the Father. Yet one has to add —in parenthesis—that Toynbee sees that the jealousness, as he calls it, of Yahweh, which at first sight is so repellent, is the one medium through which the profound truth of the unity of God has been grasped *hitherto* by human souls.[24] Given this basic contradiction between their views, however, no matter how many are the points on which they seem to correspond, the great works of Toynbee and Augustine must be totally at variance: their likeness is but superficial.

This parting of the ways is not, of course, unexpected in view of their differing spiritual odysseys and conversions: indeed it is in these odysseys, rather than the outcome, that we can see the characters of the two men more clearly manifested.

Toynbee was born a Christian, became a rationalist, and then declared himself to be a 'trans-rationalist' with a certain 'tenseness' in his feelings about Christianity. Of his *Study of History* he says that it began 'as an analytico-classificatory comparative study of human affairs and turned into a metahistorical inquiry *en route*'.[25] This recognizes the fact of Toynbee's 'conversion'. By metahistory Toynbee means metaphysics and theology, or something akin to them, and he instances Augustine's *City of God* as a classic example of metahistory.[26] Augustine's conversion was not solely the conversion of his mind from one point of view to another. Whatever be our notions of African Manicheism, it seems true that Augustine, even if his understanding of Christianity changed and developed, could count himself a kind of follower of Christ except for a brief and not very assured sceptical period immediately before his baptism in 386.[27] His understanding of the implications of Christianity then widened to allow both a *rational* content—in yielding to the predictions of cosmologists and being enamoured and set

---

22 12, 75, 9; 5, 375.   23 12, 624.   24 6, 49.   25 12.229.   26 12.228.   27 Cf. the author's *The Young Augustine*, 79.

on fire by the philosophers' commendations of the pursuit of wisdom, and in coordinating Neoplatonism with Christianity—and a *theological* content. In the end, however, while still in his early thirties, he yielded to Christ, giving theology primacy over reason, however much he might hope to co-ordinate the two:

> I, therefore, am resolved in nothing whatever to depart from the authority of Christ—for I do not find a stronger. But as to that which is sought out by subtle reasoning—for I am so disposed as to be impatient in my desire to apprehend truth not only by faith but also by understanding. . . . I feel sure at the moment that I shall find it with the Platonists, nor will it be at variance with our sacred mysteries.[28]

In so far as he departed from that position he tended to have less confidence in the Platonists.

Augustine's mind is, therefore, not open in the sense in which Toynbee's is. The latter reports this view himself:

> The openness of my mental horizon, which Voegelin notices and commends, has also been noticed by Baudet. In my view, he points out, history is an open road, in contrast to St Augustine's view that its course is predetermined. This is, I think, what Erdmann has in mind when he suggests that the unity of my book is like the unity of an expedition or a pilgrimage.[29]

Here Toynbee's most generous and positive quality, his spendthrift receptivity to every human need, to every human aspiration, to every glimmering of a solution to man's dire predicament, is manifest. His corresponding disregard of his own reputation, his humility in the face of honest criticism and even unseemly derision, should be counted to his credit. *Magni passus extra viam.* Heraclitus may be right and all things may be in a state of flux. Nevertheless life must be lived as if things were discrete, not continuous.

It is not true to say of the unity of Toynbee's book, as Erdmann does, that it is like the unity of a pilgrimage. Rather it is like the progress of many pilgrimages. On the other hand Augustine's description of his own *City of God* as a pilgrimage is true. Put it another way: Augustine's vision is intense, in depth articulated; Toynbee's is extensive and indeterminate. It is not that Toynbee has not much to teach us: he is striving at the barriers of knowledge and his work may deserve the epithet 'great'. It is rather that we are always waiting for more, perhaps also something different. Toynbee's openness is ultimately a scepticism.

This scepticism is the final source of Toynbee's many paradoxes; the un-English Englishman, the un-Christian Christian, the unempirical empiricist, the unpoetic poet, the stylist who has written some of the most unlovely passages ever written in the English language, and much else besides. Toynbee has immense respect for paradox: 'May not this be the moment to remind ourselves of the principle of *peripéteia*—"the reversal of roles"—upon which we have stumbled at an earlier stage of our inquiry? This principle of irony and paradox is mighty in operation'.[30]

28 *C. Acad.* 3, 43. 29 12, 651. 30 6, 149.

Great as is the difference between Toynbee and Augustine in their final attitudes, it is still true to say that, although Augustine is nearly always more restrained, in practice they have much in common. This is so also in their attitudes towards irony and paradox. Augustine was so impressed by the actions of Providence in his regard that he formulated a rather surprising theory of 'economy'. One can sometimes usefully understand, he suggests, the *opposite* of what a writer has meant.[31] His own experience in life had been so often the opposite of what he had anticipated, that he found nothing wonderful any longer in such surprises. He had gone to scoff at Ambrose's doctrine, and had come away shaken in his prejudices. He had read Porphyry and the Neoplatonists, the stoutest intellectual opponents of Christianity, only to be convinced of the truth of Christianity. Augustine had a weakness, perhaps as a consequence of these experiences, for a measure of make-belief. He put forward the idea, with no great show of confidence it must be said, that the sceptics of the New Academy were not only not sceptics at all but actually preserved the true positive spiritual doctrine of Plato. God, whom he describes as the Great Artifex of Great Things, composed the order of the ages as a beautiful poem, ornamenting it with antitheses, or contraries. In this way poison, when used in the right proportion, although it can kill, gives life. Therefore we must be ever conscious of our limitations in understanding. Providence justly conspires sometimes in our being deceived: *decipi iustum est.*[32]

Augustine at times in his *Confessions* appears to describe visions or mystical elevations which have been variously interpreted by scholars. Some, such as Courcelle, feel that Augustine is describing in borrowed language efforts at Neoplatonic ecstasy which were, as we would expect, unsuccessful. Others would regard such passages as Neoplatonic in inspiration and tone, it is true, but as being no more than a fantasy. But even such vitally important scenes as the final moment of his conversion in the garden at Milan— vital from the point of view of the historicity of Augustine's *Confessions*—have been plausibly interpreted, again by Courcelle among others, as being mainly fictional. Vision, fantasy, make-believe, wishful thinking are all present in one degree or another in Augustine's autobiography.

But the degree is mild in comparison with that found in Toynbee. Those who admire the reveries of Walter Mitty will find much to delight them in, for example, Toynbee's tenth volume. There he speaks of having had a sense of personal participation in the Castilian expedition to Mexico in AD 1519. Again:

> At another moment the twentieth-century reader [i.e. Toynbee] found himself in Nikítas Khoniátis' shoes, striding back, with his heart in his mouth, into the jaws of Death in the forlorn hope of trying to rescue a girl who had just been kidnapped by a Frankish soldier from among a party of Byzantine refugees that was heading for the Golden Gate in a perilous attempt to make an exodus from the ravished City.
>
> In AD 952 the writer of this study had a vivid recollection of six such experiences in which he had found himself participating in an historic past event through a momentary annihilation of the intervening time on the hypnotizing spot.[33]

31 *De utilitate credendi* 10.   32 Cf. 85f above.   33 133ff.

Nor was a higher vision denied him:

> [He] had found himself in communion, not just with this or that episode in History,
> but with all that had been, and was directly aware of the passage of History gently
> flowing through him in a mighty current, and of his own life welling like a wave in
> the flow of this vast tide.[34]

With such a *penchant* in their natures for vision and fantasy, it is only to be expected
that both authors make much use of analogy, while professing to place great reliance
upon reason. This is, once again, more remarkable in Toynbee, who draws constant
attention to what he calls his 'well-beloved method' of making an empirical survey.[35] In
point of fact, however, he tells many fables and has recourse to poetry and mythology,[36]
and he is aware of this, but insists that he can get the best of both worlds. Unluckily his
openness, detachment, or scepticism will but make him unacceptable to the scientists
and the poets. And once again he joins with Augustine and the New Testament in
commending Love as the secret of being. In this he reveals himself, as does Augustine,
a salvationist rather than an historian.[37]

The very reliance upon recurring themes, which is a notable characteristic of both
their methods of working, points to a developed and subtle artistic sensibility in both
writers. Likewise the suggestion of immensity in such grandiose themes really conceals
a most adroit exploitation of a range of knowledge of comparatively restricted propor-
tions.

Equally the clarity of outline in both the *City of God* and *Study of History* tends to
overshadow an immense prolixity and relative vagueness in the detail. The impressive
swing of complementary patterns leaves our critical faculties at least temporarily
overwhelmed: 'We can hear the beat of an elemental rhythm whose variations we have
learnt to know as Challenge-and-Response and Withdrawal-and-Return and Rout-and-
Rally and Apparentation-and-Affiliation and Schism-and-Palingenesia. This elemental
rhythm is the alternating beat of Yin and Yang'.[38]

Is pessimism implicit in such antitheses? Is dualism involved in dichotomies such as
soul and body, mind and matter, freedom and necessity, creator and creatures, God and
devil, good and bad, right and wrong—in Augustine's case, city of God and city of the
devil? Does Toynbee succumb, as some would have it, to 'profound Augustinian
pessimism'? On the whole it must be admitted that, however exaggerated current ideas
are of the pessimism of St Augustine and how insufficiently appreciated the definitely
optimistic aspects of his view of human destiny, Augustine's general notions on the
number of men who would be saved were pessimistic. I am not at all sure that Toynbee
is pessimistic in this sense, although perhaps he tends to be rather less than sanguine in
his expectation of salvation for mankind as a whole.

Ultimately both men are preoccupied with the same problem, the problem of two
cities, as has been well stressed by Pucelle.[39] This is reflected in a small way in Toynbee's
fondness for ending sections of his work with a flourishing reference to the *City of God*.[40]

34 139.   35 4, 24; 5, 210, 397.   36 4, 236; 6, 161, 377f.   37 6, 165f; 12, 652.   38 6.324.   39 *In-
ternational Philosophical Quarterly* 2 (1962), 549.   40 E.g. 5.614.

We have been concerned not so much with the *City of God* and the *Study of History* and their teaching as with the men behind these two great works. It is undeniable that in character they have a great deal in common: much of what we have had to say reinforces the impressions of others. Ultimately, however, they do differ and the difference is of immense practical consequence. Augustine, while possessing in large degree many of the tendencies that Toynbee also has, has always, so to speak, one foot on the ground. His opinions are never as extreme. He is never so detached and open as to be, in effect, without allegiance. In point of fact this difference issues in Augustine's full acceptance of Christianity with all its implications. Hence his teaching, as distinct from his natural outlook perhaps, is wholly at variance with Toynbee's. He accepts the God who tolerates no other gods. This God, Toynbee rejects. From this there emerges a long series of practical differences in their views of man's life here and hereafter.

Augustine's *City of God* is nearly always hailed as a great book—one of the world's great books. The present writer would support such a view. Is Toynbee's work great in the same way? Few professional historians would agree: many merely deride it. One cannot but regret that Toynbee does not impose more discipline upon his thoughts and their expression. If he did, the noble effort he has made to sustain his fellow men throughout their confused searching, through many creeds and systems, for a destined Omega, would meet with the careful attention its theme demands.

Index